332.024 M74we
Weverka, Peter.
Microsoft Money 98 for
dummies
(1 BOOK, 1 DISC)

Navigation Bar Buttons and Where They Take You

Clicking This Button	Takes You to . . .
Money Home	The Home screen, where you see the Chart of the Day, the Tip of the Day, and a list of bills you need to pay
Accounts	The Account Manager window, where you set up new accounts and open account registers
Bills	The Bill Calendar window, where you can record the bills you pay regularly and enlist the Money program's help in paying bills on time
Online Banking	The Home Banking & Investments window, where Money offers its online banking and online bill-paying services
Investments	The Investment Portfolio window, where you can monitor stocks, bonds, mutual funds, and other investment holdings
Budget (or Planner)	The Budget & Savings (or Goal Planner) window, where you can formulate a budget, reckon the price of a loan or mortgage, plan for retirement, calculate the cost of a college education, and estimate how investments grow over time (some features in this window are available only to users of the Money 98 Financial Suite)
Reports	The Reports & Charts window, where you can generate reports and charts that show where you stand financially
Money Insider	The Insider window, where you can scavenge for expert advice from what Microsoft calls "the nation's top money experts" (for Money 98 Financial Suite users only)
Categories	The Categories & Payees window, where the people and businesses to whom you've made payments and your categories and classifications are listed
Back	The window you looked at previously

Five Things That Every Money User Should Do

- Keep your checking account, savings account, and credit card account registers up to date

- Balance your bank accounts each month

- Create categories and subcategories so you can track your spending, income, and tax deductions

- Back up your data file to a floppy disk

- Generate a "Where the Money Goes" chart

...For Dummies: #1 Computer Book Series for Beginners

Microsoft® Money 98 For Dummies®

Recording a Transaction in an Account Register

1. **Open the register of the account you want to record a transaction in.**

2. **Click the tab — Check, Deposit, Withdrawal, or Cash Machine — that describes the transaction you intend to record.**

3. **In the transaction form at the bottom of the register, click the Number tab to move to the Number text box.**

   You can move from box to box in a transaction form by clicking or by pressing Tab or Shift+Tab.

4. **Enter a number in the Number text box, if necessary.**

5. **Enter the date in the Date text box.**

   A fast way to enter dates is to click the down-arrow to the right of the Date text box, open the mini-calendar, and click a date.

6. **Enter who you paid the money to in the Pay to text box or received the money from in the From text box.**

   If this *is not* the first time you've entered the name in the text box, simply type the first few letters to make the entire name appear.

7. **Enter the amount of the transaction in the Amount text box.**

8. **In the Category text boxes, enter a category in the left-hand text box and, if you want, a subcategory in the right-hand text box.**

9. **If you care to, write a few words in the Memo text box to describe the transaction.**

10. **Click the Enter button or press the Enter key.**

Online Services That Money 98 Offers

Service	What You Can Do
Online banking	Download records from your bank, credit card company, or brokerage house to find out which transactions have cleared. You can also download records into account registers, transfer funds between accounts, and send e-mail messages to the bank.
Online bill payment	Pay bills online. You can use this service to pay anyone, even Uncle Ernie. Processing and making a payment usually takes five days.
Online stock and mutual fund quotes	Download stock, bond, and mutual fund prices from the Internet. Current prices of the stocks, bonds, and mutual funds that you own are entered automatically in the Portfolio window.
Money Insider	Read articles on the Internet about money-management techniques (for users of the Money 98 Financial Suite only).
Microsoft Investor	Research investment opportunities. The service offers business profiles and charts, market statistics, and articles (for users of the Money 98 Financial Suite only).

...For Dummies: #1 Computer Book Series for Beginners

MICROSOFT®
MONEY 98 FOR
DUMMIES®

MICROSOFT® MONEY 98 FOR DUMMIES®

by Peter Weverka

IDG Books Worldwide, Inc.
An International Data Group Company

Foster City, CA ♦ Chicago, IL ♦ Indianapolis, IN ♦ Southlake, TX

Microsoft® Money 98 For Dummies®

Published by
IDG Books Worldwide, Inc.
An International Data Group Company
919 E. Hillsdale Blvd.
Suite 400
Foster City, CA 94404
www.idgbooks.com (IDG Books Worldwide Web site)
www.dummies.com (Dummies Press Web site)

Library of Congress Catalog Card No.: 97-80749

ISBN: 0-7645-0295-6

Printed in the United States of America

10 9 8 7 6 5 4 3 2 1

1B/RX/RR/ZX/IN

Distributed in the United States by IDG Books Worldwide, Inc.

Distributed by Macmillan Canada for Canada; by Transworld Publishers Limited in the United Kingdom; by IDG Norge Books for Norway; by IDG Sweden Books for Sweden; by Woodslane Pty. Ltd. for Australia; by Woodslane Enterprises Ltd. for New Zealand; by Longman Singapore Publishers Ltd. for Singapore, Malaysia, Thailand, and Indonesia; by Simron Pty. Ltd. for South Africa; by Toppan Company Ltd. for Japan; by Distribuidora Cuspide for Argentina; by Livraria Cultura for Brazil; by Ediciencia S.A. for Ecuador; by Addison-Wesley Publishing Company for Korea; by Ediciones ZETA S.C.R. Ltda. for Peru; by WS Computer Publishing Corporation, Inc., for the Philippines; by Unalis Corporation for Taiwan; by Contemporanea de Ediciones for Venezuela; by Computer Book & Magazine Store for Puerto Rico; by Express Computer Distributors for the Caribbean and West Indies. Authorized Sales Agent: Anthony Rudkin Associates for the Middle East and North Africa.

For general information on IDG Books Worldwide's books in the U.S., please call our Consumer Customer Service department at 800-762-2974. For reseller information, including discounts and premium sales, please call our Reseller Customer Service department at 800-434-3422.

For information on where to purchase IDG Books Worldwide's books outside the U.S., please contact our International Sales department at 415-655-3200 or fax 415-655-3295.

For information on foreign language translations, please contact our Foreign & Subsidiary Rights department at 415-655-3021 or fax 415-655-3281.

For sales inquiries and special prices for bulk quantities, please contact our Sales department at 415-655-3200 or write to the address above.

For information on using IDG Books Worldwide's books in the classroom or for ordering examination copies, please contact our Educational Sales department at 800-434-2086 or fax 817-251-8174.

For press review copies, author interviews, or other publicity information, please contact our Public Relations department at 415-655-3000 or fax 415-655-3299.

For authorization to photocopy items for corporate, personal, or educational use, please contact Copyright Clearance Center, 222 Rosewood Drive, Danvers, MA 01923, or fax 508-750-4470.

is a trademark under exclusive license to IDG Books Worldwide, Inc., from International Data Group, Inc.

About the Author

Peter Weverka is the author of ten books, including *Dummies 101: Office 97* and *Word 97 For Windows For Dummies Quick Reference,* both published by IDG Books Worldwide Inc., and *Quicken 98 For Busy People.* His humorous articles and stories (none related to computers, thankfully) have appeared in *Harper's* and *SPY.*

ABOUT IDG BOOKS WORLDWIDE

Welcome to the world of IDG Books Worldwide.

IDG Books Worldwide, Inc., is a subsidiary of International Data Group, the world's largest publisher of computer-related information and the leading global provider of information services on information technology. IDG was founded more than 25 years ago and now employs more than 8,500 people worldwide. IDG publishes more than 275 computer publications in over 75 countries (see listing below). More than 60 million people read one or more IDG publications each month.

Launched in 1990, IDG Books Worldwide is today the #1 publisher of best-selling computer books in the United States. We are proud to have received eight awards from the Computer Press Association in recognition of editorial excellence and three from *Computer Currents'* First Annual Readers' Choice Awards. Our best-selling *...For Dummies*® series has more than 30 million copies in print with translations in 30 languages. IDG Books Worldwide, through a joint venture with IDG's Hi-Tech Beijing, became the first U.S. publisher to publish a computer book in the People's Republic of China. In record time, IDG Books Worldwide has become the first choice for millions of readers around the world who want to learn how to better manage their businesses.

Our mission is simple: Every one of our books is designed to bring extra value and skill-building instructions to the reader. Our books are written by experts who understand and care about our readers. The knowledge base of our editorial staff comes from years of experience in publishing, education, and journalism — experience we use to produce books for the '90s. In short, we care about books, so we attract the best people. We devote special attention to details such as audience, interior design, use of icons, and illustrations. And because we use an efficient process of authoring, editing, and desktop publishing our books electronically, we can spend more time ensuring superior content and spend less time on the technicalities of making books.

You can count on our commitment to deliver high-quality books at competitive prices on topics you want to read about. At IDG Books Worldwide, we continue in the IDG tradition of delivering quality for more than 25 years. You'll find no better book on a subject than one from IDG Books Worldwide.

IDG BOOKS WORLDWIDE

John Kilcullen
CEO
IDG Books Worldwide, Inc.

Steven Berkowitz
President and Publisher
IDG Books Worldwide, Inc.

Eighth Annual Computer Press Awards ≥1992

Ninth Annual Computer Press Awards ≥1993

Tenth Annual Computer Press Awards ≥1994

Eleventh Annual Computer Press Awards ≥1995

IDG Books Worldwide, Inc., is a subsidiary of International Data Group, the world's largest publisher of computer-related information and the leading global provider of information services on information technology. International Data Group publishes over 275 computer publications in over 75 countries. Sixty million people read one or more International Data Group publications each month. International Data Group's publications include: **ARGENTINA:** Buyer's Guide, Computerworld Argentina, PC World Argentina; **AUSTRALIA:** Australian Macworld, Australian PC World, Australian Reseller News, Computerworld, IT Casebook, Network World, Publish, Webmaster; **AUSTRIA:** Computerwelt Österreich, Networks Austria, PC Tip Austria; **BANGLADESH:** PC World Bangladesh; **BELARUS:** PC World Belarus; **BELGIUM:** Data News; **BRAZIL:** Annuário de Informática, Computerworld, Connections, Macworld, PC Player, PC World, Publish, Reseller News, Supergamepower; **BULGARIA:** Computerworld Bulgaria, Network World Bulgaria, PC & MacWorld Bulgaria; **CANADA:** CIO Canada, Client/Server World, ComputerWorld Canada, InfoWorld Canada, NetworkWorld Canada, WebWorld; **CHILE:** Computerworld Chile, PC World Chile; **COLOMBIA:** Computerworld Colombia, PC World Colombia; **COSTA RICA:** PC World Centro America; **THE CZECH AND SLOVAK REPUBLICS:** Computerworld Czechoslovakia, Macworld Czech Republic, PC World Czechoslovakia; **DENMARK:** Communications World Danmark, Computerworld Danmark, Macworld Danmark, PC World Danmark, Techworld Denmark; **DOMINICAN REPUBLIC:** PC World Republica Dominicana; **ECUADOR:** PC World Ecuador; **EGYPT:** Computerworld Middle East, PC World Middle East; **EL SALVADOR:** PC World Centro America; **FINLAND:** MikroPC, Tietoverkko, Tietoviikko; **FRANCE:** Distributique, Hebdo, Info PC, Le Monde Informatique, Macworld, Reseaux & Telecoms, WebMaster France; **GERMANY:** Computer Partner, Computerwoche, Computerwoche Extra, Computerwoche FOCUS, Global Online, Macwelt, PC Welt; **GREECE:** Amiga Computing, GamePro Greece, Multimedia World; **GUATEMALA:** PC World Centro America; **HONDURAS:** PC World Centro America; **HONG KONG:** Computerworld Hong Kong, PC World Hong Kong, Publish in Asia; **HUNGARY:** ABCD CD-ROM, Computerworld Szamitastechnika, Internetto online Magazine, PC World Hungary, PC-X Magazin Hungary; **ICELAND:** Tolvuheimur PC World Island; **INDIA:** Information Communications World, Information Systems Computerworld, PC World India, Publish in Asia; **INDONESIA:** InfoKomputer PC World, Komputek Computerworld, Publish in Asia; **IRELAND:** ComputerScope, PC Live!; **ISRAEL:** Macworld Israel, People & Computers/Computerworld; **ITALY:** Computerworld Italia, Macworld Italia, Networking Italia, PC World Italia; **JAPAN:** DTP World, Macworld Japan, Nikkei Personal Computing, OS/2 World Japan, SunWorld Japan, Windows NT World, Windows World Japan; **KENYA:** PC World East African; **KOREA:** Hi-Tech Information, Macworld Korea, PC World Korea; **MACEDONIA:** PC World Macedonia; **MALAYSIA:** Computerworld Malaysia, PC World Malaysia, Publish in Asia; **MALTA:** PC World Malta; **MEXICO:** Computerworld Mexico, PC World Mexico; **MYANMAR:** PC World Myanmar; **NETHERLANDS:** Computer! Totaal, LAN Internetworking Magazine, LAN World Buyers Guide, Macworld Netherlands, Net, WebWereld; **NEW ZEALAND:** Absolute Beginners Guide and Plain & Simple Series, Computer Buyer, Computer Industry Directory, Computerworld New Zealand, MTB, Network World, PC World New Zealand; **NICARAGUA:** PC World Centro America; **NORWAY:** Computerworld Norge, CW Rapport, Datamagasinet, Financial Rapport, Kursguide Norge, Macworld Norge, Multimediaworld Norge, PC World Ekspress Norge, PC World Nettverk, PC World Norge, PC World ProduktGuide Norge; **PAKISTAN:** Computerworld Pakistan; **PANAMA:** PC World Panama; **PEOPLE'S REPUBLIC OF CHINA:** China Computer Users, China Computerworld, China InfoWorld, China Telecom World Weekly, Computer & Communication, Electronic Design China, Electronics Today, Electronics Weekly, Game Software, PC World China, Popular Computer Week, Software Weekly, Software World, Telecom World; **PERU:** Computerworld Peru, PC World Profesional Peru, PC World SoHo Peru; **PHILIPPINES:** Click!, Computerworld Philippines, PC World Philippines, Publish in Asia; **POLAND:** Computerworld Poland, Computerworld Special Report Poland, Cyber, Macworld Poland, Networld Poland, PC World Komputer; **PORTUGAL:** Cerebro/PC World, Computerworld/Correio Informático, Dealer World Portugal, Mac*In/PC*In Portugal, Multimedia World; **PUERTO RICO:** PC World Puerto Rico; **ROMANIA:** Computerworld Romania, PC World Romania, Telecom Romania; **RUSSIA:** Computerworld Russia, Mir PK, Publish, Seti; **SINGAPORE:** Computerworld Singapore, PC World Singapore, Publish in Asia; **SLOVENIA:** Monitor; **SOUTH AFRICA:** Computing SA, Network World SA, Software World SA; **SPAIN:** Communicaciones World España, Computerworld España, Dealer World España, PC World España, PC World Especial; **SRI LANKA:** Infolink PC World; **SWEDEN:** CAP&Design, Computer Sweden, Corporate Computing Sweden, Internetworld Sweden, it.branschen, Macworld Sweden, MaxiData Sweden, MikroDatorn, Nätverk & Kommunikation, PC World Sweden, PCaktiv, Windows World Sweden; **SWITZERLAND:** Computerworld Schweiz, Macworld Schweiz, PCtip; **TAIWAN:** Computerworld Taiwan, Macworld Taiwan, NEW ViSiON/Publish, PC World Taiwan, Windows World Taiwan; **THAILAND:** Publish in Asia, Thai Computerworld; **TURKEY:** Computerworld Turkiye, Macworld Turkiye, Network World Turkiye, PC World Turkiye; **UKRAINE:** Computerworld Kiev, Multimedia World Ukraine, PC World Ukraine; **UNITED KINGDOM:** Acorn User UK, Amiga Action UK, Amiga Computing UK, Apple Talk UK, Computing, Macworld, Parents and Computers UK, PC Advisor, PC Home, PSX Pro, The WEB; **UNITED STATES:** Cable in the Classroom, CIO Magazine, Computerworld, DOS World, Federal Computer Week, GamePro Magazine, InfoWorld, I-Way, Macworld, Network World, PC Games, PC World, Publish, Video Event, THE WEB Magazine, and WebMaster; online webzines: JavaWorld, NetscapeWorld, and SunWorld Online; **URUGUAY:** InfoWorld Uruguay; **VENEZUELA:** Computerworld Venezuela, PC World Venezuela; and **VIETNAM:** PC World Vietnam. 3/24/97

Dedication

This book is dedicated affectionately to the intersection of 24th Street and Mission Street.

Author's Acknowledgments

I would like to thank the usual suspects at IDG for giving me the chance to write this book and for helping me complete it. My thanks go especially to Acquisitions Editor Gareth Hancock, who has given me many wonderful opportunities to write books for IDG, this book included.

I also owe a big debt of gratitude to Project Editor Rev Mengle, who offered excellent suggestions for improving this book, kept everything on track, and was very cheerful throughout. I would also like to thank Senior Copy Editor Diane Smith and Copy Editor Brian Kramer for probing so tenderly with the editorial scalpel. These Hoosiers at IDG's offices in Indianapolis gave their best to my book, and for that I am very grateful.

My thanks also go to Sharon Duffy for her excellent index, and to Technical Editor Allen Wyatt, who followed doggedly in my footsteps to make sure that all the instructions in this book are completely accurate.

I would also like to thank Arlette Cox of Microsoft Corporation for helping me obtain beta copies of Money 98 and answering my questions.

Finally, thanks go to my nuclear family — Sofia, Henry, and Addie — for not going ballistic while I worked long hours to meet my deadlines.

Peter Weverka

San Francisco

September, 1997

Publisher's Acknowledgments

We're proud of this book; please register your comments through our IDG Books Worldwide Online Registration Form located at http://my2cents.dummies.com.

Some of the people who helped bring this book to market include the following:

Acquisitions, Development, and Editorial

Project Editor: Rev Mengle

Acquisitions Editor: Gareth Hancock

Media Development Manager: Joyce Pepple

Permissions Editor: Heather Heath Dismore

Copy Editors: Susan Diane Smith, Brian Kramer

Technical Editor: Allen Wyatt

Editorial Manager: Colleen Rainsberger

Editorial Assistants: Donna Love, Darren Meiss

Production

Associate Project Coordinator: Karen York

Layout and Graphics: Steve Arany, Lou Boudreau, J. Tyler Connor, Angela F. Hunckler, Todd Klemme, Anna Rohrer, Brent Savage

Proofreaders: Laura L. Bowman, Kelli Botta, Nancy Price, Janet Withers

Indexer: Sharon Duffy

Special Help: Stephanie Koutek, Proof Editor

General and Administrative

IDG Books Worldwide, Inc.: John Kilcullen, CEO; Steven Berkowitz, President and Publisher

IDG Books Technology Publishing: Brenda McLaughlin, Senior Vice President and Group Publisher

Dummies Technology Press and Dummies Editorial: Diane Graves Steele, Vice President and Associate Publisher; Mary Bednarek, Acquisitions and Product Development Director; Kristin A. Cocks, Editorial Director

Dummies Trade Press: Kathleen A. Welton, Vice President and Publisher; Kevin Thornton, Acquisitions Manager

IDG Books Production for Dummies Press: Beth Jenkins, Production Director; Cindy L. Phipps, Manager of Project Coordination, Production Proofreading, and Indexing; Kathie S. Schutte, Supervisor of Page Layout; Shelley Lea, Supervisor of Graphics and Design; Debbie J. Gates, Production Systems Specialist; Robert Springer, Supervisor of Proofreading; Debbie Stailey, Special Projects Coordinator; Tony Augsburger, Supervisor of Reprints and Bluelines; Leslie Popplewell, Media Archive Coordinator

Dummies Packaging and Book Design: Patti Crane, Packaging Specialist; Lance Kayser, Packaging Assistant; Kavish + Kavish, Cover Design

◆

The publisher would like to give special thanks to Patrick J. McGovern, without whom this book would not have been possible.

◆

Contents at a Glance

Cartoons at a Glance

By Rich Tennant

page 147

page 299

page 5

page 107

page 183

page 271

Fax: 508-546-7747 • E-mail: the5wave@tiac.net

Table of Contents

· ·

Introduction

Microsoft Money 98 has made it very easy to manage your personal finances. Well, not "very easy," but close to it. With Money 98, you don't need a bookkeeper to track your finances. You don't need an accountant or financial counselor, either. And you don't need to be a computer expert. All you need is to know how to use Money 98.

After you have read this book and started using the techniques I describe here, you will know how to record financial transactions, how much you spend in different areas, and what your net worth is. You will know what your investments (if you have any) are worth and roughly how much you owe in taxes. You will know how to print checks, generate reports and charts that show in clear terms what your spending habits are, plan for retirement, compare mortgages and loans, and analyze different kinds of investments.

Most important, you will be able to make wise financial decisions by taking advantage of the program's numerous financial analysis tools, all of which are explained in this book. And you will also make wise decisions because you will have the raw data on hand. After you record transactions in Money, the raw data is right there inside your computer. I show you how to analyze it, scrutinize it, dissect it, investigate it, and contemplate it. I show you how to admire it, too. After you read this book, you can start admiring what a financial wizard you have become.

Whom This Book Is For

This book is for users of Money 98 who want to get to the heart of the program without futzing around. Don't look in this book to find out how Money works. Look in this book to find out how *you* can manage *your finances* with Money.

I show you everything you need to know to stay on top of your finances — from recording checks and deposits to tracking investments. On the way, you have a laugh or two. And you can shed light on parts of your finances that have never seen the light of day before.

What's in This Book, Anyway?

This book is jam-packed with instructions, advice, shortcuts, and tips for getting the most out of Money. Here's a bare outline of the six parts of this book:

- ✔ **Part I: Setting Up and Starting Out:** Part I spells out everything you need to know to use Money wisely. It explains how to find your way around the Money windows, set up accounts, record transactions, categorize your spending and income, reconcile an account, and print checks.

- ✔ **Part II: Going Online with Money:** If you have a modem and you are connected to the Internet, you are invited to go online and take advantage of Money's online features. Among other high-tech tasks, Part II explains how to download bank statements over the Internet, pay bills online, and update your investment portfolio by getting security prices from the Internet.

- ✔ **Part III: Getting Your Money's Worth:** In Part III, you discover how to budget with Money, schedule bill payments so you make them on time, and do the mundane chores, such as backing up your financial data, that make Money run more smoothly.

- ✔ **Part IV: Improving Your Financial Picture:** Part IV explains how to generate reports and graphs so you see exactly where you stand financially, plan for your retirement and other future events, analyze investments and loans, track your assets and liabilities, and monitor the performance of your investments.

- ✔ **Part V: Money and the Small Business Manager:** For business managers, Part V describes how to track the bills you receive and the bills you send out, as well as handle a payroll in Money.

- ✔ **Part VI: The Part of Tens:** Each of the four chapters in Part VI offers ten tidbits of advice — advice for staying on top of your finances, improving your financial health, using Money if you are self-employed, and converting from Quicken to Money.

But wait — there's more! Turn to Appendix A to find out how to install Money, Appendix B to get basic instructions in Windows 95, and Appendix C to look up the computer and financial terms that appear in this book.

Foolish Assumptions about You

Please forgive me, but I made one or two foolish assumptions about you, the reader of this book. I assumed that

- ✔ You use a Windows operating system, either Windows 95 or Windows NT.

- ✔ You own a copy of either Microsoft Money 98 or the Microsoft Money 98 Financial Suite. (Appendix A explains how to install Money.)

- ✔ Your computer system is capable of running Money. To run the program, you need 12MB of RAM (16MB is recommended) if you have Windows 95, or 16MB of RAM (24MB is recommended) if you have Windows NT. As for your computer, you need at least a 486 or higher microprocessor; a Pentium or higher is recommended.

- ✔ You are kind to foreign tourists and small animals.

Conventions Used in This Book

I want you to understand all the instructions in this book, and in that spirit I've adopted a few conventions.

To show you how to give commands, I use the ⇨ symbol. For example, you can choose Go⇨Reports to go to the Reports & Charts window in Money. The ⇨ is just a shorthand method of saying "Choose Reports from the Go menu."

Notice how the *G* in Go and the *R* in Reports are underlined in the preceding paragraph. Those same characters are underlined in the command names in Money. Underlined letters are called *hot keys*. You can press them to give commands and make selections in dialog boxes. Where a letter is underlined in a command name or in a dialog box, it is also underlined in the step-by-step instructions in this book.

Besides pressing hot keys to give commands, you can press combinations of keys. For example, you can also go to the Reports & Charts window by pressing Ctrl+Shift+R. In other words, hold down the Ctrl key and Shift key and press the R key at the same time. Where you see Ctrl+, Alt+, or Shift+ and a key name or key names, press the keys simultaneously.

Where you see boldface letters in this book, it means to type the letters. For example, "Type **Where Did the Money Go?** in the Report name text box," means to do exactly that: Type **Where Did the Money Go?**

Dig These Special Icons

To help you get the most out of this book, I've placed icons here and there. Here's what the icons mean:

Next to the Tip icon, you can find shortcuts and tricks of the trade to make your visit to Moneyland more enjoyable.

Where you see the Warning icon, tread softly and carefully. It means that you are about to do something you may regret later.

When I explain a juicy little fact that bears remembering, I mark it with a Remember icon. When you see this icon, prick up your ears. You will find out something that you have to remember throughout your adventures with Money.

When I am forced to describe high-tech stuff, a Technical Stuff icon appears in the margin. Good news: You will find only two Technical Stuff icons in this entire book (I don't like technical stuff any more than you do). The first reader who finds both Technical Stuff icons wins a free trip to the Happyland Desert Park in Blythe, California (just kidding!).

Here and there, Money and the Money Financial Suite work differently (they better work differently — the Financial Suite costs $40 more). To mark instructions that apply only to the Financial Suite, a Money Financial Suite icon appears in the margin.

I'd Like to Hear from You!

If you have a question about using Money, a comment about this book, or a shortcut you want to share with readers of the next edition of this book, let me know. I am being held hostage at Peter_Weverka@msn.com. Send an e-mail message to that address. All messages are welcome, as they help me pass my dreary days in captivity.

Part I
Setting Up and Starting Out

The 5th Wave
By Rich Tennant

"WHAT EXACTLY ARE WE SAYING HERE?"

In this part . . .

Hello, this is your captain speaking. Thank you for flying Money. In the next six chapters, you can take off, soar above the clouds, and discover the basics of tracking your finances with Microsoft Money 98.

Please observe the "Fasten your seat belt" sign. And if I ask you to hold your breath and flap your arms to help the plane stay aloft, please do so promptly.

Chapter 1

Introducing Money

- -

In This Chapter

▶ Understanding how Money tracks your finances

▶ Starting the program

▶ Getting acquainted with the Money screens

▶ Shutting down the Money program

▶ Getting help from the Help program

- -

Chapter 1 is where you get your feet wet. Don't be shy. Walk right to the shore and sink your toes in the water. Don't worry; I won't push you from behind. Not so bad, is it?

In this chapter, you discover the various ways that Money 98 can help you stay on top of your finances. You also discover how to start the program and find your way around the Money screen. Finally, in case you get desperate, this chapter explains how to seek help with the Money Help program.

Finding Out How Money Tracks Your Finances

All the personal finance advisors agree that keeping good, accurate records is the first step toward financial security. Before you can start saving for a down payment on a house, you have to know how much you are capable of saving. Before you can tell if your investments are doing well, you have to track them carefully. If you want to make sound financial decisions, you need to know what your spending habits are and how much income you really have.

Microsoft Money 98 makes keeping accurate financial records very, very easy. After you have used the program for a while, you will know precisely what your account balances are, what your net worth is, and how much your investments — if you have investments — are worth. To find out how much you spend in different areas, all you have to do is generate a graph like the one in Figure 1-1. At tax time, you can run a report that lists and totals all your tax-deductible expenses. With Money, you can print checks, do your banking over the Internet, find out exactly what your spending habits are, compare loans and mortgages, plan for retirement, and analyze different kinds of investments.

Entering data correctly in Money is essential. Money can't do its job well unless you carefully and conscientiously enter financial data. If all you want to do is balance your savings and checking accounts, you've got it made, because Money offers lots of opportunities for double-checking the accuracy of transactions in savings and checking accounts. However, to track investments and loans, draw up a budget, or do a handful of other sophisticated things, you need to be careful when you enter the data.

Starting the Program

Starting Money is as easy as falling off a log. The following pages explain how to start Money from the Programs menu and how to start the program by double-clicking its shortcut icon. Because you can't double-click the shortcut icon until you create it, I explain how to create a shortcut icon for Money. For first-time users of Money, these pages also explain how to create a file for storing your financial records.

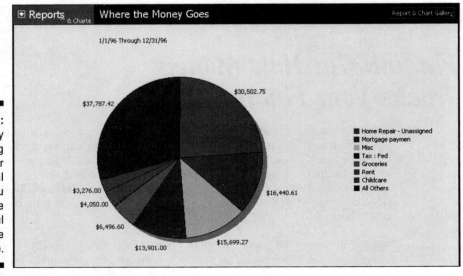

Figure 1-1:
By carefully entering your financial data, you can create meaningful graphs like this one.

Starting Money from the Programs menu

Follow these steps to start the program:

1. **Click the Start button in the lower-left corner of your screen.**

   The Start button is on the left side of the Windows taskbar. When you click it, a menu appears.

2. **Click <u>P</u>rograms on the menu.**

   Yet another menu appears with the names of computer programs.

3. **Click Microsoft Money.**

   You may have a little trouble finding Microsoft Money if a number of Microsoft programs are loaded on your computer, as is the case with the computer whose desktop is shown in Figure 1-2.

The first thing you see when you start the program is the Home screen. It looks confusing at first, doesn't it? Don't worry about that, because there is method in this madness, as you find out shortly.

The fastest way to start Money is to double-click its shortcut icon. Read on to find out how to create a shortcut icon for Money.

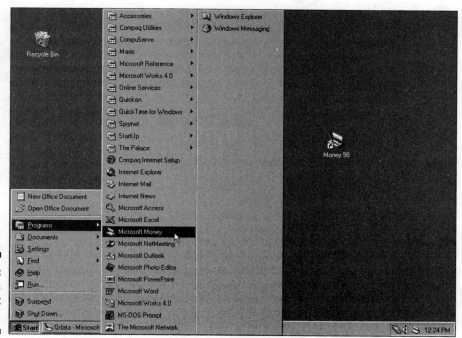

Figure 1-2:
Starting
Microsoft
Money.

If you have never used Money before

If you have never used Money before and are not upgrading from an earlier version of the program, you see the File Required dialog box after you start the program for the first time. The dialog box tells you in so many words that you need to create a new file for storing financial transactions. Follow these steps to create the file:

1. **Click the Open File button in the File Required dialog box.**

   You see the Open dialog box shown in the figure.

2. **In the File name text box, type a name for your new file.**

   File names can be many characters long (255 characters, if you want to know the whole truth) and can include blank spaces. However, a file name cannot include these characters: " / \ [ ] : ( ) * | < > = ; , ?.

3. **Click the New button.**

   You see the New dialog box. The name you typed in Step 2 appears in the File name box.

4. **Click the OK button.**

   After a moment, you see the Home screen. You're ready to go.

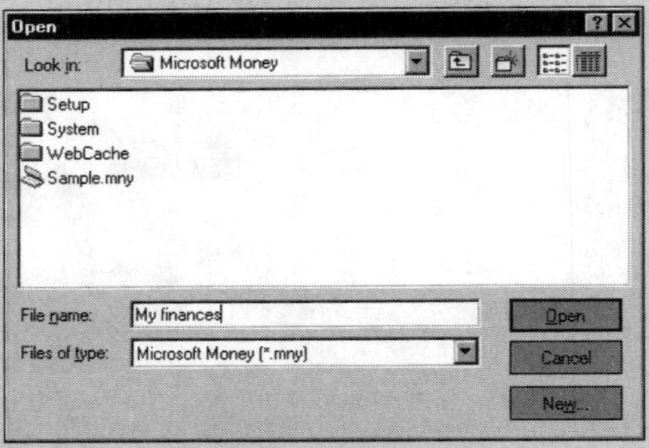

Creating a shortcut icon for Money

Besides starting at the Programs menu, you can start Money by double-clicking its shortcut icon on the desktop. As Figure 1-2 shows, the shortcut icon looks like a check book. If you intend to use the program often, do yourself a favor and create a shortcut icon. You can save a little time that way.

Follow these steps to create a shortcut icon for Money:

1. **Choose Start⇨Programs⇨Windows Explorer (or Windows NT Explorer).**

   In other words, click the Start button on the Windows taskbar, choose Programs from the menu that appears, and choose Windows Explorer from the Programs menu.

   Windows Explorer opens. Among other things, the left side of Windows Explorer lists folders on the C drive of your computer. The folders are in alphabetical order. The following three steps explain how to open the Microsoft Money folder and select the file that runs Money so you can create a shortcut to it.

2. **Find the Program Files folder and click the plus sign to its left.**

   As shown in Figure 1-3, the plus sign turns into a minus sign and all the folders in the Program Files folder appear. If you look down the list of folders, you soon find one called Microsoft Money.

3. **Click the Microsoft Money folder.**

   This time, don't click the plus sign to the left of the folder. Be sure to click the folder itself. When you do so, the folders and files inside the Microsoft Money folder appear on the right side of the Windows Explorer screen.

Figure 1-3:
Creating a shortcut icon for Money. After you create the shortcut icon, all you have to do to start Money is double-click the shortcut icon.

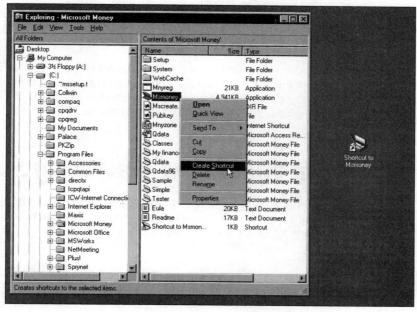

4. **Look down the list of folders and files on the right side of the screen and click the file called Msmoney.**

   Msmoney is the application file that runs whenever you run Money. Having selected the file, you are almost ready to create a shortcut to it. First, however, you may have to shrink the Windows Explorer screen so that you can see the Windows desktop. Complete Step 5 if Explorer fills your entire screen.

5. **Click the Restore button in the upper-right corner of the Windows Explorer screen.**

   The Restore button shows one square overlapping another. When you click the Restore button, you see patches of the Windows desktop, as shown in Figure 1-3.

6. **Right-click the Msmoney file and choose Create Shortcut from the shortcut menu (see Figure 1-3).**

   On the bottom of the folders and file list on the right side of the Windows Explorer screen, you see a small shortcut icon and the words "Shortcut to Msmoney." The words are highlighted.

7. **Click the highlighted words and, holding down the mouse button, drag the words and icon away from the Windows Explorer screen and onto the desktop; then release the mouse button.**

   Congratulations — you just created a shortcut icon called "Shortcut to Msmoney." Now all you have to do to start Money is double-click the shortcut icon you created.

8. **Click the Close button (the X) in the upper-right corner of the Windows Explorer to close Windows Explorer.**

You can drag shortcut icons anywhere on the desktop. You may tuck your new icon into a corner, for example. To shorten the icon's name, right-click it, choose Rename from the shortcut menu, and then type **Money 98** (or whatever you please) in the text box below the icon.

Taking a Fast Trip around the Money Screens

When they arrive in a foreign city, the first thing most people do after they find a hotel room and take a shower is go for a stroll. In the following pages, you can stroll very gingerly across the Money screens. Enjoy yourself and take your sweet time. And don't forget to put film in the camera before leaving the hotel.

The Home screen

When you start Money, the first thing you see is the *Home screen*, which is shown in Figure 1-4. The Home screen is the starting point for all your excursions in Money. If the screen looks familiar, it isn't because you visited it in a past life. No, the screen looks familiar because it's modeled after a site on the World Wide Web. Notice the splashy graphics. If you roll the mouse carefully to the right side of the Home screen, you even find a *hyperlink* — a link you can click to visit a site on the World Wide Web. In this case, you can click to visit the Money site.

Other than the gratuitous advertising that Microsoft has stuck on the right side of the Home screen, the two most important features on the screen are:

- **Tip of the Day:** Tips are there to alert you to parts of Money that you may not discover on your own.

- **Chart of the Day:** These charts offer a glimpse of your financial position — a rosy glimpse, I hope. By moving the pointer over a pie slice or bar in a chart, you can see the monetary figure that the pie slice or bar represents. The Chart of the Day changes each time you open the Money program.

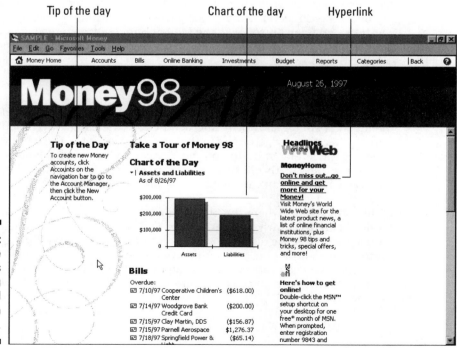

Tip of the day   Chart of the day   Hyperlink

Figure 1-4:
The Home screen is the starting point for all activity in Money.

Notice the Money Home button in the upper-left corner of the screen. No matter how far you stray from the Home screen, you can always click the Money Home button to return to the Home screen. The button is always there. Click it if you get homesick.

If you don't want the Home screen to appear first when you start the program, follow these steps:

1. **Choose Tools⇨Options.**

   The Options dialog box appears.

2. **Click the General tab.**

3. **Click the arrow to see the drop-down list under Display, and select the screen you would like to see when you start the program.**

4. **Click the OK button.**

Going from place to place: The Navigation bar, Go menu, and Back button

Besides clicking the Money Home button to return to the Home screen, you can also go from screen to screen by clicking a button on the Navigation bar, by using the Go menu, or by clicking the Back button. The Navigation bar buttons and Back button, like the Money Home button, are always available and ready to be clicked. And you can also open the Go menu whenever you wish.

The Navigation bar

The *Navigation bar* is the strip along the top of the screen right below the menu bar. (I don't know why Microsoft chose the name Navigation bar. On most ships, the navigator sits in the wheelhouse, not in the bar.) Money Home is the left-most button on the Navigation bar; the Back button is the right-most button. By clicking one of the buttons between the Money Home and Back button, you can visit other windows in Money.

Table 1-1 explains where the buttons on the Navigation bar take you. The table is here to show you what happens when you click a button and to give you a glimpse of the different tasks you can do with Money. By the way, the buttons are a little odd; they appear to be menu names and don't have rectangles you can "press" as you can the buttons in most computer programs. But they are buttons, I assure you. Try clicking one to see what I mean.

Table 1-1   Navigation Bar Buttons and Where They Take You

Clicking This Button	*Takes You to . . .*
Money Home	The Home screen, where you see the Chart of the Day and the Tip of the Day.
Accounts	The Account Manager window, where you set up new accounts and open account registers. If you have already opened an account register since you started Money, clicking the Accounts button takes you to an account register.
Bills	The Bill Calendar window, where you can record the bills you pay regularly and enlist the Money program's help in paying those bills on time.
Online Banking	The Home Banking & Investments window, where Money offers its online services. After you sign up for the services, you can pay bills over the Internet without having to write paper checks, find out which transactions have cleared a bank account, download bank statements, and transfer money between accounts.
Investments	The Investment Portfolio window, where you can monitor stocks, bonds, mutual funds, and other investment holdings.
Budget (or Planner*)	The Budget & Savings (or Goal Planner) window, where you can formulate a budget, reckon the price of a loan or mortgage, plan for retirement, calculate the cost of a college education, and estimate how investments grow over time.
Reports	The Reports & Charts window, where you can generate reports and charts that show right away where you stand financially.
Money Insider*	The Insider window, where you can rummage for expert advice from what Microsoft calls "the nation's top money experts."
Categories	The Categories & Payees window, where the people and businesses to whom you've made payments are listed. Also on this screen is the list of categories and classifications with which you describe the payments you make.
Back	The window you looked at previously.

* Only available in the Money 98 Financial Suite.

Deciding what appears on the Chart of the Day

The Chart of the Day changes day by day, but you can decide for yourself which chart appears in the Chart of the Day box by following these steps:

1. **Click the small triangle to the left side of the Chart of the Day title.**

2. **Select a chart from the list, or, to make the chart change each time you open the program, select the Change Chart Each Day option.**

The Go menu

The Go menu is an alternative to the buttons on the Navigation bar. Choose Go and a menu with a bunch of window names appears — the very same names that appear on the Navigation bar. Click a window name, and you go to that window.

The Back button

 Clicking the Back button takes you to the last screen you looked at, whatever it happened to be. Click the Back button if you hastily leave a screen and regret having done so. Money remembers the screens you visit. By clicking the Back button several times over, you can travel backward to a screen you visited several minutes before.

Shutting Down Money

When the time comes to close the Money program and get on with your real life, do one of the following:

- ✔ Click the Close button (the X in the far upper-right corner of the program window).
- ✔ Choose File➪Exit.
- ✔ Press Alt+F4.

 Veteran computer users are accustomed to saving files before exiting a program, but that isn't necessary with Money because the program saves data as soon as you enter it. If you look for a Save command or button in Money, you will look in vain — there isn't one.

When you shut down Money, the last thing you see is the Back Up dialog box shown in Figure 1-5. This dialog box makes backing up the data you just entered in Money very easy, and I strongly recommend taking advantage of it. Chapter 12 explains everything you need to know about backing up a data file. For now, click the Back Up button to be done with it.

Figure 1-5:
The Back
Up dialog
box is your
cue to
make a
backup
copy of the
Money file.

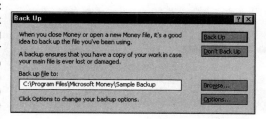

Getting Help When You Need It

From time to time, you may have to try your luck with the Help program when you don't know how to complete a task. Is the Money Help program worth using? Sometimes it is, and sometimes it isn't.

As the following pages explain, Money offers three ways to seek help:

✔ By using the Money Help program.

✔ By clicking the Help button on the Navigation bar.

✔ By pressing F1 or by right-clicking and choosing What's This? from the shortcut menu.

The Help program is a standard Windows 95 Help program. If you already know how the Contents tab, Index tab, and Find tab in Windows 95 Help programs work, you can close this book and eat a pastrami sandwich. Otherwise, read on. The pages that follow explain how the Help program works, what the Help button on the Navigation bar does, and how to get help with on-screen options.

Asking the Help program for assistance

Go to the Help program when you want comprehensive instructions for doing a task. To open the Help program, choose Help⇨Help Topics. The Help program window shown in Figure 1-6 appears. On the window are three tabs for finding the instructions you need: Contents, Index, and Find.

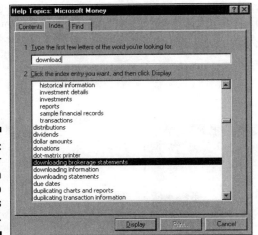

Figure 1-6:
Looking for
help on
the Help
program's
Index tab.

✔ **Contents tab:** The Contents tab works like a book's table of contents. Beside each topic is a book icon. Double-click the icon and you see a list of subtopics, each with a question mark by its name. By double-clicking a question mark or clicking it and then clicking Display, you can get instructions.

✔ **Index tab:** My favorite is the Index tab, which works like the index at the back of a book. Click the Index tab and type a few letters that describe the subject that puzzles you. The alphabetical list of index topics scrolls down so you can see which topics are available. If a topic strikes your fancy, double-click it or click it and then click the Display button. You see an instruction list or other help feature.

✔ **Find tab:** The Find tab is the least efficient means of getting instructions, but sometimes you have to resort to it if the Contents and Index tabs fail. The Find tab is for searching for specific words in Help files. For example, if you need help with currency conversions, type **currency** on the Find tab. A list of topics whose instructions include the word *currency* appears at the bottom of the dialog box. Click a topic and then click Display.

The Help program appears in its own window. As such, you can maximize it, minimize it, or drag it into a corner. In fact, you may try dragging the Help program window into a corner of the screen and reading its instructions as you do a task. Appendix B explains how to minimize, maximize, and drag windows.

Menu commands in instruction windows

After you arrive at an instruction window, you can take advantage of the menu commands in the Help program window to do the following nifty things:

✔ **Printing:** To print an instruction list and perhaps tack it to a bulletin board so you don't have to search for it again, choose File⇨Print Topic and click OK in the Print dialog box.

✔ **Copying:** Copy instructions to the Clipboard by choosing Edit⇨Copy or pressing Ctrl+C. To copy only a few lines, drag the cursor over them before choosing the Copy command.

✔ **Bookmarking:** Try bookmarking the instruction lists that you go to often. That way, you can find them in a hurry. To bookmark an instruction list, choose Bookmark⇨Define, enter a name in the Bookmark Define dialog box, and click OK. To go to an instruction list that you bookmarked, pull down the Bookmark menu and choose a bookmark name.

✔ **Going backward:** The Help program keeps track of the screens you visit on your journey to find the right set of instructions. Click the Back button to revisit screens you visited before.

Getting help with a screen or window

 Another way to seek help is to click the Help button, the question mark on the right side of the Navigation bar. Clicking the Help button yields a list of topics that pertain to the screen or window you are in. For example, I clicked the Help button in the Categories & Payees window and got the topics shown in Figure 1-7.

Move the pointer over a topic that interests you and click. You see a step-by-step list of instructions for completing a task.

To return to the list of topics, click the Back button in the Help window. Sometimes the instructions you get by clicking the Help button aren't detailed enough. Try appealing to the more powerful Help program. To get there, click the Contents or Index button in the Help window. The section, "Asking the Help program for assistance," in this chapter explains how the Contents and Index tabs work.

Getting help with on-screen options

Last but not least, you can get explanations of options in dialog boxes and on windows by pressing F1 or by right-clicking and choosing What's This? from the shortcut menu. If you press F1 or choose What's This?, a box appears and describes the option that you want to know about.

Click to go to the Help program's
Contents or Index tab.

Click a topic to see step-by-step instructions.

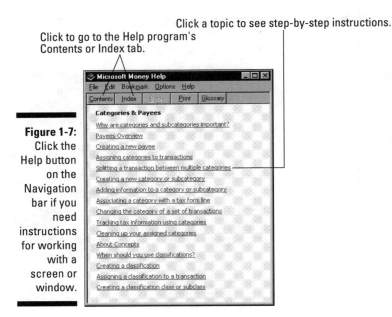

Figure 1-7:
Click the
Help button
on the
Navigation
bar if you
need
instructions
for working
with a
screen or
window.

The only way to get an explanation of a button is to right-click it. You can't select a button and press F1 because the only way to select a button is to click it, and that activates the button. In Figure 1-8, I right-clicked the Don't Back Up button in the Back Up dialog box and chose What's This? from the shortcut menu. The Help box tells me that clicking the button closes the dialog box without creating a backup file.

Figure 1-8:
You can get
brief
explanations
of options
and buttons
in dialog
boxes
and on
windows.

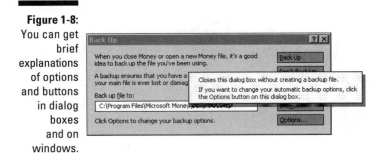

Chapter 2

Setting Up Your Accounts

. . . .

In This Chapter

▶ Understanding how accounts and registers record financial activity

▶ Identifying the thirteen kinds of accounts

▶ Setting up a checking and savings account

▶ Listing account numbers, contact persons, and the like

▶ Changing account names and types

▶ Setting up a credit card account

. . . .

Chapter 1 gets you going with Money. In this chapter, you get down to the nitty-gritty: how to set up accounts so that you can track financial activity.

In this chapter, you discover how to set up savings, checking, and credit card accounts. You also find out about Money files, how to put an account on the Favorites menu, and how to change account names and account types.

Accounts and Registers for Recording Financial Transactions

The first step in tracking your financial activity is to set up an account for each thing you want to track — a checking account, a savings account, an IRA. When most people hear the word "account," they think of savings accounts, checking accounts, and other kinds of bank accounts. But accounts in Money are a little more than that. For example, you can create a house account for tracking the value of a house. And you can create a credit card account for tracking credit card charges.

When you set up an account, you are asked to name the kind of account you want. Money offers thirteen kinds of accounts. Table 2-1 describes the different kinds of Money accounts and mentions where you can turn to read more about them.

Table 2-1	The Thirteen Kinds of Accounts
Account	*What the Account Is for*
Asset	Tracking the value of things that you own — real estate, a truck, a baseball card collection. Asset accounts can be useful for finding out your net worth. See Chapter 16.
Bank	Recording transactions made to a bank account, but not a savings account, checking account, or line of credit.
Cash	Recording cash payments and tracking petty cash accounts. See Chapter 18.
Checking	Recording activity in a checking account. See "The Basics: Setting Up Checking, Savings, and Credit Card Accounts" in this chapter. Chapter 3 explains how to record transactions in checking accounts.
Credit card	Recording credit card purchases, usurious finance charges, and credit card payments. See "The Basics: Setting Up Checking, Savings, and Credit Card Accounts" in this chapter. Turn to Chapter 3 as well.
House	Tracking how much equity is in a house and determining a house's market value. See Chapter 16.
Investment	Tracking the value of something you own and intend to sell later for a profit — stocks, bonds, securities, annuities, treasury bills, precious metals, real estate investment trusts (REITs), and unit trusts. See Chapter 17.
Liability	Tracking debts for which you don't have to pay interest — income taxes owed and private loans, for example. See Chapter 16.
Line of credit	Recording payments made with a *debit card* — a charge card that debits, or deducts money from, a bank account. See "The Basics: Setting Up Checking, Savings, and Credit Card Accounts" in this chapter and read Chapter 3 as well.
Loan	Tracking debts for which you have to pay interest, such as mortgages and car loans. See Chapter 16.

Account	What the Account Is for
Other	Recording transactions that — you guessed it — don't fit neatly in the other twelve categories. *Hmmm.* I've been wracking my brain for an example of an account that doesn't fit into the other twelve categories, and for the life of me I can't think of one. Maybe this account is where laundered money is kept.
Retirement	Tracking tax-deferred retirement plans, such as 401(k)s, Keoghs, SEPs (Simplified Employee Pensions), and IRAs. See Chapter 17.
Savings	Recording activity in a savings account. See "The Basics: Setting Up Checking, Savings, and Credit Card Accounts" in this chapter. Chapter 3 explains how to record transactions in a savings account.

Each time you set up an account, Money creates a new register for recording transactions. As all bookkeepers know, a *register* is a place for recording income and expenses, withdrawals, deposits, payments, and the like. Figure 2-1 shows a credit card account register for recording purchases, finance charges, and payments to the card issuer.

Registers look different, depending on what kind of account you have set up, but all have places for recording transaction dates and transaction amounts. Registers also show balances. The *balance* is the amount of money in the account, or, in the case of an asset, liability, or investment account, the value of the thing being tracked.

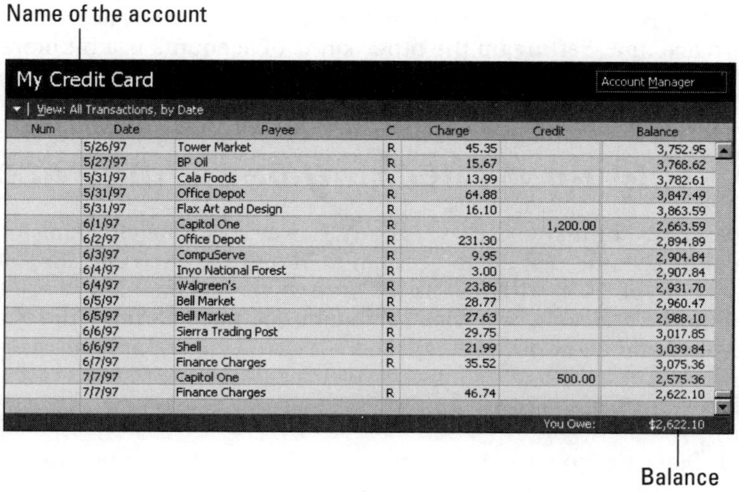

Name of the account

Figure 2-1:
A credit
card
account
register.

Balance

A word about Money files

When you install Money, the program gives you the opportunity to create a file for storing your transactions. Chances are that file is the only one you need, but some rare birds do require a second file. Create more than one file if:

- You intend to use Money to track your personal finances and your business finances, and you want to keep the two separate. Self-employed people don't necessarily need a second file. I'm self-employed, and I use the same file to track my personal and business transactions. But if you run a small business, you absolutely

need a separate file. The basic idea is: If you submit a separate tax return for your business and yourself, you need two Money files.

- Someone besides yourself uses your computer to track his or her finances with Money.
- You track someone else's finances.

Chapter 18 explains how to create a second file. Chapter 18 is the first of three chapters that explain the whys and wherefores of managing a small business with Money.

The Basics: Setting Up Checking, Savings, and Credit Card Accounts

Enough, already. Now that you've glimpsed the big picture and know what an account and register are, you can create an account. In the next sections, you find out how to set up a checking account, savings account, and credit card account. Setting up the other kinds of accounts is a bit more complicated and is explained elsewhere in this book (Table 2-1 mentions where).

Setting up a checking or savings account

Everybody, or just about everybody, has at least one checking and one savings account. Set up an account in Money for each checking and savings account you keep with a bank. Be sure to get out the paperwork before you set up the checking or savings account. You need to know the account number and a few other details.

Follow these steps to set up the account:

1. **Starting from the Home screen, click the Accounts button.**

   You land on the Account Manager window (if you don't get there straight away, click the Account Manager button in the upper-right corner of the screen).

My Checking Account

After you are done creating your new account, its name and a passbook icon appear on this screen.

2. Click the New Account button.

You can find this button along the bottom of the window. When you click it, you see the first of several New Account dialog boxes like the one shown in Figure 2-2. Each dialog box asks a nosy question about your account.

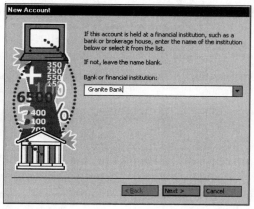

Figure 2-2:
To set up a new account, fill out a bunch of dialog boxes like this one.

3. Enter the name of the bank or financial institution in which you keep the account, and click the Next button.

If you have another account with the bank and have set up an account in Money for tracking it, you can enter the bank's name by clicking the down-arrow and selecting a bank name from the drop-down list.

4. In the next dialog box, select the type of account you want to create — Checking or Savings — and then click Next.

Table 2-1 explains what the account types are. You can also read their descriptions in the dialog box.

5. Type a descriptive name for the account and then click the Next button.

The name you type will appear on the Account Manager window. Enter a descriptive name so you can distinguish this account from the others you set up in Money.

6. In the next dialog box, select the option that best describes why you opened the account; then click Next.

Money offers four ways to classify the account. These classifications are used for budgeting and for devising saving plans, among other reasons.

7. **Enter the account number and click Next.**

   The dialog box you see next asks for the balance (how much money is in the account).

8. **Enter a figure for the account balance and click Next.**

   Knowing the balance isn't as important as you may think because you can change the starting balance after the account has been set up by changing the first entry in the register.

   More power to you if you know the starting balance and you have diligently kept records so that you can enter past transactions and bring the account up-to-date. But if you don't know the opening balance, either enter the balance from your last bank statement or make an estimate. Chapter 3 explains the ins and outs of starting balances.

9. **Either select I have no other accounts or I have other accounts and click the Next button.**

   This dialog box wants to know if you keep other accounts at the same bank where you keep this account.

   Clicking I have no other accounts takes you to the Account Manager window, where you see a new passbook icon and the account name you entered in Step 5.

   Clicking I have other accounts takes you to the dialog box for selecting an account type. Follow Steps 4 through 9 again to give Money the lowdown on the next account.

Telling Money about the account details

Before you put away the paperwork and say good-bye to the account you set up, take a moment to acquaint Money with the details. As Figure 2-3 shows, the program has a special Account Details window for entering a bank's telephone number, an account's minimum balance, and anything else you care to enter.

The Account Details window is a handy place to store bank telephone numbers and other information. If you lose your passbook or ATM card and need to call the bank, for example, you can get the number from the Account Details window. The window also has a check box for making an account appear on the Favorites menu.

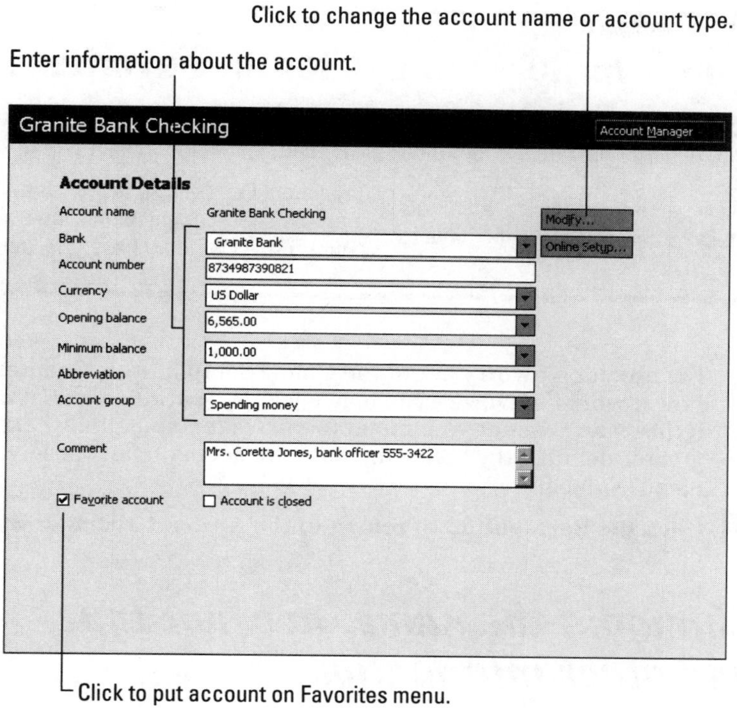

Click to change the account name or account type.

Enter information about the account.

Granite Bank Checking

Account Manager

Account Details

Account name   Granite Bank Checking   Modify...

Bank   Granite Bank   Online Setup...

Account number   8734987390821

Currency   US Dollar

Opening balance   6,565.00

Minimum balance   1,000.00

Abbreviation

Account group   Spending money

Comment   Mrs. Coretta Jones, bank officer 555-3422

☑ Favorite account   ☐ Account is closed

Figure 2-3:
Keep information about accounts on the Account Details window, where you can get it in a hurry.

Click to put account on Favorites menu.

Follow these steps to get to the Account Details window and enter the pertinent information:

1. **Starting from the Account Manager window, click the name of the account whose Account Details window you want to see.**

   To get to the Account Manager window, choose Go➪Accounts or press Ctrl+Shift+A.

2. **Either right-click the account icon and choose Go to Details from the shortcut menu or choose Edit➪Go to Details.**

   You see the Account Details window (refer to Figure 2-3).

3. **Enter information about your account in the window.**

   In Figure 2-3, I entered a telephone number and the account's minimum balance, among other things.

Choosing favorite accounts for the Favorites menu

Checking accounts, credit card accounts, and other accounts that you have to dig into on a regular basis are good candidates for "favorite" status. The names of favorite accounts appear on the Favorites menu. All you have to do to open a favorite account is click Favorites and the name of the account.

To make an account a favorite account, click the Favorite account check box on the Account Details window (refer to Figure 2-3).

For now, don't worry about the Online Setup button. Chapter 7 explains how it works. However, you may click the Favorite account check box if this is an account you intend to open a lot, something I explain in greater detail in the "Choosing favorite accounts for the Favorites menu" sidebar.

4. **Click the Back button to return to the Account Manager window.**

Changing the name, account type, and other information

Suppose that you got it wrong. Suppose that you gave the account the wrong name or told Money that a checking account was a savings account. All is not lost. You can fix these grievous errors by returning to the Account Details window and clicking the Modify button.

Follow these steps to change the name and other information about an account:

1. **Go to the Account Manager window.**

   To get there, choose Go⇨Accounts or press Ctrl+Shift+A.

2. **Double-click the icon that represents the account that needs a change.**

   Double-clicking opens the account register. You can also open an account register by clicking its icon and then clicking the Go to Account button.

3. Click the Details button.

You land in the Account Details window (refer to Figure 2-3). From here, you can change the account number, the minimum balance, and other trivia. However, to change the account name or account type, you need to click the Modify button.

4. Click the Modify button.

The Modify Account dialog box appears, as shown in Figure 2-4.

Figure 2-4:
To change the account name or account type, click the Modify button in the Account Details window.

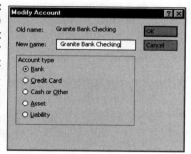

5. Make the necessary changes in the dialog box.

If you need to change the account's name, simply type a new one in the New name field. To change the account type, click an Account type button.

If you want to change account types but can't find a radio button on the list for the account type you want, you're out of luck. In its wisdom, Money puts radio buttons in the Modify Account dialog box only for accounts to which your account can be changed. Camels can't fly, nor can credit card accounts, for example, be changed into investment accounts.

6. Click OK to return to the Account Details window.

7. Click the Back button to return to the Account Manager window.

If all you want to do is change the name of an account, the fastest way is to select the account on the Account Manager window and either choose Edit⇔Rename or right-click and choose Rename from the shortcut menu. Then type a new name for the account in the box below its icon.

Setting up an account to track credit card and line of credit transactions

Except for filling out an extra dialog box or two, setting up a credit card or line of credit account works the same way as setting up a checking or savings account. Set up a credit card or line of credit account for each credit card and each line of credit you have. When you set up the account, Money asks how much you owe and whether you want to be reminded when the credit card or line of credit bill is due.

Money also asks for the name of the account from which you will pay the credit card or line of credit bill. Therefore, set up the checking or other kind of bank account with which you will pay the bill before you set up the credit card or line of credit account.

Get out your last credit card or line of credit statement and follow these steps to set up a credit card or line of credit account:

1. **Place the finger of your right hand on this page and, with your left hand, turn back several pages to the "Setting up a checking or savings account" section.**

2. **Follow Steps 1 through 7 (but not Step 4) of the instructions for setting up a checking or savings account.**

   In other words, go to the Account Manager window, click the New Account button, enter the name of the bank or credit card issuer, select Credit Card or Line of Credit as the account type, enter a descriptive name for the account, and enter the account number.

   That brings you to the dialog box shown in Figure 2-5, where Money asks how much you owe. I hope that you are all paid up and owe nothing, but if you resemble the average citizen, you owe the bank or credit card issuer some money.

3. **Enter 0 if the credit card or line of credit is paid in full; otherwise enter how much your last statement says that you owe, and then click Next after you are done.**

4. **Select the Credit card or Charge card option and click Next.**

   This dialog box asks whether your account will track a credit card or charge card. As the dialog box explains, charge cards have to be paid in full each month, but you can carry debt from month to month with a credit card.

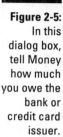

Figure 2-5:
In this
dialog box,
tell Money
how much
you owe the
bank or
credit card
issuer.

Select the Credit card option if the account will track credit card spending or a line of credit. Otherwise, select Charge card. If yours is a credit card that doesn't have to be paid in full but you intend to pay it off each month, click the Always pay entire balance each month check box.

What happens next depends on whether the account will track a credit card or charge card.

If the account will track a charge card, skip ahead to Step 6.

If the account will track a credit card or line of credit, the dialog box that appears asks you to list the interest rate you will be charged for carrying debt, as Figure 2-6 shows.

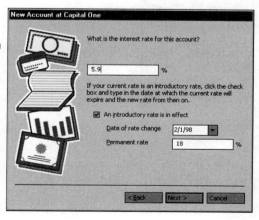

Figure 2-6:
In this
dialog box,
list the
interest rate
you will be
charged for
carrying
debt on a
credit card.

5. **Tell Money what rate of interest you will be charged for using the credit card and then click Next.**

   List the interest rate in the first % box. If the rate is a temporary, introductory rate, click the An introductory rate is in effect check box and enter the permanent rate and the date that the temporary rate expires. Money needs this information for the Debt Reduction Planner and other features designed to help you manage debt.

6. **In the dialog box that follows, enter the maximum amount that you can charge on your credit or charge card; then click Next.**

   The next dialog box is kind of misleading. It seems to say that if you pay your credit card bill in full each month, you should click the second radio button. But you should do no such thing. Click the second radio button only if you *don't* want to track the charges you run up on your credit card.

   Be sure to click the first radio button if you intend to track individual transactions for tax purposes or to find out where you spend your hard-earned income.

7. **Click the first or second radio button and then click Next.**

   As shown in Figure 2-7, the next dialog box asks if you want to put the monthly credit card or line of credit payment on the Bill Calendar. Chapter 11 explains how the Bill Calendar works. For now, all you need to know is that the Bill Calendar reminds you when bills are due. The notice appears on the Home screen where you can see it each time you start Money.

Figure 2-7:
From this dialog box, you can add the credit card or line of credit payment to the Bill Calendar and maybe pay the bill on time.

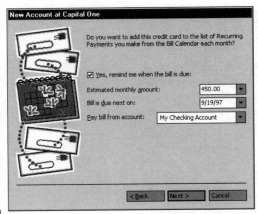

8. **If you want the bill to appear on the Bill Calendar, make sure that the Yes, remind me when the bill is due check box is checked; enter an estimate of how much you owe in an average month; and enter a date in the Bill is due next on box.**

I strongly recommend clicking the Yes, remind me when the bill is due check box, because credit cards and lines of credit can get very, very expensive if you don't work to pay them off or you forget to pay them on time. Banks charge outrageous interest rates on lines of credit and credit cards. A reminder to pay the bill can help keep you from being squeezed by creditors.

Credit card and line of credit bills fall due on the same day each month. Each month, Money reminds you five days before the payments are due.

9. **In the Pay bill from account drop-down list, select the account — probably a checking account — from which you will pay the bill, and then click Next.**

10. **Either select I have no other accounts and click Next to be done with it, or select I have other accounts and click the Next button.**

Capital One
Credit Card

Selecting I have no other accounts takes you to the Account Manager window, where you see a credit card icon and the name of your new account. Selecting I have other accounts takes you back to the dialog box for choosing an account type.

While your credit card or line of credit account is highlighted in the Account Manager window, right-click it and select Go to Details from the drop-down list. Then, in the Account Details window, at least enter the telephone number of the credit card issuer or bank. You may need the number, for example, if you must report a lost credit card. The "Telling Money about the account details" section earlier in this chapter explains how the Account Details window works.

Chapter 3

Recording Your Financial Activity

- -

- -

*T*his chapter tackles the four or five things you have to do each time you run the Money program. It explains how to record deposits, withdrawals, payments, and charges in registers. You also find out how to record a transfer of money between accounts, how to move around in a register, and how to find transactions in large registers. This chapter describes how to delete and void transactions. Finally, for the man or woman who likes to leave behind a wide paper trail, this chapter explains how to print a register.

Accomplish the tasks described in this chapter and you are well on your way to becoming an ace user of the Money program.

The Basics: Recording Transactions in Savings and Checking Registers

After you set up an account (the subject of Chapter 2), you're ready to start recording transactions in the account's register. A *register* is the place where checks, payments, deposits, charges, and withdrawals are recorded. Figure 3-1 shows a checking account register. Like all registers, this one has places for numbering transactions, recording transaction dates, and viewing balances.

Check number

Date of transaction

Running balance

My Checking Account

Account Manager

View: All Transactions, by Date

Num	Date	Payee	C	Payment	Deposit	Balance
ATM	6/15/97	Withdrawal	R	20.00		3,383.29
1768	6/16/97	McKesson Water Products		32.55		3,350.74
1769	6/16/97	Raymond Katz DDS		11.40		3,339.34
1770	6/16/97	Sallie Mae		296.56		3,042.78
1771	6/16/97	Kaiser Permanente		225.00		2,817.78
1772	6/16/97	San Francisco Tax Collector		1,294.94		1,522.84
ATM	6/16/97	Withdrawal	R	300.00		1,222.84
	6/18/97	Service Charge	R	20.24		1,202.60
	6/19/97	tricom systems, inc.			1,085.00	2,287.60
1773	6/23/97	Lilli Lanier		60.00		2,227.60
1774	6/25/97	Pacific Supply		55.90		2,171.70
ATM	6/26/97	Withdrawal		200.00		1,971.70
1775	6/27/97	Adu Larsen		40.00		1,931.70
1776	6/29/97	SF Bay Area Educator's Credit Uni		196.00		1,735.70
ATM	6/29/97	Withdrawal		200.00		1,535.70
	6/30/97	SFUSD			1,978.72	3,514.42
1777	6/30/97	Bank of America		1,640.10		1,874.32
1778	7/1/97	Floorcraft		26.37		1,847.95
					Ending Balance:	$3,545.08

Figure 3-1: Financial transactions are recorded in account registers like this one.

Ending balance

The following sections explain how to record transactions in savings and checking account registers. Everybody, or almost everybody, has a savings or checking account, so that's a good place to start. These sections explain how to open an account register and view it in different ways. You also find out how to record deposits, withdrawals, and checks, as well as how to record a transfer of money from one account to another. The basic techniques for recording transactions that you discover here apply to all the accounts you set up in Money.

Opening an account register

Money offers several different ways to open account registers. The first step is to go to the Account Manager window. You can get there from one of three ways:

Account Manager

- ✔ Choose Go➪Accounts.
- ✔ Click the Account Manager button (if you are looking at a register).
- ✔ Press Ctrl+Shift+A.

The Account Manager window, shown in Figure 3-2, is Account Central as far as Money is concerned. On the window is an icon for every account you've set up. To open an account register:

  ✔ Double-click an account icon.

  ✔ Click an account icon and then click the Go to Account button.

  ✔ Select an account from the Accounts drop-down list.

Which of these methods for opening an account register works best? How should I know? All I know is, you shouldn't try them all at once.

Recording checks, deposits, and withdrawals in registers

Several tabs are at the bottom of the Account Register window. Figure 3-3 shows the five tabs in a checking account register. Which tabs appear depend on which type of account you are working with. Here are the common tabs for checking or savings accounts:

  ✔ **Check.** Use this tab to tell Money when you write a check.

  ✔ **Deposit.** Record all deposits to an account, including those made at a cash machine, on this tab.

Open a register from the Accounts menu   Or double-click an account icon

Figure 3-2: You can open any account register from the Account Manager window.

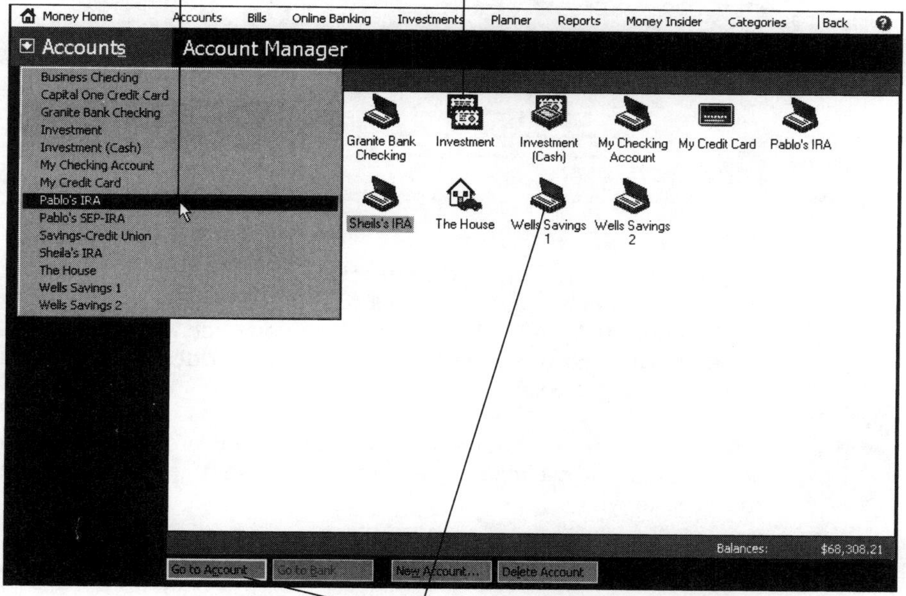

Or click an account icon and then click this button

✔ **Transfer.** Shifting money from one account to another? Tell Money here.

✔ **Withdrawal.** Taking money out of the account? Stealing from yourself isn't really stealing, but so you don't feel guilty, let Money know how much on this tab.

✔ **Cash Machine.** Use this tab to record cash machine withdrawals made from the account. "Wait," you're asking, "why does Money want you to record cash machine withdrawals on the Cash Machine tab, but not cash machine deposits?" Good question. When you find out the answer, let me know.

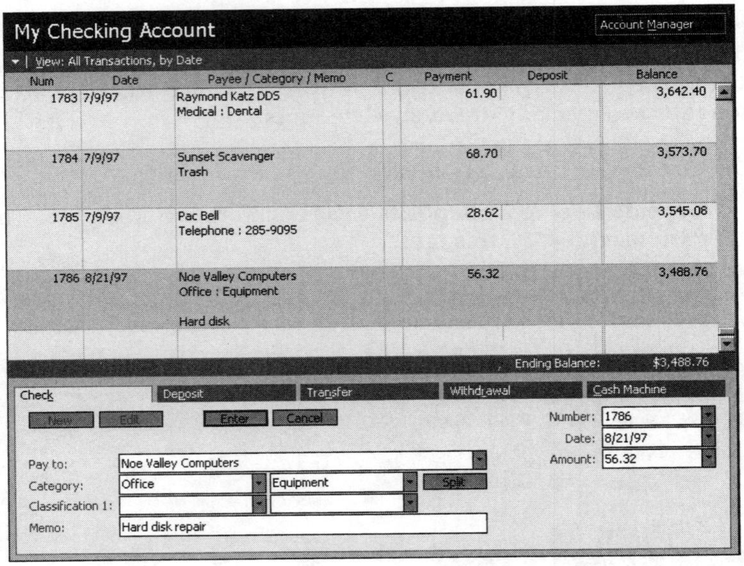

Figure 3-3:
Recording a
transaction
in an
account
register.

My Checking Account					Account Manager
▼	View: All Transactions, by Date				
Num	Date	Payee / Category / Memo	C	Payment	Deposit	Balance
1783	7/9/97	Raymond Katz DDS Medical : Dental		61.90		3,642.40
1784	7/9/97	Sunset Scavenger Trash		68.70		3,573.70
1785	7/9/97	Pac Bell Telephone : 285-9095		28.62		3,545.08
1786	8/21/97	Noe Valley Computers Office : Equipment Hard disk		56.32		3,488.76

Ending Balance: $3,488.76

Check | Deposit | Transfer | Withdrawal | Cash Machine

New | Edit | Enter | Cancel

Number: 1786
Date: 8/21/97
Amount: 56.32

Pay to: Noe Valley Computers
Category: Office | Equipment | Split
Classification 1:
Memo: Hard disk repair

The first step in recording a transaction is to click a tab. Click the Check tab to record a check you wrote. Click Cash Machine to record an ATM (automatic teller machine) withdrawal. When you click a tab, a *transaction form* appears with text boxes and drop-down lists for describing the transaction. Figure 3-3 shows a Check transaction form.

TIP

If no tabs appear on your screen, open the View menu (it's right below the account name) by clicking it and select Transaction Forms, the last entry on the drop-down list.

Follow these steps to record a check, deposit, withdrawal, or cash-machine withdrawal in a register:

1. **Open the register of the account you want to record a transaction in (see the "Opening an account register" section earlier in this chapter).**

2. **Click the tab that describes the transaction you intend to record.**

   Click Check, Deposit, Withdrawal, or Cash Machine.

3. **Enter a number in the Number text box, if necessary.**

   To move from place to place on a transaction form, either click elsewhere or press Tab or Shift+Tab.

   Only checks require a number, but you can enter deposit slip and withdrawal slip numbers if you want to track deposits and withdrawals carefully (the Cash Machine form does not have a Number text box). Money keeps track of check numbers and puts the next available check number in the Number text box, but you can enter a number of your own if you want to.

4. **Enter the date in the Date text box, if necessary.**

   Money puts today's date in the Date text box, so you don't need to do anything if you are recording a transaction you completed today.

   A fast way to enter the date is to click the down-arrow to the right of the Date text box and make the mini-calendar appear. If the calendar shows the right month, simply click a day. Otherwise, click the arrows on either side of the month name to go backward or forward month by month, and then click a day.

5. **Enter who you paid the money to in the Pay to text box or received the money from in the From text box.**

   The Deposit form has a From text box instead of a Pay to text box.

   If this *is not* the first time you have entered the name in the text box, all you have to do is type the first few letters to make the entire name appear. Or you can click the down-arrow beside the text box, scroll through the list of people or businesses you entered on past occasions, and click a name to enter it, as shown in Figure 3-4. Money remembers all the people and businesses to whom you paid or from whom you received payments. You don't have to keep entering the same names over and over again.

   For deposits, enter the name of the person or business who wrote you the check or checks you deposited. For withdrawals, enter **Cash** if you withdrew cash from the bank. For cash machine withdrawals, Money enters the word Cash automatically.

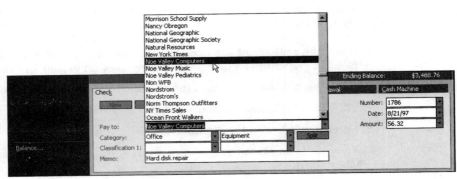

Figure 3-4:
One way to
enter a
name in the
Pay to or
From text
box is to
select it
from the
drop-down
list.

If you entered the name in the register before, the amount you last paid or received appears in the Amount text box. Not only that, but the category and subcategory that you assigned to the last transaction you recorded with the person or company appear in the Category text boxes. You may not have to change the amount or category choices. If this transaction is identical to the one you recorded last time, your work is almost done.

6. **Enter the amount of the transaction in the Amount text box.**

To enter a round number, you don't have to enter the decimal point or trailing zeroes. In other words, to enter $21.00, all you have to type is **21**. Money adds the zeroes for you.

Try clicking the down-arrow to the right of the Amount text box. When you click it, you see a mini-calculator. Use that calculator to total checks for a deposit, for example. When you press the equals key, the total is entered directly into the Amount text box.

7. **In the Category text boxes, enter a category in the left-hand text box, and, if you want, a subcategory in the right-hand text box.**

Creating and choosing the right categories and subcategories is so important I devote all of Chapter 4 to the subject. By assigning categories and subcategories to income and expense transactions, you can discover where you spend your hard-earned money and where it comes from — critical information if you itemize on tax forms.

For now, all you need to know is that you can enter a category or subcategory by typing the first few letters of its name. Soon you see the name in its entirety. You can also click the down-arrow to open a drop-down list and select a name from there.

Expense categories are at the top of the drop-down list. Payments made by check require an expense category. Deposits require an income category, which are found in the middle of the drop-down list.

8. **If you care to, write a few words in the Memo text box to describe the transaction.**

   Write a memo if for any reason you may come back to the account register in the future, see the transaction, and not know what it was for.

9. **Click the Enter button or press the Enter key.**

Don't be alarmed if the transaction you just entered doesn't appear on the register's last line. Transactions appear in date order. The "How's your view of the register?" section later in this chapter explains how to display transactions in different ways.

By the way, if you start recording a transaction but decide to do it later or start all over, click the Cancel button. The Edit button is for altering a transaction that you entered already. The "Changing, or editing, a transaction" section later in this chapter explains how to do that.

Do you have to record past transactions?

I'm sorry to say it, but almost everyone has to record at least a few transactions from the past. When you set up an account, you have to list or estimate a balance. If you followed Money's recommendation and entered the closing balance from your last bank statement, you have to enter all the transactions that didn't appear on that statement because they didn't clear the bank. In other words, if you wrote a check on June 30 and it didn't appear on the statement that you received on July 15, you have to enter that check in order to make your account balance.

To enter uncleared transactions, either use your own records or wait until next month's statement arrives and use it to record the absent transactions.

If you intend to use Money to help with tax returns, you'll need to record transactions back to the beginning of your tax year, usually January 1. If today is September 30 or December 2, you have a great deal of work to do — or you can wait until next year to use Money in earnest. All I can tell you by way of encouragement is that Money makes it easy to enter transactions, as this chapter and the next one show.

You can always change the opening balance of an account by changing the amount of the initial deposit. Knowing the opening balance is easy if you just opened the account, but tracking an account you've had for a while requires a little detective work. You have to find out how much money was in the account as of the starting date you entered when you set it up. That isn't easy. Rather than dig through old records, you may simply tinker with the initial deposit until the ending balance of the account matches the one on your last bank statement.

Splitting transactions that don't fit in one category

Suppose that you try to record a transaction in a register but it doesn't fit in a single category. For example, suppose that you write a check to the Old Country Store to buy motor oil, a blouse, and a rocking chair. The transaction wouldn't fall neatly in the Automotive, Clothing, or Household: Furnishings category. And suppose that you deposit two checks at once, one from your place of work and one from the New Jersey Lottery Commission. To record a transaction like that, you *split* it. Money offers the Split button on the transaction form for that very purpose. Follow these steps to split a transaction:

1. **Record the transaction as you normally would.**

   If, like me, you don't have and have never had a good sense of what's normal, follow Steps 1 through 6 in the preceding section, "Recording checks, deposits, and withdrawals in registers."

   Split

2. **Instead of selecting a category and subcategory on the transaction form, click the Split button.**

   You see the Split Transaction dialog box shown in Figure 3-5. The Category list is already open so you can select the first category.

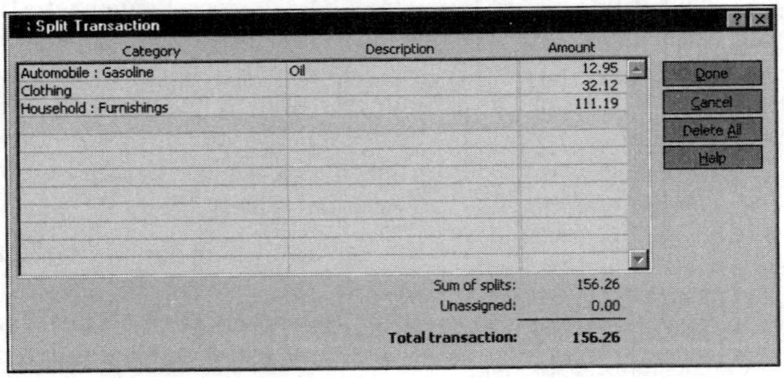

Figure 3-5: Splitting a transaction that doesn't fit into a single category.

Category	Description	Amount
Automobile : Gasoline	Oil	12.95
Clothing		32.12
Household : Furnishings		111.19

Sum of splits: 156.26
Unassigned: 0.00
Total transaction: 156.26

3. **For the first item in the bundle that you purchased or deposited, select a category on the first line of the dialog box, and, if necessary, a subcategory from the drop-down list as well.**

4. **If you care to, enter a description in the Description text box on the first line.**

5. **In the Amount text box on the first line, enter the cost of the first item or the amount of the first check you deposited.**

6. **Repeat Steps 3 through 5 for each item you purchased or each check you deposited.**

   After you are done, the Sum of splits figure in the lower-right corner of the Split Transaction dialog box should equal the Total transaction figure, and the Unassigned figure should be 0.00. If the figures don't add up, tinker with the numbers in the Split Transaction dialog box until they do.

7. **Click the Done button to return to the transaction form.**

8. **Make sure that the transaction form is filled out properly and then click the Enter button.**

In registers, transactions that have been split bear the word "Split" in the Category text box. Figure 3-6 shows a split transaction in a register. To see how a transaction in a register was split, click the transaction, then click the transaction form, and then click the Split button to open the Split Transaction dialog box.

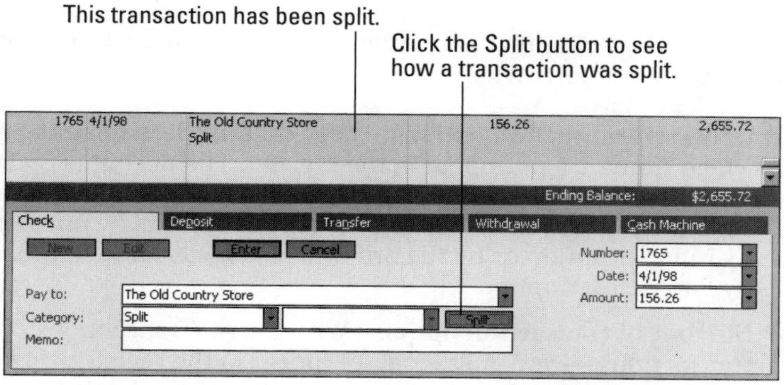

Figure 3-6:
When you split a transaction, the word Split appears in the register where a category name usually appears.

This transaction has been split.

Click the Split button to see how a transaction was split.

| 1765 4/1/98 | The Old Country Store Split | 156.26 | 2,655.72 |

Ending Balance: $2,655.72

Check Deposit Transfer Withdrawal Cash Machine

New Edit Enter Cancel

Number: 1765
Date: 4/1/98
Amount: 156.26

Pay to: The Old Country Store
Category: Split Split
Memo:

How's your view of the register?

Try using the View menu in the Account Register window like a TV remote control device to change channels when you get bored. As Figure 3-7 shows, you can change views by clicking the triangle beside the word View and making a choice from the drop-down list. No, the views are not especially exciting, but I've seen worse on TV.

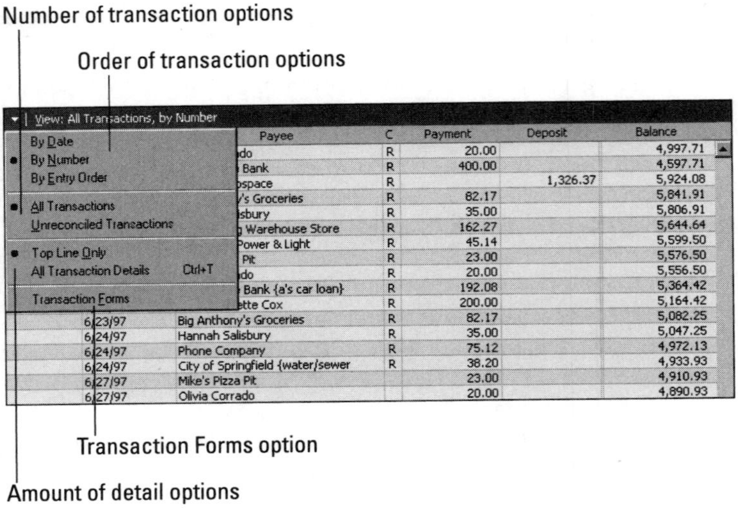

Number of transaction options

Order of transaction options

Figure 3-7:
The View
menu offers
many
different
ways to
arrange
transactions
on-screen.
Here, only
the first line
of each
transaction
is shown.

	Payee	C	Payment	Deposit	Balance
By Date	do	R	20.00		4,997.71
By Number	Bank	R	400.00		4,597.71
By Entry Order	pspace	R		1,326.37	5,924.08
All Transactions	's Groceries	R	82.17		5,841.91
Unreconciled Transactions	sbury	R	35.00		5,806.91
	Warehouse Store	R	162.27		5,644.64
Top Line Only	Power & Light	R	45.14		5,599.50
All Transaction Details Ctrl+T	Pit	R	23.00		5,576.50
	do	R	20.00		5,556.50
	Bank {a's car loan}	R	192.08		5,364.42
Transaction Forms	tte Cox	R	200.00		5,164.42
6/23/97	Big Anthony's Groceries	R	82.17		5,082.25
6/24/97	Hannah Salisbury	R	35.00		5,047.25
6/24/97	Phone Company	R	75.12		4,972.13
6/24/97	City of Springfield {water/sewer}	R	38.20		4,933.93
6/27/97	Mike's Pizza Pit		23.00		4,910.93
6/27/97	Olivia Corrado		20.00		4,890.93

View: All Transactions, by Number

Transaction Forms option

Amount of detail options

Different kinds of registers offer different kinds of views. However, the options fall into four categories:

- **Order of transaction options:** These options determine the order by which transactions appear in the register. The default is By Date, which arranges transactions in date order as they are arranged on bank statements, but you can also arrange transactions by number with the By Number option or by the order in which *you* entered them with the By Entry Order option.

- **Number of transaction options:** With the All Transactions option, all transactions — you guessed it — appear in the register. However, to make only transactions that have not cleared the bank appear, select the Unreconciled Transactions option. How to clear transactions in a register is the subject of Chapter 5.

- **Amount of detail options:** To see more transactions on-screen, click the Top Line Only option. As Figure 3-7 demonstrates, only the first line of each transaction is shown. Select the All Transaction Details option or press Ctrl+T to see all parts of transactions, including categories and memo descriptions.

- **Transaction Forms option:** With the Transaction Forms option, you can decide for yourself whether or not the transaction form appears at the bottom of the screen and takes up valuable space.

Transferring money between accounts

Sometimes good luck comes your way; you earn a few extra dollars, so you transfer money from your checking account to a savings account or investment account. And sometimes, in a fit of panic, you have to transfer money from a savings account to a checking account to cover a couple of large checks. When you transfer money between real-life bank accounts, record the transfer in your Money account registers as well.

Follow these steps to record a transfer of money from one account to another:

1. **Open the register of the account from which you will transfer the money.**

   In other words, to transfer money from a checking to a savings account, open the checking account register.

2. **Click the Transfer tab.**

   You see the transaction form shown at the bottom of Figure 3-8.

Figure 3-8:
Transferring money between accounts (bottom) and what a transfer looks like in a register (top).

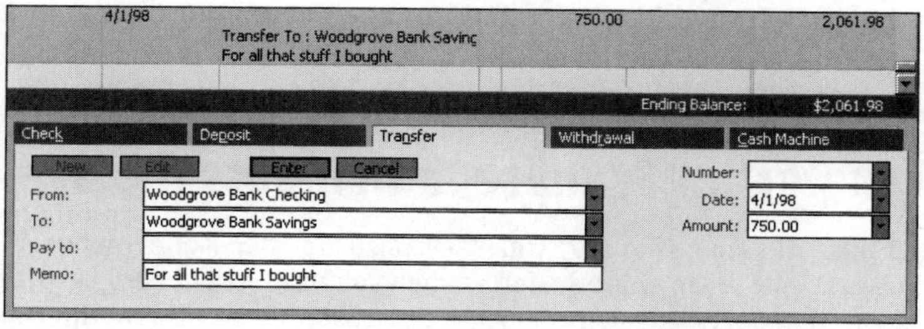

3. **Enter the date the transfer was made in the Date text box.**

4. **In the Amount text box, enter the amount of the transfer.**

5. **Click the down-arrow on the To drop-down list and select the account that is to receive the money you are transferring.**

   All the accounts you set up in Money appear on the To drop-down list. The name of the account from which you are transferring the money should already appear in the From text box. Leave the Pay to text box empty when you transfer money between bank accounts.

6. Optionally, enter a few words to describe the transaction in the Memo text box.

7. Click the Enter button or press the Enter key.

The top of Figure 3-8 shows what a money transfer looks like in an account register. The amount you transferred is deducted from one account and added to the other.

Recording Transactions in Credit Card and Line of Credit Accounts

If you slogged through the previous few pages and discovered how to record checking and savings account transactions, you may experience déjà-vu in the next few pages. Entering credit card and line of credit transactions is mighty similar to recording transactions made in savings and checking accounts.

Besides keeping credit cards at home, one way to keep credit card spending under control is to diligently record charges as you make them. As the amount that you owe in the credit card register gets larger and larger, you will be discouraged from spending so much with your credit card.

Transferring is more than meets the eye

It seems odd at first, but Money requires you to transfer funds not only when you transfer funds between bank accounts, but also when you pay credit card bills or contribute to IRAs or other kinds of investments. Think of it this way: If you open an IRA and you write a $1,000 check for a contribution to your IRA, that $1,000 still belongs to you. You haven't really spent it. All you have done is transfer it from one account (checking) to another account (the retirement account with which you track the value of your IRA). Therefore, when you open a new account, you record the initial deposit as a transfer from your checking account to the new account.

You also transfer money between accounts when you pay a credit card bill. Here's how it works: Each time you record a charge in a credit card account, the charge is added to the amount of money that you owe. Suppose that at the end of a month your account shows that you owe $200 because you charged $200 worth of items. To pay the $200 that you owe, you record a check for $200 to the credit card issuer, but in the register the $200 is shown as a transfer from your checking account to your credit card account. After the transfer is complete, the $200 that you owed is brought to zero. The section, "Recording a credit card payment," explains how to pay credit card bills.

Recording credit card and line of credit charges

Credit card and line of credit account registers have a Charge form for recording charges. You can see a Charge form in Figure 3-9. Like the Check form, the Charge form has places for entering a transaction date, amount, payee name, category, subcategory, and memo. All the drop-down lists and keyboard tricks work the same way on a Charge form and a Check form.

To fill in the Charge form, follow these steps:

1. **Open the account register.**
2. **Click the Charge tab.**
3. **Enter a reference number (optional).**
4. **Enter the charge date.**
5. **Enter the business you purchased the item from.**
6. **Enter the amount of the charge.**
7. **Select a category and, if necessary, a subcategory, too.**
8. **Enter a description (optional).**
9. **Click the Enter button (or press Enter).**

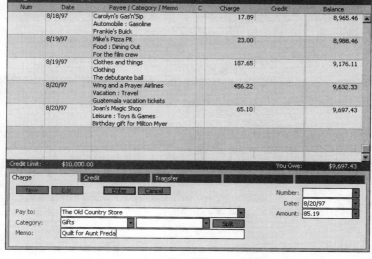

Figure 3-9:
Record credit card and line of credit transactions exactly as you would record a check.

Credit card and line of credit accounts track what you owe, not what you have. Don't forget this all-important detail. In the credit card register shown in Figure 3-9, you can clearly see the words `You Owe` where the words `Ending Balance` appear in a savings or checking account register. In effect, the `You Owe` number is a negative number. It represents an amount you will have to pay out of your checking account one of these days.

The fast but dicey way to record credit card charges

Here's a little trick for people who don't use their credit cards a great deal: Rather than record the charges in a credit card account, simply record them in your checking account by splitting the payment to the bank or credit card issuer.

To see how this works, compare Figure 3-9 to the figure in this sidebar. The same charges are listed and categorized in the register in Figure 3-9 and the Split Transaction dialog box in this figure. In each example, the same payee names, expense categories, and amounts are recorded in Money. In this figure, however, the user has recorded the charges by splitting the payment that he or she makes to the credit card issuer. See the "Splitting transactions that don't fit in one category" section earlier in this chapter.

Splitting credit card payments is not for everybody. If you don't pay the bill in full each month, you can't do it. And if you make a lot of credit card charges, recording them in a credit card account is easier than recording them in the relatively small Split Transaction dialog box.

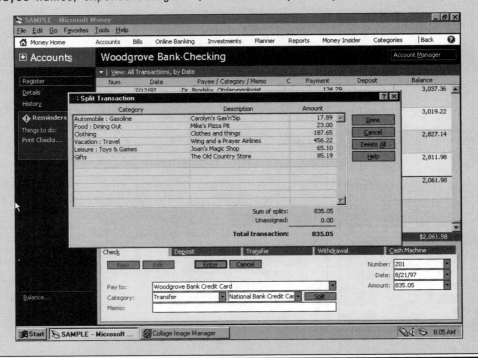

Recording a credit

If, for whatever reason, you receive a credit from a bank or credit card issuer, perhaps because you overpaid or you disputed a bill, you can record that as well in the credit card account register. To do so, click the Credit tab and fill in the blanks in the Credit form. The Credit form works exactly like the Charge form.

For a category, I suggest choosing Other Income. Be sure to describe the credit in the Memo text box. Credits tend to look very mysterious on reports and registers. By describing them, you know exactly what they are and why they were issued to you.

Recording a credit card payment

Take note of how much of the debt you intend to pay, and then follow these steps to make a payment to the bank or card issuer:

1. **Open the register of the account from which you intend to make the payment. (See the section, "Opening an account register," earlier in this chapter.)**

   Probably a checking register.

2. **Click the Transfer tab at the bottom of the Account window.**

   You see the Transfer form shown in Figure 3-10. Looks familiar, doesn't it? Earlier in this chapter, the "Transferring money between accounts" section explains the ins and outs of the Transfer form (and the sidebar, "Transferring is more than meets the eye," explains the mystery of why you transfer money between accounts to satisfy a credit card debt).

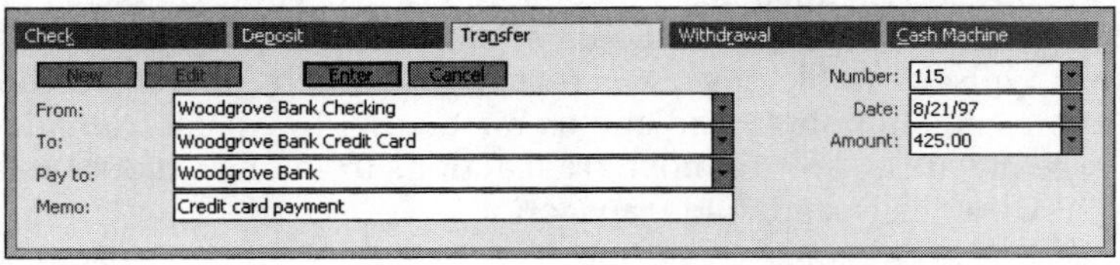

Figure 3-10:
Paying all
or part of a
credit card
bill.

Check	Deposit	Transfer	Withdrawal	Cash Machine

New	Edit	Enter	Cancel

		Number:	115
From:	Woodgrove Bank Checking	Date:	8/21/97
To:	Woodgrove Bank Credit Card	Amount:	425.00
Pay to:	Woodgrove Bank		
Memo:	Credit card payment		

3. **Enter a check number in the Number text box if the number that appears there isn't correct.**

   Even though you are transferring money, the bank or card issuer that you are about to pay doesn't see it that way. The bank or card issuer wants a real-life check with a number on it.

4. **In the Date text box, enter the date that you wrote or will write on the check.**

5. **Enter the amount of the check in the Amount text box.**

   I hope that you can pay off the entire credit card or line of credit bill; but if you can't, Money doesn't care. Money continues to track what you owe from month to month.

6. **Click the down-arrow in the To text box and select the name of the credit card or line of credit account for which you are making the payment.**

   In other words, to pay the bill for a Visa card that you track in an account called My Visa, select My Visa from the drop-down list.

7. **In the Pay to text box, enter the name of the bank or card issuer that appears or will appear on the check.**

   For example, if the check is written to City Bank, make sure that City Bank appears in the Pay to text box.

8. **If you care to, write a few descriptive words in the Memo text box.**

9. **Click the Enter button or press Enter.**

   The amount you paid is deducted from the checking account. Meanwhile, the You Owe amount in the credit card or line of credit register decreases or is brought to zero.

Before you make a credit card or line of credit payment, reconcile the credit card or line of credit account. Chapter 5 explains how.

Fixing Mistakes in Registers

Everybody makes mistakes, and absolutely everybody makes mistakes when they enter transactions in account registers. Most people do not have an expert typist's nimble fingers or sureness of touch. Therefore, the following sections explain how to find and fix mistakes, how to get from place to place in large registers, how to move transactions from one account to another, and how to delete and void transactions.

Finding a transaction so you can fix it

Suppose that you made a terrific blunder somewhere in a register but aren't sure where. You categorized a transaction incorrectly, entered a transaction in the wrong account, or misspelled a name. Suppose that you did it many times over. How can you fix the errors quickly without wasting an entire morning?

Fortunately, editing your transactions is easy in Money. But before you can fix errors, you have to find them. Read on to find out how to get around quickly in a register and how to find transactions with the Tools⇨Find⇨Transactions command.

It helps to see more transactions on-screen when you are looking for a transaction. To see more transactions, open the View menu in the upper-left corner of the register and click Top Line Only (or press Ctrl+T) to see only the first line of transactions. While you're at it, click Transaction Forms to remove the forms from the bottom of the register window.

Moving around in an Account Register

One way to find a transaction is to eyeball the account register. With this technique, you put the register on-screen, move around in it like mad, and hope you find the transaction you are looking for. Table 3-1 presents keyboard and scroll bar techniques for getting around quickly in an account register.

Table 3-1	Keyboard and Scroll Bar Techniques for Moving around in Registers
Press/Click/Drag	*To Go*
Ctrl+Home	To the first transaction in the register.
Ctrl+End	To the last transaction in the register.
↑ or ↓	To the previous or next transaction in the register.
PgUp or PgDn	Up or down an entire screenful of transactions.
Scroll bar arrows	To the preceding or next transaction. Click the arrow at the top of the scroll bar to go up; the one at the bottom to go down.
Scroll bar	Up or down an entire screenful of transactions. With this technique, you click on the scroll bar but not on the arrows or the scroll box. Click above the scroll box to go up; click below to go down.
Scroll box	Willy-nilly through the register. Drag the *scroll box,* the elevator-like object in the middle of the scroll bar, to go up or down very quickly.

Searching with the Find command

The surest way to pinpoint a transaction or a bunch of similar transactions is to choose the Tools⇨Find⇨Transactions command (or press Ctrl+F). The Find command looks for transactions in all the registers, not just the one that is open, so you don't have to be in a specific register to start looking for transactions.

Follow these steps to look for transactions in your account registers:

1. **Choose Tools➪Find➪Transactions.**

   You see the Find Transactions dialog box with its six tabs, as shown in Figure 3-11. You can also press Ctrl+F to choose the command.

2. **As necessary, fill out tabs in the Find Transactions dialog box.**

   Fill out one tab or a combination of tabs. Table 3-2 describes how to fill out the six tabs in the Find Transactions dialog box. By the way, if you set up a classification, its name appears on a tab as well so you can search for transactions that were classified a certain way.

Table 3-2	Searching for Transactions in the Find Transactions Dialog Box
Tab	**What It Is for**
Text	For searching for specific words. For example, if you are searching for a check on which you wrote "Damn the torpedoes" on the Memo line, type **Damn the torpedoes** in the Find transactions with this text box.
Account	For choosing which accounts to search in. To search in specific accounts, click the Selected accounts radio button and then click the names of the accounts you want to search.
Date	For searching in specific date ranges. Either click the Range down-arrow and select a time period from the drop-down list, or enter a From and To date in the text boxes.
Categories	For searching in specific categories. Click an option button to narrow the search to a certain type of category, and then click the names of the categories you want to search in. Click the Show subcategories check box to narrow the search to subcategories. (Chapter 4 explains more about fixing categorization errors.)
Payee	For searching for specific payees. Click the Selected payees option button and then click the name of the payee or names of the payees for which you recorded transactions.
Details	For searching by transaction type (payments, deposits, transfers) and reconciliation status (unreconciled and reconciled), as well as by date.

3. **Click the Find button.**

   As Figure 3-11 shows, the transactions that met your criteria appear below the dialog box. Examine the transactions and click the scroll bar, if necessary, to find the one you are looking for.

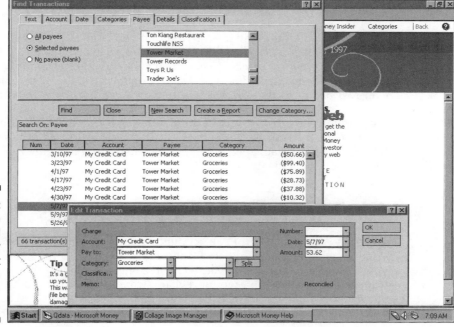

Figure 3-11:
Use the
tabs to tell
Money
what
transaction
you are
looking for.

Try clicking the Num, Date, Account, Payee, or Category button in the middle of the dialog box to arrange the transactions in a new way. For example, clicking the Date button arranges the transactions in date order. Clicking Payee arranges them in alphabetical order by payee.

4. Double-click a transaction if you want to change it in any way.

When you double-click, you see the Edit Transaction dialog box shown on the bottom of Figure 3-11. Change part of the transaction and click the OK button.

5. Click Close to close the Find Transactions dialog box, or click New Search to conduct another search of the registers.

By the way, Money offers two more commands for looking for transactions in investment and loan accounts: Tools⇨Find⇨Investment Transactions and Tools⇨Find⇨Loan Transactions. Use them to find lost-sheep investment and loan transactions. The commands work like the Tools⇨Find⇨Transactions command but don't present as many tabs in the Find Transactions dialog box.

Changing, or editing, a transaction

All right, so you found the transaction that you entered incorrectly. What do you do now? If you are staring at the transaction in an account register, either double-click it or click it and then click the Edit button on the transaction form. Then go right into the transaction form, fix the mistake in whatever text box or drop-down list it is located in, and click the Enter button.

If you found the error by way of the Tools⇨Find⇨Transactions command, double-click the transaction in the Find Transactions dialog box. When the Edit Transaction dialog box appears (see the bottom of Figure 3-11), repair the transaction and click OK.

Voiding and deleting transactions

To strike a transaction from an account register, either delete or void it. What's the difference? A deleted transaction is erased permanently from your financial records. It may as well have never happened. But a voided transaction stays in the account register, where the word ****VOID**** clearly shows that you entered the transaction but voided it later on. What's more, a voided transaction can be "unvoided."

Void a transaction when you want to keep a record of having made it. For example, if you start writing check number 511 but accidentally enter the wrong payee name, void the check instead of deleting it. That way, the account register records what happened to check number 511 and you know that the check wasn't lost or stolen. Likewise, if you stop payment on a check, void it (and explain on the Memo line why you stopped payment).

History records what happened to voided transactions, but deleted transactions are lost forever in the prehistoric murk.

Voiding a transaction

Follow these steps to void a transaction:

1. **Click the transaction in the register.**
2. **Choose Edit⇨Mark As⇨Void.**
3. **Click the Enter button or press the Enter key.**

   You can also right-click a transaction and choose Edit⇨Mark As⇨Void to void it.

After a transaction has been voided, the word ∗∗VOID∗∗ appears in the balance column of the register, and an R (for Reconciled) appears in the C (for Cleared) column to show that the transaction has cleared. Figure 3-12 shows a voided transaction in a register. Chapter 5 explains what reconciling is.

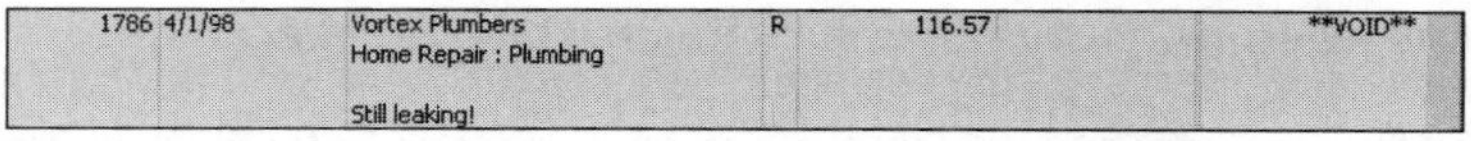

Figure 3-12:
A voided
transaction.

1786	4/1/98	Vortex Plumbers Home Repair : Plumbing	R	116.57	∗∗VOID∗∗
		Still leaking!			

To unvoid a transaction, click it in the register and choose Edit⇨Mark As⇨Void all over again, and click OK when the warning message tells you that you are messing with a reconciled transaction. The Void command is what is known in computer jargon as a *toggle* — something you can turn on and off like a toggle switch. The term comes from the ancient Romans, who used to toggle their togas when going in or out of the baths.

Deleting a transaction

Follow these steps to delete a transaction:

1. **Click the transaction in the register.**

2. **Press the Del key, choose Edit⇨Delete, or right-click and choose Delete from the shortcut menu.**

3. **Click Yes when Money asks if you really want to go through with it.**

If you try to delete a transaction that is marked as cleared in the register (an R appears in the C column), Money warns you that deleting the transaction could upset your account balance and put the account out of sync with bank records. I strongly suggest clicking Cancel in the dialog box. Very likely, the transaction was cleared because it appeared on bank records, so it should appear on your records as well. Investigate the matter before deleting the transaction.

You cannot delete an online payment that has been sent to Online Services. You can, however, send instructions to cancel the payment, as long as you do so within a couple of days of sending it. See Chapter 8.

Moving transactions from one account to another

Suppose that an error you discover has nothing to do with incorrect categories, amounts, or payee names. Suppose that you committed the grievous error of entering a transaction in the wrong account register. Before you are put in leg-irons, move the transaction to the correct account.

Money gives you two ways to move transactions between accounts:

- **From an account register:** If you found the errant transaction in a register, either click it and then choose Edit⇨Move to Account or right-click it and choose Move to Account on the shortcut menu. You see the Move Transaction dialog box. In the Move the transaction to drop-down list, select the name of the account to which you will move the transaction and then click the OK button.

- **From the Edit Transaction dialog box:** If you found the errant transaction by way of the Tools⇨Find⇨Transactions command (the "Searching with the Find command" section a few pages back explains how), double-click it to open the Edit Transaction dialog box (refer to the bottom of Figure 3-11). Then click the down-arrow on the Account drop-down list box and select the name of the account that the transaction rightfully belongs in.

I'm sorry to report that you can't move more than one transaction at a time between accounts. And you can't move transactions between different Money files — can't be done, I'm afraid.

Printing a Register

Besides fretting over income taxes in April, you also have to print all your account registers from the previous year. Your accountant, if you have one, wants to see them. Even if you don't have an accountant, you should still print the account registers and tuck them away with copies of your income tax forms. Leaving behind a paper trail in case posse members from the IRS come to track you down is important.

Follow these steps to print all or part of an account register:

1. **Open the account register that you want to print. (See the "Opening an account register" section earlier in this chapter.)**

2. Choose File⇨Print or press Ctrl+P.

You see the Print Report dialog box shown in Figure 3-13. Theoretically, you can print part of a register from this dialog box by entering page numbers in the From and To text boxes. However, it is impossible to tell by looking at a register what page you are on or how many pages are in the register altogether. Oh well, so much for printing a handful of pages, although you can blindly try your luck with the From and To text boxes if you want.

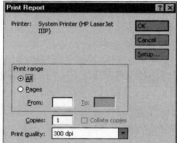

Figure 3-13:
Printing an
account
register.

3. If you want to try your luck with printing less than the entire register, click the Pages radio button and enter page numbers in the From and To text boxes.

4. Click OK.

If the register doesn't print correctly, the problem could be because Money and your printer aren't yet on speaking terms. See the "Printing Reports and Charts" section near the end of Chapter 13 for more information.

To solve the problem of printing part of a register, create an Account Transactions report and customize it so that only transactions from a certain year or time period appear. See Chapter 13.

Chapter 4

Categorizing Your Spending and Income

. . . .

In This Chapter

▶ Identifying categories, subcategories, and classifications

▶ Creating your own categories and subcategories

▶ Creating tax-related categories for tax-reporting purposes

▶ Setting up a classification

▶ Recording transactions by category, subcategory, and classification

▶ Reassigning transactions to different categories

▶ Changing and deleting category and subcategory names

. . . .

*Y*ou've probably withdrawn money from an ATM machine, noticed the dwindling account balance, and asked yourself, "Where did the money go?" Or perhaps you balanced a checking account and scratched your head, asking, "Why did I write so many checks?"

Money can help you find out. By assigning each transaction to a category, you can discover a great deal about your spending habits and sources of income. You can generate a report or graph and find out how much you spent on clothing and dining and office supplies. You can find out how much you earned in interest income and how much you earned from different clients. You can even find out how much you are allowed to deduct for income tax purposes.

This chapter explains how to categorize and classify transactions in account registers. I give advice about choosing categories and show you how to create meaningful categories that work for you. You also explore how to rename categories, delete categories, and recategorize a transaction. You may still have to write the same number of checks, but at least you'll have a better idea why.

Looking at the Ways to Categorize Income and Spending

Money offers three ways to categorize a financial transaction. In order of importance, they are:

- ✔ **By category.** By assigning transactions to categories, you can create neat-looking charts that give you the big spending picture, as shown in Figure 4-1. (See Chapter 13 for more about charts.)

- ✔ **By subcategory.** Divide a category into subcategories when you want to closely examine spending or income. The report in Figure 4-2 shows three month's worth of expenses in three Automobile subcategories. Given how much was spent in the Maintenance subcategory, you can conclude that the person who generated this report needs a new car.

- ✔ **By classification.** Most people don't need to bother with classifications, but they can be useful for tracking things such as rental properties. As the owner or manager of an apartment building or office building, you need to know precisely how much income the property generates and how much it costs to maintain. The only way to track income and costs, which fall in lots of different categories and subcategories, is to create a classification.

Figure 4-3 shows a monthly income report on a classification called Properties. In the report, you can clearly see the amount of rental income the properties generated altogether, the amount each property generated, and the amount each unit in each property generated.

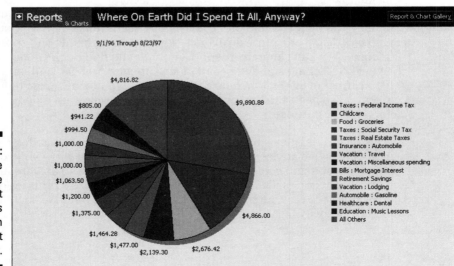

Figure 4-1: Each slice in this pie chart represents spending in a different category.

Figure 4-2:
This report
shows
spending
in the
Automobile
subcate-
gories.

Subcategory	Total
Automobile	
Gasoline	497.25
Loan Interest	180.70
Maintenance	2,750.89
Total Automobile	3,428.84

Figure 4-3:
Classifica-
tions are
useful for
tracking
rental
property
income and
expenses.

1020 Lakeshore Drive	
Apt. 1	340.00
Apt. 2	850.00
Apt. 3	812.85
Total 1020 Lakeshore Drive	2,002.85
17 Screed Street	
Apt. A	400.00
Apt. B	475.00
Apt. C	510.00
Total 17 Screed Street	1,385.00
4127 – 23rd Street	1,050.00
Grand Total	4,437.85

Actually, Money also offers a fourth way to categorize a transaction, if you count the tax-related status. By giving a category tax-related status, you can tell Money to include categories and subcategories in tax reports like the one in Figure 4-4. An accountant may need two or three hours to examine account registers, find all the tax-related transactions, and total them — time that you will be charged for. Money can do it in about six seconds.

Figure 4-4:
You can
gather data
about tax-
related
transactions
in reports
like
this one.

Income Categories	
Wages & Salary	
Gross Pay	47,100.00
Total Wages & Salary	47,100.00
Total Income Categories	47,100.00
Expense Categories	
Bills	
Mortgage Interest	1,063.50
Total Bills	1,063.50
Charitable Donations	700.00
Childcare	4,866.00
Healthcare	
Dental	1,098.09
Physician	134.29
Total Healthcare	1,232.38
Taxes	
Federal Income Tax	9,890.88
Medicare Tax	548.40
Real Estate Taxes	1,477.00
Social Security Tax	2,139.30
Total Taxes	14,055.58
Total Expense Categories	21,917.46
Grand Total	25,182.54

Setting Up Your Own Categories and Subcategories

Money gives you a set of generic categories and subcategories so you can start entering transactions right away. To see the complete list, click the Categories button on the Navigation bar. The list is fine and dandy, but sooner or later you have to give serious thought to which categories and subcategories suit you, especially if you use Money to manage a business or track tax-deductible expenses. If you don't see what you need in the generic lists, then create your own!

Sit down and compose a list of all the categories and subcategories you need for your business or personal finances *before* you begin creating categories and subcategories. That way, you get it right from the start and you lower the odds of having to recategorize transactions later on.

Money offers two different ways to create categories and subcategories. You can make them up as you go along with the fast but dicey method, or you can thoughtfully create them all at once with the slow but thorough method. The following sections describe the thorough way and the fast way to create categories and subcategories.

Creating a new category

Follow these steps to set up a new category:

1. **Click the Categories button on the Navigation bar or choose Go⇨Categories.**

   That takes you to the Categories & Payees window shown in Figure 4-5. While you're viewing the window, you may want to scroll down the list of categories and subcategories and examine the ones that are already there. Expense categories appear at the top of the list and Income categories appear at the bottom.

   In Figure 4-5, I chose Categories, Subcategories, and Tax Information from the View menu, but the View menu offers other ways of displaying categories and subcategories. Try experimenting with the other views when you have a minute or two to spare.

2. **Click the New button along the bottom of the screen.**

   The New Category dialog box asks if you want to create a new category or add a subcategory.

Click here to change view of categories

Category   Subcategories

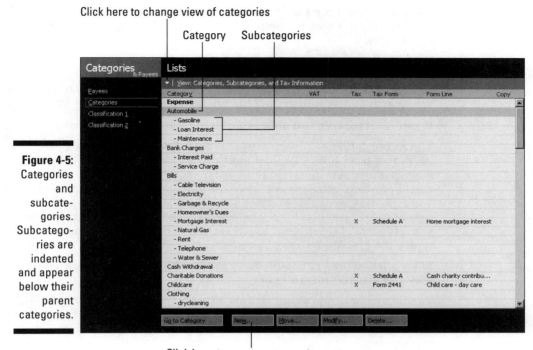

Figure 4-5:
Categories
and
subcate-
gories.
Subcatego-
ries are
indented
and appear
below their
parent
categories.

Click here to create a new category

3. **The Create a new category? radio button is already selected, so click the Next button.**

4. **Type a name for the category in the Name box.**

   The name you enter appears on the drop-down list when you record transactions, so be sure to choose a meaningful name.

5. **Click the Income or Expense radio button and click the Next button.**

6. **Select a concept from the list.**

   A *concept* is a broad means of defining the category. Money uses concepts to make calculations in the Tax Estimator, Home Worksheet, and other features (see Chapter 14). When you click a concept, a description appears on the right side of the dialog box.

7. **Click Finish.**

   There it is — your new category alive and kicking on the Categories & Payees window.

8. **Make sure that the new category is highlighted on-screen and then click the Go to Category button (you can find it along the bottom of the window).**

   You see the Categories window like the one in Figure 4-6. You can also get here by double-clicking a category on the Categories & Payees window. The window presents a bunch of different amenities, but for now you are interested in the Abbreviation and Comment text boxes.

9. **If you want to, enter an abbreviation in the Abbreviation box.**

   The Abbreviation box represents an alternative way to assign a category to a transaction. Besides selecting a category from the drop-down list on the transaction form or typing the first few letters of the category name, you can type a two- or three-letter abbreviation. After you type the two or three letters and press Tab to move to the next part of the transaction form, Money enters the entire category name for you. (Big deal, I say. It's not as if selecting from the drop-down list or typing the first few letters of a category name is very difficult.)

10. **Enter a few words of commentary in the Comment box to describe why you created this category.**

    The Comment box is worth visiting. Enter a few words to describe the category and why you created it. That way, if you forget what the new category is for, you can always come back to the Categories window and find out.

11. **Click the Include on Tax Reports check box if you want transactions made under this category to be calculated in tax reports.**

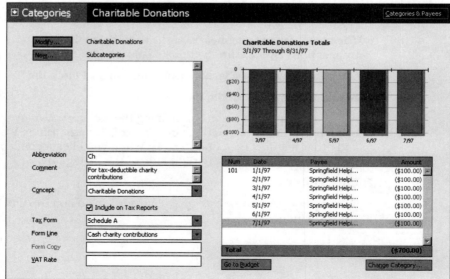

Figure 4-6:
The left side of the Categories window offers options for entering an abbreviation and giving the category tax-related status.

12. Click the Back button to return to the Categories & Payees window.

Your new category is ready and waiting to be assigned to a transaction. While you are in the Categories & Payees window, you may want to create a few more categories. To create subcategories for your new category, see the next section, "Creating a new subcategory," and begin at Step 3.

Creating a new subcategory

The best way to create a new subcategory is to go straight to the Categories & Payees window and start from there. Follow these steps:

1. Click the Categories button on the Navigation bar or choose Go⇨Categories to go to the Categories & Payees window.

2. If necessary, click the Categories button on the window to view categories.

3. Click the category that is to be the parent category of the subcategory you want to create.

In other words, to create a subcategory of the Education category, scroll to and click Education in the Categories & Payees window.

4. Either double-click the category name or click the Go to Category button.

The Categories window appears (refer to Figure 4-6). The name of the category you chose appears at the top of the window. The names of subcategories, if there are any for the category, are listed in the Subcategories scroll list. Scroll down the list to see the other categories.

5. Click the New button.

You see the New Subcategory dialog box. Make sure that the correct category name appears in the Subcategory for box.

6. Enter a name for the subcategory in the Name text box and click the Next button.

7. Select a concept.

Concepts are another one of those bold attempts by Microsoft to do your thinking for you. The concept you select can be used by the Tax Estimator and other features to help run your life.

8. Click the Finish button.

Check it out — your new subcategory appears on the Subcategory scroll list on the Categories window. Either start all over (at Step 5) to create another subcategory, or leave the Categories window by clicking the Back button.

The fast but dicey way to set up categories

The sections "Creating a new category" and "Creating a new subcategory" explain the thorough way to handle categories, but you can also create categories on the fly without visiting the Categories & Payees window. Follow these steps:

1. **Enter the entire transaction in the register except for the category and subcategory.**

   In other words, enter numbers or letters in the Number, Date, Amount, Pay To, From, and Memo text boxes. Chapter 3 explains how to enter a transaction in a register.

2. **Click the Category text box if you want to create a new category; to create a new subcategory, select the parent category in the Category box, and then press Tab or click the Subcategory text box to move the cursor there.**

The Subcategory text box is located to the right of the Category box.

3. **Type the name of the new category or subcategory.**

   Be sure to enter a descriptive name.

4. **Press the Tab key.**

   You see the New Category dialog box. I hope that it looks familiar.

5. **Make sure that the name you entered appears correctly in the dialog box, and then click the Next button.**

6. **Select a concept.**

7. **Click the Finish button.**

   The name of the category or subcategory you created takes its place on the Category or Subcategory drop-down list so you can select it in the future.

Getting Ready for Tax Time with Tax-Related Categories

Giving a category tax-related status when you create it is one thing. But how do you give an existing category tax-related status? Simply, that's how.

The following pages explain how to give a category or subcategory tax-related status. They also explain how to assign a category or subcategory to a line item on a tax form. As shown in Figure 4-7, Money offers the Tax Software Report that connects category and subcategory totals to specific income tax forms (W-2, Schedule A, and so on). The Tax Software Report makes filling out income tax forms easier. All you have to do is get the figures from the report and plug them into the right places on the tax forms. However, to make the process work, you have to know more about the tax forms than most people know or care to know.

Figure 4-7:
The Tax
Software
Report
presents
figures for
use in
preparing
federal
income tax
returns.

☐ Reports & Charts	Tax Software Report

3/1/97 Through 8/23/97

Tax Form Line	Amount
SCHEDULE A	
Doctors, dentists, hosp.	918.64
Real estate tax	1,899.00
Cash charity contributions	500.00
Home mortgage interest	5,414.88
FORM 2441	
Child care - day care	3,450.00
W-2	
Salary	31,400.00
Federal Withholding	6,593.92
Soc Sec Tax Withholding	1,426.20
Medicare Tax Withholding	365.60

Telling Money that a category is tax-related

Follow these steps to give an existing category or subcategory tax-related status so that it is figured into tax reports:

TIP

1. **Click the Categories button on the Navigation bar or choose Go⇨Categories to get to the Categories & Payees window.**

Let others do the work

Don't bother to keep tax records when others do it for you. Employers, for example, keep careful track of their employees' federal income, state income, Social Security, and Medicare tax-deduction information. Why keep those numbers yourself when your employer pays someone to do it? Besides, you have to use your employer's numbers when you file your income tax return.

Similarly, you can track tax-deductible mortgage interest payments, but why bother? At the start of the year, the bank sends you a statement that indicates how much you paid in interest. So only keep track of tax-related income and expenses with Money that no one tracks for you.

2. **If necessary, click the <u>C</u>ategories button to view the list of categories.**

   Now the Categories & Payees window lists categories and subcategories. Tax-related categories show an X in the Tax column.

   If you don't see a Tax column on your screen, click the View menu triangle and choose Categories, Subcategories, and Tax Information.

3. **Find and double-click the category or subcategory that needs tax-related status.**

   You see the Categories window, the left side of which is shown in Figure 4-8. You can also get to this screen by clicking a category or subcategory and then clicking the Go to Category button.

4. **Click the Inc<u>l</u>ude on Tax Reports check box.**

5. **Click the Back button to return to the Categories & Payees window.**

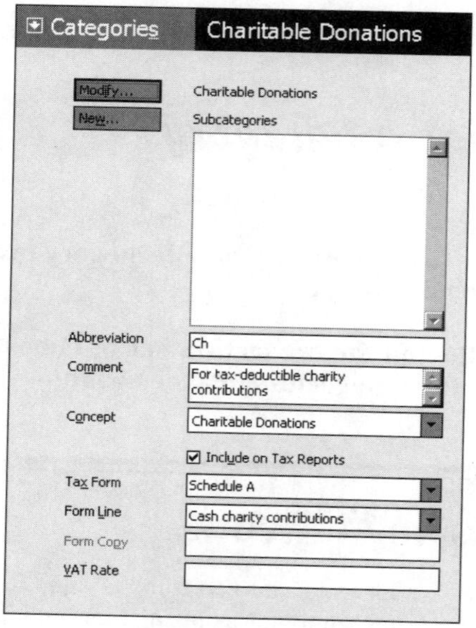

Figure 4-8:
The area
near the
Include on
Tax Reports
check box
in the
Categories
window is
where you
tell Money
about a
category's
tax status.

Categories	Charitable Donations
Modify...	Charitable Donations
New...	Subcategories

Abbreviation: Ch
Comment: For tax-deductible charity contributions
Concept: Charitable Donations
☑ Inc<u>l</u>ude on Tax Reports
Ta<u>x</u> Form: Schedule A
Form <u>L</u>ine: Cash charity contributions
Form Co<u>p</u>y:
<u>V</u>AT Rate:

Tagging categories to tax form line-items

Being able to tag categories and subcategories to tax forms (W2, Schedule B, Form 1040) is a neat idea, but you have to know the tax forms well to pull it off. You have to know, for example, that tax-exempt interest is reported on the Interest Income line of the Schedule B form. Who besides a tax accountant knows that?

If you want to be able to run Tax Software Reports, study your income tax returns from past years to see which forms and form lines to assign to the categories and subcategories that you use. Or speak to an accountant about it. Beware that the tax forms change yearly, so what goes on one line one year may go somewhere else the next. Where possible, the generic categories and subcategories that Money creates are automatically assigned tax forms and form lines. You can see what they are by glancing at the Tax Form and Form Line columns on the Categories & Payees window (refer to Figure 4-5).

Follow these steps to assign tax forms and line items to a category or subcategory:

1. **Click the Categories button on the Navigation bar or choose Go⇨Categories to go to the Categories & Payees window.**

2. **If necessary, click the Categories button or press Ctrl+Shift+C to display categories on-screen.**

3. **Find the category or subcategory that needs to be tagged and double-click it.**

   The Categories window appears (refer to Figure 4-8).

4. **Make sure that the Include on Tax Reports check box is checked, and if it isn't, click it.**

5. **Click the down-arrow on the Tax Form drop-down list and select a tax form.**

6. **Click the down-arrow on the Form Line drop-down list and select the form line on which the income or expense is reported.**

7. **If you use multiple forms (more than one W2, for example) to report your income, enter the number of forms you use in the Form Copy text box.**

8. **Click the Back button to return to the Categories & Payees window.**

Setting Up and Defining a Classification

At the beginning of this chapter, I explain that a classification is an umbrella grouping under which you track income and expenses in many different categories and subcategories. You can only create two classifications in each Money file. When you generate some kinds of reports, you can ask Money to tell you everything it knows about transactions that were assigned a certain classification.

The following pages explain how to set up a new classification. You also find out how to define the *classes* and *sub-classes* that go into the classification. Figure 4-9 shows classes and sub-classes. When you enter a transaction, you select a class and sub-class from special drop-down lists on the transaction form. In Figure 4-9, the user has named the classification Properties, the class in question is the building at 1020 Lakeshore Drive, and Apt. 2 is the sub-class. The transaction records a check that was written to cover plumbing repairs done to Apartment 2 at 1020 Lakeshore Drive.

Classification name that you choose

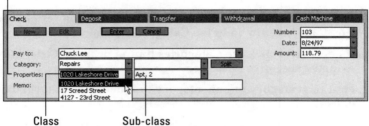

Figure 4-9: Choosing a class from the drop-down list.

Class   Sub-class

Setting up a classification

Like categories and subcategories, the starting point for setting up a classification is the all-purpose Categories & Payees window. Follow these steps to set up a classification:

1. **Click the Categories button on the Navigation bar or choose <u>G</u>o⇨<u>C</u>ategories.**

   You see the Categories & Payees window.

2. **Click the Classification <u>1</u> button.**

   You see the Add Classification dialog box shown in Figure 4-10.

3. **At the bottom of the dialog box, either select one of Money's names by clicking a radio button or click the last radio button and enter an original name for the classification.**

   Money's six suggestions for naming the new classification appear next to the six radio buttons. If you click the Properties radio button, for example, the new classification is called Properties, and the word *Properties* appears on your transaction forms, as it does in Figure 4-9.

   If you don't like Money's suggestions for a name, you can always click the last radio button and enter a name of your own in the text box.

Figure 4-10:
To name the classification, either select a name or click the last radio button and enter your own choice for the name.

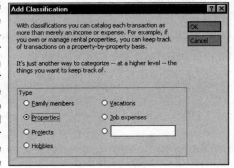

4. **After you select or enter a name, click OK.**

   You return to the Categories & Payees window, where the name you chose or entered appears on the left side of the window on a button below the Categories button.

The next step is to define classes and perhaps sub-classes for the new classification. By the way, if you set up two classifications in a Money file, you get two sets of classification drop-down lists on the transaction forms that appear in account registers.

Defining the classes and sub-classes

Follow these steps to define the classes that appear on the first classification drop-down list on transaction forms:

1. **If necessary, click the Categories button on the Navigation bar or choose Go⇨Categories to open the Categories & Payees window.**

2. **Click the classification button that is named after the classification to which you want to add the classes.**

   In other words, to create classes for the Properties classification, click the Properties button. The Categories & Payees window lists classes and sub-classes in the classification, if you have already created any, as shown in Figure 4-11.

3. Click the New button.

You see the New Class or Sub-Class dialog box shown in Figure 4-11. Under Add, make sure that the first radio button is selected.

4. Enter a name for the item in the Name text box and click OK.

The name you entered appears in the Categories & Payees window.

Figure 4-11 shows a Categories & Payees window with several classes and sub-classes. For the figure, I clicked the View menu triangle and chose Properties and Sub-Classes so I could see all the classes and sub-classes in my Properties category.

Figure 4-11:
Classes and
sub-classes
for a
classification
called
Properties,
as well as
the New
Class or
Sub-Class
dialog box
for creating
classes
and sub-
classes.

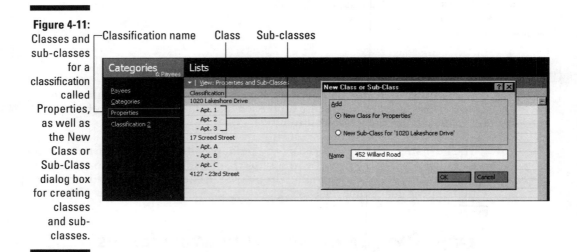

The steps for defining the sub-classes that appear on the second classification drop-down list (refer to Figure 4-11) are going to be very familiar:

1. If necessary, click the Categories button on the Navigation bar or choose Go⇨Categories to go to the Categories & Payees window.

2. Click a classification button on the left side of the window to see the list of classes in the classification.

3. Click the class under which you want to define a sub-class.

For example, to define a sub-class called Apt. 1 that is to be subordinate to the 1020 Lakeshore Drive class, click 1020 Lakeshore Drive.

4. Click the New button.

The New Class or Sub-Class dialog box appears (refer to Figure 4-11).

5. Under **A**dd, click the New Sub-Class for radio button.

6. Enter a name for the sub-class in the **N**ame text box and click OK.

If you're in a hurry, you can also create new classes and sub-classes directly from a transaction form. To do so, click a classification text box, type the name of the new class or sub-class, and press the Tab key. You see the Create New (Classification Name) dialog box with the name you entered inside it. Edit the name if necessary, and then click OK.

Correcting Transactions Recorded in the Wrong Category

Don't feel foolish if you recorded transactions in the wrong category or subcategory. It happens all the time. Lucky for you, Money offers a special button called Move for reassigning all the transactions in one category to another category. And if only a handful of transactions need to be reassigned, you can use the Find command to reassign transactions one at a time.

The Move button is very powerful indeed. When you reassign all the transactions in one category to another category with the Move button, you delete the first category as well. For example, suppose that you assigned the Vacation category to a bunch of transactions when you should have assigned the Leisure category. If you use the Move button to move all Vacation transactions to the Leisure category, you delete the Vacation category from the Categories & Payees list as well. Only use the Move button when you want to drop one category altogether and move all its transactions elsewhere.

Another thing about the Move button: If you attempt to move transactions in one category to another category and the category you want to move includes subcategories, the subcategory assignments are lost when you make the move. However, you can move subcategory assignments from one subcategory to another subcategory with the Move button.

Moving all transactions from one category to another category

To change category or subcategory assignments throughout your account registers, follow these steps:

1. **Click the Categories button on the Navigation bar or press Ctrl+Shift+C to go to the Categories & Payees window.**

2. **If necessary, click the Categories button on the window to make the categories and subcategories appear.**

   To see the categories and subcategories, you may need to open the View menu and choose Categories and their Subcategories.

3. **Scroll down the list and click the name of the category or subcategory whose transactions you want to reassign.**

   For example, if you erroneously assigned transactions to the Education: Kids subcategory when you should have assigned them to the Childcare category, click the Education: Kids subcategory on the list.

   Remember, the category or subcategory you select is deleted from the Payees & Categories window after you are done reassigning the transactions.

4. **Click the Move button.**

   You see the Move Transactions dialog box shown in Figure 4-12. This is where you tell Money where to reassign the transactions in the category or subcategory you chose in Step 3. The text box on the left is for selecting a category and the text box on the right is for selecting a subcategory, if necessary.

Figure 4-12:
Use the
Move
Transactions
dialog box
to reassign
transactions
to a
different
category
and
subcategory.

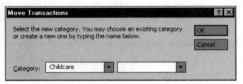

5. **In the Category text box on the left, select the category to which you want to reassign the transactions.**

6. **If you want to reassign the transactions to a subcategory, select it from the subcategory text box on the right.**

7. **Click OK.**

On the Categories list, the category or subcategory you chose in Step 3 has been deleted. Meanwhile, all transactions in your registers that were assigned the old category or subcategory are assigned the one you chose in Steps 5 and 6.

Reassigning transactions to new categories one at a time

Instead of making a wholesale reassignment of one category or subcategory to another, you may decide to examine transactions one at a time and choose which ones need reassigning. To do that, you have to search for transactions in the account registers, examine each transaction, and then either choose a new category and subcategory or move on without moving the transaction.

The "Finding a transaction so you can fix it" section in Chapter 3 explains everything you need to know about finding transactions. However, here are shorthand instructions for finding and fixing transactions that were assigned the wrong category or subcategory:

1. **Choose Tools⇨Find⇨Transactions or press Ctrl+F.**

   You see the Find Transactions dialog box shown at the top of Figure 4-13. The figure shows the results of the search.

2. **Click the Categories tab.**

3. **Click the Selected categories radio button.**

4. **If you are looking for a subcategory, click the Show subcategories check box.**

5. **Scroll through the list of categories and subcategories and click the one that needs fixing.**

6. **Click the Find button.**

   A list of transactions that were assigned the category or subcategory you chose appears at the bottom of the dialog box (see Figure 4-13).

7. **Double-click the first transaction on the list that needs reassigning, and, in the Edit Transaction dialog box, select a new category or subcategory, if necessary; then click OK or Cancel.**

   Figure 4-13 shows the Edit Transaction dialog box. It works exactly like a transaction form.

   By the way, when you double-click a transaction that has been reconciled, Money beeps and warns you not to change the amount of the transaction you are about to edit. Don't worry about the warning. You are concerned with the category assignment, not the amount of the transaction.

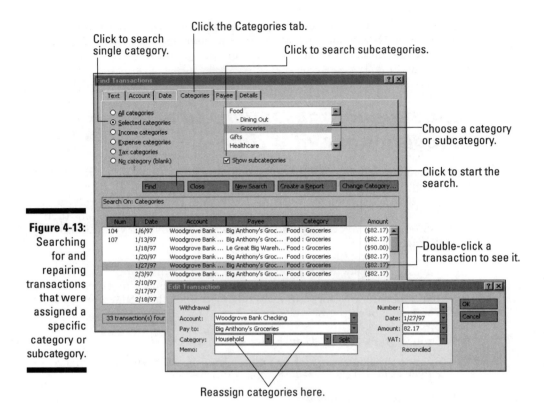

Click to search single category.

Click the Categories tab.

Click to search subcategories.

Choose a category or subcategory.

Click to start the search.

Figure 4-13: Searching for and repairing transactions that were assigned a specific category or subcategory.

Double-click a transaction to see it.

Reassign categories here.

8. **Double-click the other transactions on the list and investigate them as well.**

9. **Click the Close button in the Find Transactions dialog box after you are done reassigning transactions.**

Renaming and Deleting Categories and Classifications

After you have worked with Money for a while and you have refined the list of categories and classifications that you want to work with, you can delete unnecessary categories and classifications. And if a category or classification name isn't descriptive enough, you can rename it. The following sections explain how to delete and rename categories, subcategories, and classifications.

After you have renamed a category or classification, transactions throughout the account registers that were assigned the old category or classification name are automatically given the new name. So when you rename, you also change the names of category, subcategory, or classification assignments throughout your registers.

Renaming a category or subcategory

Follow these steps to rename a category or subcategory:

1. **Click the Categories button on the Navigation bar or choose** **Go**➪**Categories to go to the Categories & Payees window.**

2. **If necessary, click the Categori**e**s button on the window to see the list** **of categories and subcategories.**

   If you don't see subcategory names but need to see them, choose Categories and their Subcategories from the View menu.

3. **Scroll down the list and click the category or subcategory whose** **name you want to change.**

4. **Click the Mod**i**fy button or right-click and choose** **R**ename.

   You see either the Modify Category dialog box or the Modify Sub-Category dialog box shown in Figure 4-14.

5. **Enter a name in the New** **n**ame text box and click OK.

Figure 4-14:
Changing
the name of
a category
or
subcategory.

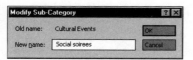

Renaming a classification

Follow these dance steps to change the name of a classification:

1. **Click the Categories button on the Navigation bar or choose** **Go**➪**Categories to open the Categories & Payees window.**

2. **Click the button on the left side of the window that is named after the** **classification whose name you want to change.**

3. **Click the Rename Classification button.**

   The button is located in the lower-left corner of the screen. The Re-name Classification dialog box appears.

4. **Enter a name in the New name text box and click OK.**

   Back in the Categories & Payees window, the button you clicked in Step 2 has a new name. Classification assignments throughout your account registers have new names as well.

Deleting a category or subcategory

When you no longer need a category or subcategory, you can delete it. However, be careful, because if you delete a category or subcategory to which transactions are assigned, the transactions lose their category assignments. In other words, you end up with transactions to which no category is assigned — and that defeats one of the primary reasons people use Money, to categorize their spending and income to find out where the money came from and where it went.

Try to delete a category or subcategory to which categories are assigned and you see the Delete Category dialog box shown in Figure 4-15. From this dialog box, you can assign transactions to a different category before you delete the category in question, but do you really want to do that? Suppose that some transactions belong in one category and others belong in another category. No, reviewing the transactions one at a time before you delete the category to which they are assigned is wiser. Earlier in this chapter, the "Reassigning transactions to new categories one at a time" section explains how to review transactions before you change their category or subcategory assignments.

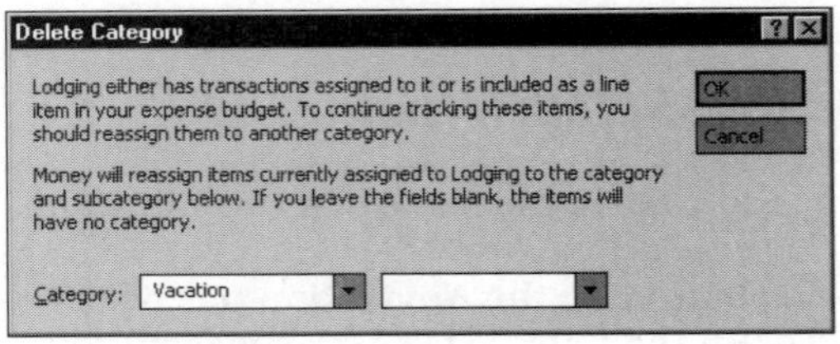

Figure 4-15:
If you try to delete a category to which transactions in your registers are still assigned, this dialog box appears.

Delete Category   ? X

Lodging either has transactions assigned to it or is included as a line item in your expense budget. To continue tracking these items, you should reassign them to another category.

> OK
>
> Cancel

Money will reassign items currently assigned to Lodging to the category and subcategory below. If you leave the fields blank, the items will have no category.

Category: [Vacation   ▼]   [▼]

After you have reviewed the transactions whose category you want to delete, follow these steps to delete a category or subcategory:

1. **Click the Categories button on the Navigation bar or choose Go⇨Categories to open the Categories & Payees window.**

2. **Click the Categories button on the window, if necessary, to see the list of categories and subcategories.**

   If you intend to delete a subcategory, you may need to choose Categories and their Subcategories from the View menu to see subcategories.

3. **Scroll through the list and click the category or subcategory you want to delete.**

4. **Click the Delete button or right-click and choose Delete from the shortcut menu.**

That's all she wrote — the category is gone from the Categories & Payees window. However, if you try to delete a category with subcategories underneath it, a dialog box warns you that deleting a category also deletes its subcategories. If you try to delete a category to which transactions are assigned, you see the Delete Category dialog box shown in Figure 4-15.

Whatever you do, don't delete a category with subcategories. Investigate the matter first and find out if you need the subcategories for tracking your finances.

A fast way to remove deadwood categories

When you install Money on your computer, the program gives you a bunch of generic categories that you may or may not need. Very likely, you don't need many of them. To quickly remove them, you can use a special button called Remove Unused Categories. After you click the button, Money removes all categories and subcategories on the Categories list to which no transaction has been assigned.

Follow these steps to remove deadwood categories that take up space on the Categories list:

1. **Choose Tools⇨Options to open the Options dialog box.**

2. **Click the Categories tab.**

3. **Make sure that a check mark appears in the Ask me before removing each category check box, and if a check mark doesn't appear, click the check box.**

4. **Click the Remove Unused Categories button. A dialog box asks if you want to remove a certain category.**

5. **Click Yes or No.**

6. **Keep clicking Yes or No until all deadwood categories and subcategories have been axed.**

Deleting a classification

After you delete a classification, all transactions throughout the registers that were assigned the classification are no longer assigned to it. Therefore, I suggest that you think twice before deleting a classification. Think twice and think hard. Going back through the registers and reassigning transactions to a classification that you deleted is hard work to be avoided.

Follow these steps to delete a classification that you no longer need:

1. **Click the Categories button on the Navigation bar or choose Go⇨Categories to open the Categories & Payees window.**

2. **Click the button on the left side of the window that is named after the classification that you want to delete.**

3. **Click the Delete Classification button.**

   You can find this button in the lower-left corner of the window. A dialog box warns you of the drastic nature of what you are about to do.

4. **Ignore the dialog box and click Yes to delete the classification.**

   Back on the Categories & Payees window, the classification button now has the generic name Classification 1 or Classification 2, and all class and sub-class names have disappeared from the screen.

You can delete a class or sub-class by right-clicking it and choosing Delete.

Chapter 5

Reconciling, or Balancing, an Account

- -

In This Chapter

▶ Finding out what reconciling is and how to do it in Money

▶ Reconciling a savings or checking account

▶ Recognizing and fixing reconciliation problems

▶ Using the AutoReconcile feature to fix reconciliation problems

▶ Reconciling a credit card account

- -

*U*ntil I started using Money, I never *reconciled,* or balanced, my checking or savings account. But Money makes balancing an account very easy indeed. No kidding, you can do it in four or five minutes.

This chapter explains what reconciling is, how to reconcile the transactions in your records with the bank's records, and what to do if you can't get an account to reconcile. Because reconciling a credit card account can be slightly tricky, you can find instructions in this chapter for reconciling credit card accounts as well as checking and savings accounts. Bon voyage!

How Reconciling Works

Reconciling is your opportunity to examine your records closely and make sure that they are accurate. When you reconcile an account, you compare your record's to the bank's, fix discrepancies if you find any, enter transactions that appear on the statement that you forgot to enter in the register, and click in the C (for Cleared) column next to each transaction that appears both in the register and on the bank statement.

What does "reconcile" mean, anyway?

In financial terms, *reconcile* means to compare one set of records to another for the sake of accuracy. When you reconcile an account in Money, you compare the transactions on the statement that the bank or brokerage house sent you to the transactions you entered in the Money register.

If you find a discrepancy between your records and the bank's, you can be pretty sure

that the error was made on your side. Banks don't err very often when recording financial transactions. Yes, bank lines move too slowly and banks have been known to nickel and dime their customers with all kinds of petty charges, but banks are sticklers for accuracy. If you find a discrepancy between your records and the bank's, change your records to match those of the bank's.

In an account register, transactions that have *cleared the bank* — transactions that have been reconciled — show an R (for Reconciled) in the C (for Cleared) column, as shown in Figure 5-1. In the figure, you can see that some of the transactions have cleared the bank and some are still waiting to be cleared.

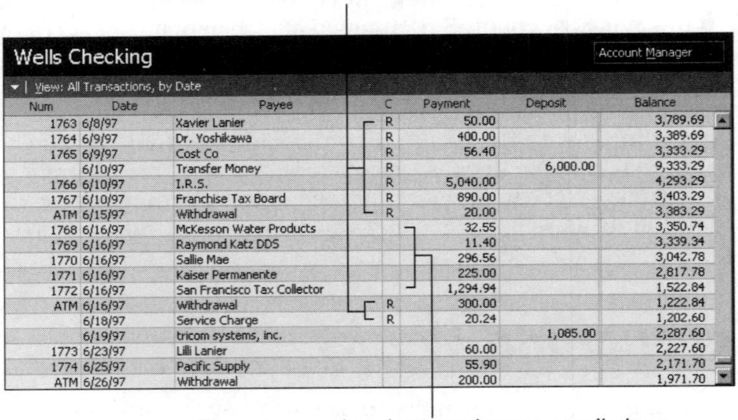

These transactions have cleared the bank.

Figure 5-1:
Transactions that have cleared the bank and been reconciled show an R in the register's C (for Cleared) column.

These transactions have not been reconciled yet.

Reconciling an Account

Reconciling an account is a two-step business. First, you tell the program how much money in interest the account earned (if it earned any) and how much you had to pay the bank for checks, ATM withdrawals, and other service charges (if you had to pay anything). Then you move ahead to the Balance dialog box, where you make your records jibe with the bank's and click off each transaction that appears both on your bank statement and in the register.

Before you begin comparing the register to the bank statement, lay the bank statement flat on the desk. And you may want to put checks in numerical order (if you intend to reconcile a checking account) and put your ATM slips in data order (you *have* been saving your ATM slips, haven't you?). With a little luck, you may be able to reconcile without having to glance at checks and ATM slips. But if something goes amiss, you may have to examine the paperwork closely.

Telling Money which transactions cleared the bank

Follow these steps to tell Money which transactions cleared the bank and reconcile an account:

1. **Open the account that you intend to reconcile.**

   To open the account, click the Accounts button to open the Account Manager window, click the Accounts arrow on the left side of the screen, and then select the account you want to open from the drop-down list.

2. **Click the Balance button in the lower-left corner of the screen.**

   You see a Balance dialog box like the one in Figure 5-2. The dialog box lists the name of the account you are reconciling after the word "Balance" in the title bar, so the account I'm reconciling in Figure 5-2 is called Business Checking. This dialog box is where you enter information from the bank statement. The Starting balance text box shows the amount of money in the account as of the last time you reconciled it (or the account's opening balance if you recently opened the account).

3. **If necessary, enter the date listed on the bank statement in the Statement date text box.**

4. **In the Ending balance text box, enter the closing balance from the bank statement.**

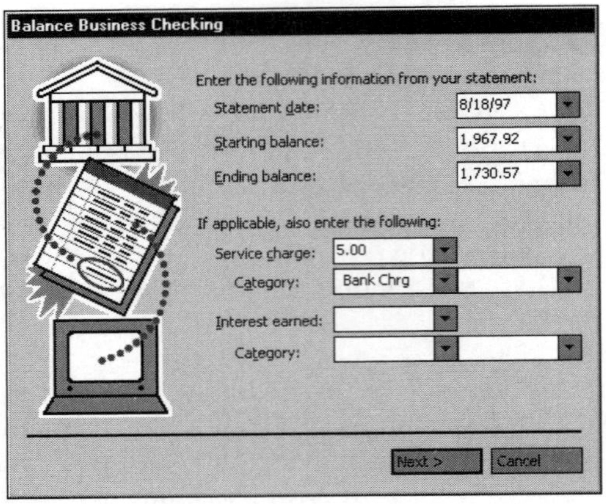

Figure 5-2:
The
Balance
dialog box,
where you
tell Money
what the
bank told
you.

5. **If you have to pay a service charge, enter it in the Service charge text box, and categorize the service charge as well.**

Banks, like mosquitoes, like to bite customers and charge all sorts of miscellaneous fees. The fees appear on bank statements. You may get charged for ordering checks or calling for information or using an ATM or sneezing too loudly. Scour the statement for evidence of service charges and enter the sum of those charges in the Service charge box. For a category, choose Bank Charges: Service Charge, or something similar. (And for more on categorizing, turn to Chapter 4.)

6. **In the Interest earned text box, enter an amount if the account earned any interest, and categorize the interest payment as well.**

You may use the Int Inc (Interest Income) category, for example.

7. **Click the Next button to move ahead to the Balance Account window shown in Figure 5-3.**

Only transactions in the register that have not been reconciled appear in the window. If you entered a service charge and/or interest payment in the Balance dialog box (in Steps 5 and 6), the amounts already appear in the window along with a C, to show that they have been cleared.

In Figure 5-3, the account has been reconciled successfully. You can tell by looking at number 2 (Try to get balance difference to zero) on the left side of the window. There, the sum of the cleared transactions ($1,730.57) and the sum of the transactions on the statement ($1,730.57) are equal. When you click the C column in the register to clear transactions, the Cleared amount changes. The Statement amount does not change. It comes from the Balance dialog box (refer to Figure 5-2), where you entered it in the Ending balance text box.

Click here when a transaction also appears on the bank statement.

Figure 5-3:
Compare
transactions
in the
register
to the
transactions
on the bank
statement;
click in the
C column
next to
each
transaction
that
appears in
both places.

	Accounts	Business Checking							Account Manager

Balance Account

1. Click the "C" column to clear transactions from your statement.

Cleared so far:

0 Deposits	0.00
7 Payments	237.35

2. Try to get balance difference to zero:

Cleared:	1,730.57
Statement:	1,730.57
Difference:	0.00

☑ Click here to add or edit transactions

3. Click Next:

[Next >] [Postpone]

View: Unreconciled Transactions, by Number

Num	Date	Payee	C	Payment	Deposit	Balance
	7/16/97	tricom systems, inc.			890.00	2,857.92
	7/22/97	Wells Fargo	C	5.00		2,852.92
116	5/30/97	Rooftop PTA	C	50.00		2,802.92
117	5/30/97	Rooftop PTA	C	30.00		2,772.92
118	5/30/97	Rooftop PTA	C	20.00		2,752.92
119	6/16/97	Pac Bell	C	40.08		2,712.84
120	6/16/97	Pac Bell	C	42.27		2,670.57
121	6/16/97	Dept. of Parking and Traffic	C	50.00		2,620.57
122	7/1/97	Advantage Enterprises		195.05		2,425.52
123	7/16/97	Bronsteins' Music		97.00		2,328.52

Ending Balance: $2,328.52

Check	Deposit	Transfer	Withdrawal	Cash Machine

[New] [Edit] [Enter] [Cancel]

Number: 121
Date: 6/16/97
Amount: 50.00

Pay to: Dept. of Parking and Traffic
Category: Parking ticket
Classification 1:
Memo: 908830440 and 906738151

Cleared

8. **Examine your bank statement and click the C column next to each transaction on the statement that also appears in the register.**

   As you click transactions, the Cleared figure and Statement figure gradually fall in line with each other. If all goes well, they show the same amount and the Difference figure shows 0.00, as in Figure 5-3. The next section in this chapter explains how you can fix mistakes in the register while you reconcile. The section after that offers strategies for recognizing and fixing reconciliation problems.

   If you have trouble finding a transaction in the register, click the View arrow and select By Date or By Number. By Date lists transactions in date order, and By Number lists them in numerical order on the Num column.

9. **Click the Next button after the account has been reconciled.**

   A Congratulations screen appears and tells you that your account is balanced.

10. **Click the Finish button on the Congratulations screen.**

    Back in the register, all those Cs in the Balance Account window turn to Rs in the register. The transactions you clicked off in the Balance Account window have cleared the bank and have been reconciled with your records.

If the reconciling business makes you tired or you find something better to do, click the Postpone button. Later, you can pick up where you left off by clicking the Balance button on the Account window.

Fixing mistakes as you reconcile

Glancing at the bank statement, you discover that you made a mistake when you entered a transaction in a register. Or perhaps you forgot to enter a transaction altogether. It happens. Cash withdrawals from ATM machines, which are usually made at the spur of the moment, often fail to get recorded in account registers.

To enter a new transaction or edit one you already entered, Money offers the small check box on the left side of the Balance Account window beside the words "Click here to add or edit transactions." When you click this check box, transaction forms appear at the bottom of the window, as shown in Figure 5-3. Use the forms to enter or edit a transaction in the register. Before you can edit a transaction, you have to select it in the register.

Help! The Darn Thing Won't Reconcile!

Not being able to reconcile a bank account is frustrating. You pore over the bank statement. You examine checks and ATM slips. You gnash your teeth and pull your hair, but still the thing won't reconcile. No matter how hard you try, the Difference figure that lists the difference between the cleared amount and the statement amount cannot be brought to 0.00.

To help you get out of the jam you are in, Money offers techniques for recognizing and fixing reconciliation problems. Money also has a gizmo called AutoReconcile that may or may not be able to help you reconcile your bank account.

A checklist of things to do if you can't reconcile

If an account won't balance, a number of different things could be wrong. The following list explains how to recognize and fix reconciliation problems.

✔ **A transaction was not entered.** The primary reason that accounts don't reconcile is because a transaction that is listed on the bank statement has not been entered in the register. To find out whether you are suffering from this particular problem, look for a transaction on the bank statement that is equal to the Difference amount on the Balance Account window. If the Difference amount is $30.00, chances are you forgot to record a $30.00 transaction in the register. Look for a $30.00 transaction on the bank statement and, if necessary, record it in the register.

✔ **An amount in the register is incorrect.** Another reason that accounts don't reconcile is because amounts were entered incorrectly in the register. This problem is a sticky one and is hard to track down. Look for transposed numbers and numbers entered backwards. For example, $32.41 and $34.21 look alike at a glance, but there is a difference of $1.80 between the numbers. (An old accountant's trick: If the difference between what you have and what you should have is divisible by 9, you probably transposed a number.) To fix an incorrect entry, click the transaction and then click the check box called Click here to add or edit transactions. Transaction forms appear at the bottom of the window. Change the amount on a transaction form.

✔ **A transaction was entered twice.** Look for duplicate transactions in the register. If a transaction was entered twice, delete one of the transactions by right-clicking it and choosing Delete from the shortcut menu.

✔ **The Ending (Statement) balance is incorrect.** If you enter the Ending balance incorrectly in the Balance dialog box (refer to Figure 5-2), you cannot reconcile an account no matter how hard you try. Compare the Statement figure on the Balance Account window to the ending balance on your statement. If the figures do not match, you need to return to the Balance dialog box (refer to Figure 5-2) and enter a correct Ending balance figure. To do so, click the Postpone button to return to the Accounts window, click the Balance button, and then click Next. You see the Balance dialog box again, where you can enter a correct Ending balance this time.

✔ **A service charge or interest earned is incorrect.** Besides entering the Ending balance incorrectly, you may have entered an incorrect amount in the Service charge or Interest earned text box in the Balance dialog box (refer to Figure 5-2). Compare the interest and service charges on your statement to the ones on the Balance Account window. If an amount is incorrect, click it, click the check box called Click here to add or edit transactions, and enter a correct figure on the transaction form.

✔ **The bank statement was not flipped over.** I'm embarrassed to admit it, but one or two times I wasn't able to reconcile an account because I forgot to turn over the bank statement and examine the transactions on the other side of the page — very stupid of me. I couldn't understand why the account wouldn't reconcile until I turned the page and noticed a bunch of other transactions that needed addressing.

Many bank statements include a total of all debits (payments) and a total of all credits (deposits). By comparing these numbers to the numbers on the Balance Account window (refer to Figure 5-3), you can quickly see if you are out of agreement on your deposits or your payments.

Money's AutoReconcile gizmo

If, despite your detective work, you can't find the problem that keeps your account from reconciling, you can always try your luck with Money's AutoReconcile gizmo. This contraption scours the register for transactions that it thinks were entered incorrectly and gives you the chance to enter them correctly so that the account can be reconciled.

Follow these steps to try out the AutoReconcile gizmo:

1. **Click Next on the Balance Account window.**

   Click Next even though the account has not been reconciled. The Balance dialog box appears. It tells you that the account isn't in balance and asks what you want to do about it.

2. **Click the Use AutoReconcile to help find the error radio button and click Next.**

   If Money can find what it thinks is an error, it displays the Possible Error dialog box shown in Figure 5-4.

3. **Read the description of the error and click Yes or No to change the transaction in question or let it stand.**

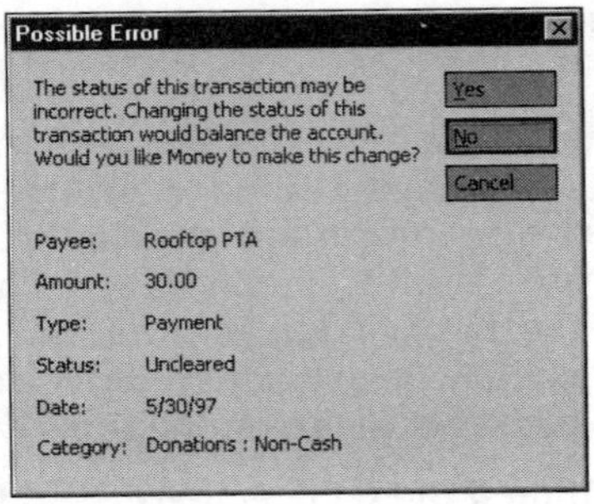

Figure 5-4:
If you can't reconcile an account, try using the AutoReconcile gizmo to locate transactions that were entered incorrectly.

Possible Error

The status of this transaction may be incorrect. Changing the status of this transaction would balance the account. Would you like Money to make this change?

Yes

No

Cancel

Payee:	Rooftop PTA
Amount:	30.00
Type:	Payment
Status:	Uncleared
Date:	5/30/97
Category:	Donations : Non-Cash

Reconciling a Credit Card Account

Reconciling a credit card account is done in much the same way as reconciling a checking or savings account. The only difference is in the Balance dialog box (refer to Figure 5-2), where you tell Money how much the statement says that you owe.

When you reconcile an account, you clear credits as well as charges made to your credit card. Before you start reconciling, make sure that the credits the card issuer owes you have been entered in the credit card register.

Lay the credit card bill flat on your desk and follow these steps to reconcile a credit card account:

1. **Open the credit card account that you intend to reconcile.**

2. **Click the Balance button.**

   You see the Balance dialog box shown in Figure 5-5. The amount you owed as of the last time you reconciled the account appears in the Total amount you owed last month text box.

3. **In the Statement date text box, enter the date on your credit card statement.**

4. **In the Total amount you owe this month text box, enter the total amount that the statement says that you owe, including service and interest charges.**

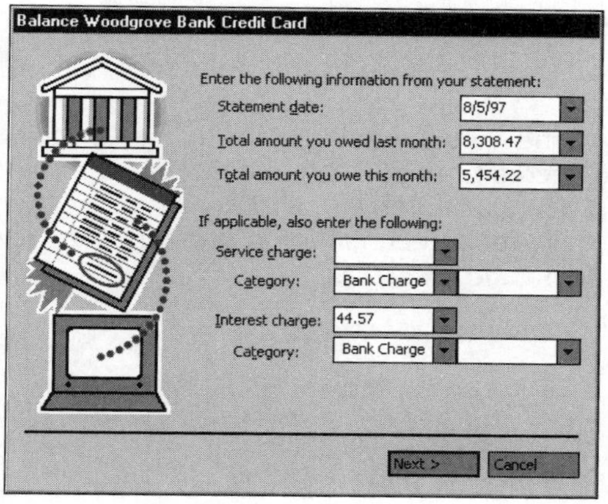

Figure 5-5:
When you reconcile a credit card account, start by telling Money how much you owe this month.

5. **In the Service charge text box, enter the service charges, if any, that you were charged for, and categorize the expense in the Category text box.**

   Some credit card issuers charge an annual fee. An annual fee falls under the Service charge heading, although most issuers don't levy service charges. They don't have to because they can take it out of your hide in exorbitant monthly interest charges, which brings up Step 6.

6. **In the Interest charge text box, enter the amount you must pay in interest to service the credit card debt.**

   Most people don't pay off their credit card debt each month, so they have to pay an interest charge. And if you take out cash advances, you have to pay interest for those, too.

7. **Click the Next button.**

   You see the Balance Account window, which lists all transactions in the register that have not been reconciled. If the Balance Account window looks familiar, that is because it looks like and works exactly like the Balance Account window for reconciling savings and checking accounts.

8. **Examine your credit card statement and click the C column next to each transaction on the statement that also appears in the register.**

   To change the amount of a charge or credit, click it in the register and then click the check box called Click here to add or edit transactions. That step brings up the transaction forms so that you can alter the transaction.

9. **Click the Next button after the account is reconciled.**

   A Congratulations screen appears.

10. **Click the Finish button on the Congratulations screen.**

Guess what? You can use the same techniques for fixing reconciliation problems in credit card accounts as you can in checking and savings accounts. See the "Help! The Darn Thing Won't Reconcile!" section earlier in this chapter to find out how to fix reconciliation problems or use the AutoReconcile gizmo to find and fix errors.

Chapter 6

Writing and Printing Checks

· ·

In This Chapter

▶ Identifying the different kinds of checks

▶ Ordering checks

▶ Preparing your printer to print checks

▶ Recording checks that you intend to print in registers

▶ Printing practice checks

▶ Printing a full or partial sheet of checks

▶ Reprinting checks that didn't print correctly

· ·

*N*ot every Money user needs to print checks. Checks are expensive for one thing. An order of 500 checks can cost between $72 and $90, depending on the kind of check you order, whereas most banks charge about $15 for that many checks. So printing checks with Money costs five to six times as much as writing checks by hand.

But printing checks with Money can save time, especially if you run a small business and print lots of checks. When you write a check by hand, you have to write it twice (once when you record it in a register and once when you scribble on the paper check). When you print a check with Money, you only enter it once when you record it in a register. The printer handles the rest. What's more, you can *batch-print* checks (print a dozen or so at once). Small business owners that print lots of payroll checks or monthly expense checks ought to seriously consider printing checks with Money.

Another advantage of printing checks is being able to itemize the payment on the check stub. As long as you print checks on wallet-size or voucher checks (I explain those shortly), you can itemize the payment by splitting it (discussed in Chapter 3). The split-transaction information appears on the check stub.

But the best reason for printing checks has nothing to do with saving time or itemizing — it has to do with appearances. Printed checks are more professional-looking. They make a good impression on creditors and clients.

A printed check says, "I mean business," whereas a handwritten check with spidery lettering says, "Thank you kind sir or madam for honoring my little check." Everyone who works in a profession where appearances count — supermodels, for example — ought to print checks.

This chapter explains everything you need to know about printing checks — from choosing the right type of checks, ordering checks, telling your printer how to print checks, to adjusting checks that don't print correctly. You also discover how to record checks in a register, print a full sheet or a partial sheet of checks, and print addresses on checks.

By the way, if you came to this chapter to find out how to record a check in a register, you came to the wrong place. You should be in Chapter 3.

Deciding What Kind of Check to Order

Your first decision is what kind of check to order. The choices are wallet-size, standard business, or voucher checks. Checks and check envelopes are available in standard as well as European sizes. Table 6-1 compares and contrasts the three types of checks. The checks are printed on sheets and are loaded in the printer like sheets of paper. The table explains how many checks are on each sheet.

Table 6-1			Checks for Use with Money	
Name	*Size*	*Checks per Sheet*	*Cost per 500/ Cost per Check**	*Description*
Wallet-size	2.83" x 8.5"	3 checks	$72.50/14.5¢	The smallest check. It includes a 2.5" perforated stub for tracking expenses. This check is for individuals, not businesses. Standard colors: blue or green.
Standard business	3.5" x 8.5"	3 checks	$78.50/16¢	The largest check. It does not include a stub, although you can list tax-deductible expenses on the Memo line. For small businesses. Standard colors: blue or green, plus security watermark.

Name	Size	Checks per Sheet	Cost per 500/ Cost per Check*	Description
Voucher	3.5" x 8.5"	1 check	$89.50/18¢	Includes ample room — two-thirds of a page — for listing expenses. For small businesses that need to itemize checks in detail. Standard colors: blue, burgundy, gray, or green, plus security watermark.

* Prices listed here are from Microsoft Money Checks, are for standard-color checks, and are current as of September 1997. Premier-color checks, which come in a variety of colors, cost an additional $14 per 500 checks. You can buy checks in sets of 250, 500, 1,000, or 2,000. Different vendors offer different prices for checks.

Ordering the Checks

Once you know how many checks you want and in what size, your next step is to contact Microsoft Money Checks, the company that handles check orders. Third-party vendors also offer checks. Be sure to find out if they work with Money 98.

Get in touch with Microsoft Money Checks by phone or fax at the following numbers:

✔ **By phone:** 800-432-1285. To help decide whether you want the checks, ask the friendly human to send a brochure and throw in a few sample checks for you to experiment with.

I recommend calling the company because the friendly human on the other side of the phone connection can likely answer all your questions. Perhaps checks are available in soft lilac, paprika, icy periwinkle, and the other chichi colors whose names grace clothing catalogues. I'm too scared to ask.

✔ **By fax:** 800-531-1931. In the box that Money comes in you may find an order form, but if it isn't there, you can generate a form. Choose Help⇨Ordering Checks and click the Click here to order checks hyperlink. That step takes you to information about ordering checks, including the address of Microsoft Money Checks in case you want to mail the form, not fax it. To get to the order form, click the Microsoft Money checks order form hyperlink. You see a Help window with the order form on it. Click the Print button and click OK in the Print dialog box.

Choosing a starting number for the checks

When you choose a starting number for the checks, be sure to choose one that won't conflict with the numbers on checks you write by hand. Bankers frown and even call you on the telephone when you write two checks with the same check number. And if you try to record two checks with the same number in a checking register, a dialog box asks if you really want to do that.

Writing checks with duplicate numbers is a *faux pas,* but it is easy to do when you write checks and print checks from the same account. Your spouse, check book in hand, could be on a shopping spree while you are at home printing checks. Or you could write a few checks from the check book, forget to record

them in Money, and then print checks with the same numbers without thinking about it.

To keep from writing checks with duplicate numbers, choose a starting number for the printed checks that is far, far removed from the check numbers in your check book. For example, if the checks in your check book are numbered 600 to 650, choose 1501 as the starting check number for printed checks. That way, you can't write and print checks with duplicate numbers.

Printing the checks you order isn't absolutely necessary. You can always tear one off and write it by hand when you buy a pillbox hat at the thrift store or pay for a pizza.

Whether you order the checks by phone or fax, you need to give Microsoft Money Checks the following information, most of which is found on the face of a check:

- ✓ Your name, address, and phone number.
- ✓ Your bank's name and the city, state, and zip code in which it is located.
- ✓ Your bank's *fractional number.* When you deposit a check, you usually list the first four numbers of the fractional number on the deposit slip. Here is an example of a fractional number: 66-55/4321.
- ✓ Your checking account number.
- ✓ The starting check number. See the sidebar "Choosing a starting number for the checks" to find out the ins and outs of choosing a number.
- ✓ The size of the checks — wallet, standard business, or voucher.
- ✓ Whether yours is a laser printer or a continuous-feed printer.

Getting Your Printer Ready to Print Checks

To print checks, Money and your computer have to be on speaking terms. They have to understand each other and be able to work together. And your printer has to know which kind of check to print — a wallet-size check, standard business check, or voucher check.

Very likely, Money and your printer have already been introduced. When you install Money, the program gets information about your printer from the operating system, Windows 95. You probably don't have to tinker with the printer settings, but you do need to tell the printer what kind of check to print.

Follow these steps to open the Check Setup dialog box and tell your printer everything it needs to know to print checks:

1. Choose File⇨Print Setup⇨Check Setup.

You see the Check Setup dialog box shown in Figure 6-1.

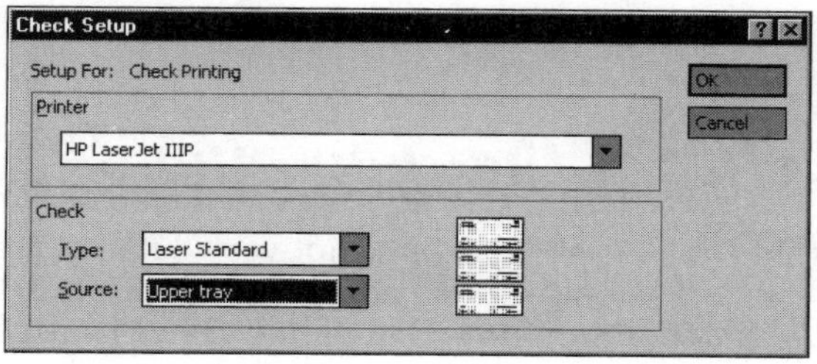

Figure 6-1:
Use the Check Setup dialog box to tell Money about your printer and the style of check that you intend to print.

2. In the Printer drop-down list, select which printer to print the checks with, if necessary.

More than one printer appears on the drop-down list if you or someone else set up a second or third printer to work with your computer. Select the printer from which you will print the checks.

3. **Click the down-arrow on the <u>T</u>ype drop-down list and select which style of check you will print on.**

   Select an option from the top of the list if you have a laser printer. Choices for continuous-feed printers, also known as pinwheel printers, appear on the bottom of the list. (If you migrated to Money from Quicken, additional choices appear on the Type drop-down list for printing on Quicken check forms. See Chapter 24.)

4. **If necessary, click the down-arrow on the <u>S</u>ource drop-down list and select the tray through which you will feed checks to the printer.**

   Don't bother with the Source drop-down list if your computer has only one tray.

5. **Click OK to close the Check Setup dialog box.**

At Last — Time to Print the Checks

So far in this chapter, you have been reading about the preliminaries. Everything you've read about until now takes place before you print checks. But now the moment of truth has arrived. It is time to print the checks!

The following pages explain how to record a check before printing, print a practice check, make adjustments, print a full sheet or a partial sheet of checks, print one check or several checks at a time, and include an address on a check in case you want to mail it in a window envelope.

Recording checks that you intend to print

Recording a check that you intend to print is not very different from recording a handwritten check. The only difference is that you select Print this transaction from the Number drop-down list on the Check transaction form instead of entering a check number, as Figure 6-2 shows.

Chapter 3 explains everything you need or care to know about recording a check, but here are the raw details:

1. **Open the checking account register from which you want to write the check.**

2. **Click the Chec<u>k</u> tab.**

3. **From the Number drop-down list, select Print this transaction.**

4. **Enter the date that you want to appear on the check in the Date text box.**

These checks have not been printed yet

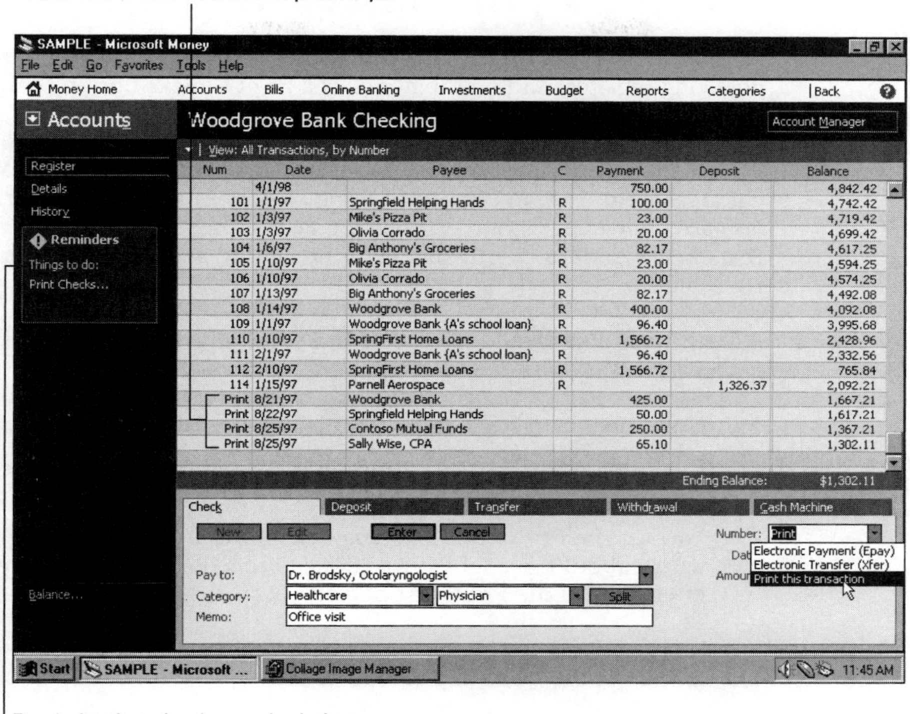

Figure 6-2:
Select
Print this
transaction
from the
Number
drop-down
list to
record a
check you
want to
print.

Num	Date	Payee	C	Payment	Deposit	Balance
	4/1/98			750.00		4,842.42
101	1/1/97	Springfield Helping Hands	R	100.00		4,742.42
102	1/3/97	Mike's Pizza Pit	R	23.00		4,719.42
103	1/3/97	Olivia Corrado	R	20.00		4,699.42
104	1/6/97	Big Anthony's Groceries	R	82.17		4,617.25
105	1/10/97	Mike's Pizza Pit	R	23.00		4,594.25
106	1/10/97	Olivia Corrado	R	20.00		4,574.25
107	1/13/97	Big Anthony's Groceries	R	82.17		4,492.08
108	1/14/97	Woodgrove Bank	R	400.00		4,092.08
109	1/1/97	Woodgrove Bank {A's school loan}	R	96.40		3,995.68
110	1/10/97	SpringFirst Home Loans	R	1,566.72		2,428.96
111	2/1/97	Woodgrove Bank {A's school loan}	R	96.40		2,332.56
112	2/10/97	SpringFirst Home Loans	R	1,566.72		765.84
114	1/15/97	Parnell Aerospace	R		1,326.37	2,092.21
Print	8/21/97	Woodgrove Bank		425.00		1,667.21
Print	8/22/97	Springfield Helping Hands		50.00		1,617.21
Print	8/25/97	Contoso Mutual Funds		250.00		1,367.21
Print	8/25/97	Sally Wise, CPA		65.10		1,302.11

└Reminder that checks need printing

5. **Enter the name of the person or business you are paying in the Pay To text box.**

   If you have paid this person or party before, you can enter the payee's name by typing the first couple of letters and pressing the Tab key.

6. **Enter the amount of the check in the Amount text box.**

7. **Describe the transaction by selecting a category and subcategory.**

8. **Click the Enter button (or press Enter).**

The check number is entered in the register automatically after the check is printed. Until the check number is entered, the word `Print` appears in the `Num` column of the register, as shown in Figure 6-2, and the Reminders notice tells you that checks in the register need printing.

When you split a check payment, the split-transaction information appears on the voucher, or stub, of the check, provided that you're printing on wallet-size or voucher checks. (Wallet-size and voucher checks include a stub.)

Printing a practice check

After you have recorded a check, the Reminders notice appears beside the checking register. And on the notice is a Print Checks button that you can click to print checks. You are ready to go.

Rather than print on a real check, insert one of the practice checks that came inside the Money 98 box or a thin piece of paper into the printer. After you are done experimenting, you can lay the sheet of paper over a sheet of real checks and hold both sheets to the light to see if the text landed in the right places.

Follow these steps to do a test run and see if your printer handles checks correctly:

1. **Open the checking register if it is not already open.**

2. **Click the Print Checks button on the Reminders notice or choose File⇨Print Checks.**

   You see the Print Checks dialog box shown in Figure 6-3. For now, don't worry about the confusing options in this dialog box. You are only interested in the Print Test button.

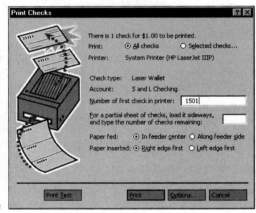

Figure 6-3: Printing a check to make sure that the printer handles checks correctly.

3. **Make sure that no number appears inside the text box called For a partial sheet of checks.**

   True, the option is actually called "For a partial sheet of checks, load it sideways, and type the number of checks remaining." But that's a mouthful, so I'm going to call this and other options with longwinded names by shorter, abbreviated names. Hope you don't mind.

Wallet and standard business checks come in sets of three per page. If you print only the first or first and second check in the set, you are left with a partial sheet with only one or two checks. The "Printing partial sheets of checks" section later in this chapter explains how to print a partial sheet of checks.

4. Click the Print Test button.

5. Click Cancel to close the Print Checks dialog box.

Money prints a check with a bunch of Xs on it and the words `This is a VOID check`. How does it look? If all is well, you don't need to read the next part of this chapter. It explains how to realign checks so that they print correctly.

As the "Printing partial sheets of checks" section later in this chapter explains, to print a partial sheet of checks you have to load it into your printer as if you were loading an envelope. If you want to test how partial sheets print, follow the instructions here but enter a **1** or a **2** in the For a partial sheet of checks text box in Step 3. Then tear off a practice check or two (or cut off part of the practice piece of paper you are using), load the partial sheet (or partial sheet of paper) in your printer, and click the Print Test button.

Making adjustments to the text alignment

So everything is slightly out of whack on your check? You can do something about that if you are using a laser printer. You can visit the Print Checks tab in the Options dialog box and change the vertical and horizontal alignment settings. (If you're using a dot-matrix printer, you can fix the problem the old-fashioned way by adjusting the sprockets on the printer.)

Take note of roughly how far out of position the text is, and then do the following to realign the text so that it falls correctly on your checks:

1. Click the Print Checks button on the Reminders notice to the left of the register, or choose File➪Print Checks to see the Print Checks dialog box.

2. Make sure that no number appears in the text box labeled For a partial sheet of checks.

3. Click the Options button.

As shown in Figure 6-4, you see the Print Checks tab in the Options dialog box. You can also get here by choosing Tools➪Options and then clicking the Print Checks tab.

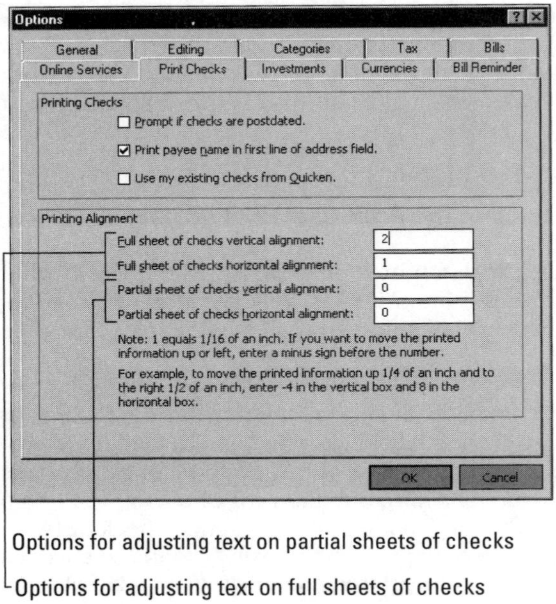

Figure 6-4:
If you have
a laser
printer, you
can use the
Print
Checks tab
to adjust
where text
falls on
sheets of
checks.

Options for adjusting text on partial sheets of checks

Options for adjusting text on full sheets of checks

At the bottom of the tab are four text boxes for changing the horizontal (side to side) and vertical (up and down) alignment of text on sheets with all three checks and on partial sheets. The horizontal boxes move the text left or right on the check. The vertical boxes move it up or down.

4. Enter a number or numbers in the text boxes.

Enter a **1** to move text by a sixteenth of an inch, a **2** to move it by an eighth (two-sixteenths) of an inch, or a **3** to move it three-sixteenths of an inch.

To move text side to side, click in one of the horizontal text boxes and enter a positive number to move the text toward the right or a negative number to move it toward the left.

To move text up or down, click one of the vertical boxes and enter a positive number to move the text down or a negative number to move it up.

5. Click OK after you are done.

You return to the Print Checks dialog box.

6. Click the Print Test button.

I hope the check prints correctly this time. If it doesn't, return to the Options dialog box and keep trying. As the prelate said to the layman, "Persistence and perseverance made a bishop of his reverence."

Printing a full sheet of checks

Take note of the number on the first check, load a sheet or two of checks into the printer, and then follow these steps to print on a full sheet of checks:

1. **Open the checking register and either click the Print Checks button on the Reminders notice or choose File⇨Print Checks.**

   You see the Print Checks dialog box (refer back to Figure 6-3).

   The top of the dialog box indicates how many checks need printing and how large a bite the checks will take out of your checking account. If the bite is too large, you can always click the Selected Checks radio button and tell Money to print a few checks, not all of them.

2. **If necessary, enter a new check number in the Number of first check in printer text box.**

   The Number of first check in printer text box lists what Money thinks is the next available check number. This number could be wrong. Compare it to the first paper check you loaded in the printer and enter a new number, if necessary.

3. **Make sure that no number appears inside the text box called For a partial sheet of checks.**

   To print a full sheet of checks, that box should be empty.

4. **Click the All Checks radio button to print all the unprinted checks in the register; click the Selected Checks button to pick and choose which ones to print.**

   Clicking the Selected Checks radio button opens the Select Checks dialog box shown in Figure 6-5. To begin with, all the checks are selected, or highlighted, in the dialog box.

   To print a handful of these checks, either click the Select None button to unselect all the checks and then click each one you want to print, or simply click each check you *don't* want to print to take its highlighting away and unselect it.

5. **Click OK.**

   You return to the Print Checks dialog box.

Figure 6-5:
Pick and
choose
which
checks to
print in this
dialog box.
It opens
automatically
when you
click the
Selected
Checks
radio
button.

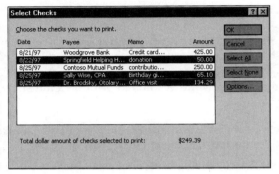

6. **Click the Print button.**

   The Print Checks dialog box shows you the numbers of the checks that "should have printed correctly." Examine the checks to see if they printed correctly.

7. **Click the Finish button if the checks printed correctly; click Reprint if they didn't print correctly.**

   If, woe is me, you have to click the Reprint button, turn a couple pages ahead to the "Whoops! My Checks Didn't Print Correctly" section. That section explains what to do next.

Compare the numbers on the printed checks to the numbers in the Num column of the checking register to make sure that the numbers match. Be sure to sign the checks.

Printing partial sheets of checks

Wallet-size and standard business checks come three to a sheet, which makes printing them slightly problematic. After you print the first check on the sheet, for example, you are left with two blank checks. It would be a shame to waste them, so Money offers options in the Print Checks dialog box for printing on partial sheets.

However, to take advantage of the partial sheet options, you may have to get out the dreary manual that came with your printer. You have to find out how your printer accepts envelopes. Find out whether envelopes are fed to your printer in the center or along the side of the paper tray. Find out as well whether envelopes are fed right-edge first or left-edge first. The settings that apply to envelopes also apply to partial sheets of checks.

The previous section in this chapter, "Printing a full sheet of checks," explains how to print checks. The only difference between printing a full sheet and a partial sheet of checks is that you have to do three important things in the Print Checks dialog box (refer to Figure 6-3):

✔ **Enter the number of remaining checks on the partial sheet in the text box called For a partial sheet of checks, load it sideways, and then type the number of checks remaining.**

✔ **Select the Paper fed radio button that describes where on the paper tray the paper is fed to your printer.**

✔ **Select the Paper inserted radio button that describes which edge of the paper is inserted in your printer.**

As someone who writes and edits computer books, I shouldn't admit it, but I have a phobia of printers. I hate them. Rather than dicker with the options for printing on partial sheets of paper, I always try to print checks three at a time. That way I never have to agonize over the partial sheet options. It's easy enough to find a second or third bill that needs paying and use it to round out a check sheet. And if I can't find a second or third bill, I simply tear out the extra checks, carry them to a store, and use them like handwritten checks.

Including addresses on checks

As long as an address is on file for a person or business to which you write a check, the address appears on the check. As Chapter 11 explains, Money gets addresses from the Payee Details window.

To enter an address for a payee, follow these steps:

1. **Click the Categories button on the Navigation bar or choose Go➪Categories to see the Categories & Payees window.**

2. **Click the Payees button.**

   You see a list of payees.

3. **Either double-click the payee for whom you want to enter an address or click the payee and then click the Go to Payee button.**

   You see the Payees window, with boxes for entering addresses and other kinds of juicy information.

4. **Enter an address.**

   The address you enter appears on printed checks.

Whoops! My Checks Didn't Print Correctly

If you had to click the Reprint button in the Print Checks dialog box because your checks didn't print correctly, all is not lost; Money gives you a second chance to print the checks. When you click the Reprint button, the Select Checks to Reprint dialog box shown in Figure 6-6 appears. From this dialog box, you tell Money which checks to reprint.

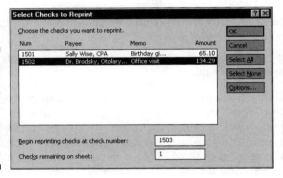

Figure 6-6:
Telling
Money
which
checks
need
reprinting.

Before you reprint wallet-size or standard business checks that didn't print correctly, you may have to load the sheets sideways in your printer. Wallet-size and standard business checks come three to a sheet, so you have to load them sideways when only one or two checks remain on a sheet. "Printing partial sheets of checks," earlier in this chapter, explains all the issues that pertain to printing on partial sheets.

After you click the Reprint button in the Print Checks dialog box, follow these steps to reprint checks:

1. **Click the checks that need reprinting.**

   As you click each check in the Select Checks to Reprint dialog box, the check is highlighted, as Figure 6-6 shows.

2. **Make sure that the number in the Begin reprinting checks at check number text box is correct, and if it isn't, enter a new number.**

   This number should match the number on the first check that is loaded in your printer.

3. **Make sure that the number in the Checks remaining on sheet text box is correct, and enter a new number if necessary.**

4. Click the OK button.

The Print Checks dialog box appears.

5. Examine your checks and click the Finish button if the checks printed correctly; click Reprint if they didn't print correctly.

As someone who has had to battle with printers, I hope that you don't have to click the Reprint button again.

Be sure to write VOID on checks that didn't print correctly and file them away with your canceled checks. That way, you have a record of what happened to them.

And on the subject of checks that didn't print correctly, what happens if you have to reprint three or four checks and you end up with a three- or four-check gap in the checking register? If you are a stickler for keeping good records, enter a transaction in the checking register for each check that needed reprinting and void it. In other words, if you botched check 1501 and reprinted it, enter a check transaction, give it number 1501, and then choose Edit⇨Mark As⇨Void to void it.

Part II
Going Online
with Money

The 5th Wave — By Rich Tennant

IN A BIZARRE MIX-UP, KEN BALANCES A BUS SCHEDULE INSTEAD OF HIS CHECKBOOK, AND THEN CONTINUES BY BOOKING A SEAT FOR HIM AND LAVERNE IN THE LOCAL BANK'S SAFE DEPOSIT BOX.*

©RICHTENNANT

*From that time forward, Laverne handled their financial affairs.

In this part . . .

Part II is dedicated to Buck Rogers, that citizen of the future who banks online and pays all his bills in digital cash. You won't catch Buck Rogers standing in line at a bank or ATM machine. You won't see him reconciling his bank accounts from a measly paper statement. You won't see him thumbing through the newspaper in search of a stock quote because Buck Rogers downloads stock quotes from the Internet.

If you have a modem and you are connected to the Internet, you're invited to go online and make like Buck Rogers. Here's your chance to take advantage of the Money program's many online features. This part of the book explains how.

Chapter 7

Getting Ready to Go Online

● ●

In This Chapter

▶ Exploring the online services that Money offers

▶ Getting the equipment and services you need to bank online

▶ Disabling, canceling, or changing the status of an online account

● ●

*T*he makers of Money 98 are betting that people will soon rely on home computers to do their banking, in the same way that people rely on ATM machines to do most of their banking today. Not so long ago, ATM machines were regarded with suspicion: "What if the machine shortchanges me?" However, most people don't think twice about using ATMs nowadays, and someday they probably won't think twice about banking online, either.

This chapter explains the steps you must take before you can start banking online. I describe the online services and the equipment that you need, and show you how to find out if your bank offers the services and how to sign up for them. Oh, and this chapter also explains how to cancel the services in case cyber-banking isn't for you.

Reviewing the Online Services That Money Offers

The Money program's online services enable you to do everything from pay your bills to investigate potential investments. Table 7-1 describes the Money online services.

Table 7-1	The Online Services That Money Offers
Service	*What You Can Do*
Online banking	Download records from your bank or credit card company to find out which transactions have cleared the bank (and then balance the account, if you so choose). You can also transfer funds between accounts and send e-mail messages to the bank or credit card company. Records that you download are entered automatically in the account register, which saves you some of the trouble of entering the records yourself. You can also download brokerage statements. *Cost:* Varies from institution to institution. My bank charges $3 per month and offers a free two-month trial period. See Chapter 8.
Online bill payment	Pay bills online. You can use this service to pay anyone, even Uncle Ernie. *Cost:* Varies from bank to bank. My bank charges $5 per month for the first 25 payments (that's 20 cents per payment, which is cheaper than the 32-cent stamp it takes to mail a payment). After the first 25, payments cost 40 cents apiece. See Chapter 8.
Online stock and mutual fund quotes	Download stock, bond, and mutual fund prices from the Internet. Current prices of the stocks, bonds, and mutual funds in your portfolio are entered automatically in the Portfolio window. By using this service, your portfolio is always up-to-date. *Cost:* Free. See Chapter 9.
Money Insider	Read articles on the Internet. From the Contents window, click a topic. Then click Headlines or Internet Links, click the title of an article that interests you, and go on the Internet to read it. *Cost:* Free. See Chapter 9.
Microsoft Investor	Research investment opportunities. The Investor offers business profiles and charts, market statistics, and articles. *Cost:* Some of the services, such as stock trading, require a paid subscription. Money users can get a free 6-month trial subscription to some of the services. See Chapter 9.

By the way, Money offers two more amenities that fall in the online category:

- **Money Web site:** Choose Help⇨Microsoft on the Web⇨Microsoft Money Home Page to visit the Money Web site. There you find advice for using Money and even a place to ask questions about the Money features that baffle you.

- **Technical support:** Choose Help⇨Microsoft on the Web⇨Online Support to get answers to technical questions about using Money.

Before you can start banking or paying bills online, you have to sign up with your bank. After you sign up, the bank sends you a startup kit that includes a PIN (personal identification number) identical to the PINs used in automatic teller machines. You have to supply a PIN number whenever you make an online transaction.

To make an online transaction, you record it in Money and then you give instructions to send it into cyberspace. When you bank online — when you download bank records or transfer funds between accounts — a connection is made directly to your bank's computers.

When you pay a bill online, the payment order is sent to the On-Line Services Corporation. Its computers contact your bank's computers and withdraw the money necessary for the payment. Then the On-Line Services Corporation either sends a paper check or an electronic funds transfer to the payee.

You can download up-to-date prices of stock quotes and mutual fund shares directly from the Portfolio window. As long as you enter the correct ticker symbol for the mutual fund or stock you want to update, the stock's price is updated.

Is online banking safe?

Occasionally, you read in the newspaper about an evil, twisted computer genius who crashes into others' computers and steals credit card numbers, account numbers, and the like. And stories like that make you wonder if banking online is safe.

Banking online is safe. It's safe because banks and corporations such as Microsoft want it to be safe. Companies have poured millions of dollars into security measures to make banking on the Internet safe.

If you use an ATM card, you take a bigger risk than you do when you bank online. The odds that a thief will take your ATM card or demand your card's PIN number are higher than the odds that an evil hacker will steal your bank account's PIN number and use it to clean out your bank account.

Laying the Groundwork

I'm afraid that getting online isn't as easy as counting one, two, three. Before you can start exploring cyberspace, you have to complete two or three irksome little chores. Sorry about that.

The following sections explain what equipment you need to go online, how to introduce your modem and browser to Money, how to investigate whether your bank offers online services, how to sign up for the services, and how to set up an account so you can go online with it.

The good news is you only have to complete these irksome little chores once.

The equipment you need

Before you even think about going online with Money, make sure that your computer is connected to or includes a modem. A *modem* — the word stands for "modulator/demodulator" — is a hardware device for sending and receiving files and messages over the telephone lines.

You also need a browser. A *browser* is a computer program that connects to Web sites and displays Web pages ("browser" is not a contraction of the word "brown-noser," by the way). When you installed Money, you also installed Internet Explorer 3.02, the browser made by the Microsoft Corporation, so a browser is already installed on your system.

Telling Money about your modem, browser, and Internet connection

Before you can go online with Money, you need to formally introduce the program to the Internet service provider (the ISP) and browser that you use and make sure that Money understands the settings under which your modem operates.

Chances are Money already knows everything it needs to know about your browser, modem, and modem connection because it got the information from its cousin, Windows, when you loaded Money. However, making sure that Money and your modem are on speaking terms never hurts. And if you change Internet service providers, install a new modem, install a new browser, or connect on a laptop computer from a new location, you have to tell Money. Follow these instructions to make sure that Money and your modem are on speaking terms:

1. **Choose Tools⇨Update Internet Information.**

   You see the Connecting to the Internet dialog box.

2. **Select the means by which you connect to the Internet:**

   - **Have Money connect to the Internet using my Internet service provider from the list below:** If the Internet service provider you use is on the list, select this option and select your provider's name.

   - **Access the Internet via a Local Area Network:** Select this option if your computer is on a network.

   - **Manual:** Select this option if you use CompuServe, America Online (AOL), or another online service provider. These services don't make use of the Windows Dial-Up networking device.

   - **Proxy Server:** With some ISPs and on certain networks, you have to enter the address of a proxy server. If that's the case, click this option and enter the server's address and port.

3. **Click OK.**

   You see the Internet Connection dialog box shown in Figure 7-1.

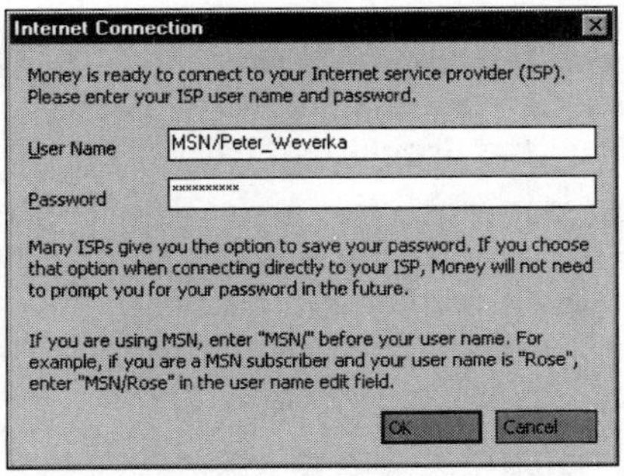

Figure 7-1:
Telling
Money
your user
name and
password.

4. **Enter your user name and password and click OK.**

   By entering your user name and password here, you won't have to do it each time you connect to the Internet.

   Money does a test run to see if it can connect to the Internet. If the connection is successful, you see the Connecting dialog box and Money downloads information from the Internet.

If all goes well, the Call Summary dialog box tells you that your call completed successfully. If all didn't go well, a message box tells you that `access is denied.` You are in a state of denial. Try again and see if you can get it right the second time.

5. Click Close.

Finding out whether your bank or credit card company offers online banking services

After you have found out whether you can connect to the Internet from Money, you need to find out whether your bank or credit card company offers online banking services. Most, but not all, banks and credit card companies offer the services.

To find out if your bank or credit card company offers online services, follow these steps:

1. **Click the Online Banking button on the Navigation bar or choose Go⇨Online Banking.**

2. **Click the arrow in the upper-left corner of the Online Banking & Investments window and select the name of the financial institution you want to investigate from the drop-down list.**

   Figure 7-2 shows how. If the institution you want to investigate isn't listed, you didn't enter its name correctly when you set up the account (discussed in Chapter 2). Go to the Account Details window and change bank names, if necessary.

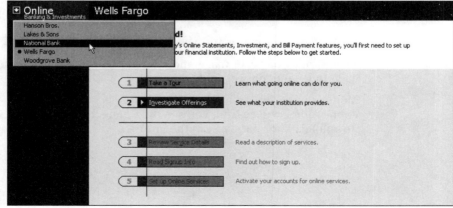

Figure 7-2: Choosing the bank whose online services you want to investigate.

You land in the Get Connected! window. Why the exclamation point? I mean, is going online that exciting?

3. Click the Investigate Offerings button.

You see the first of several so-called wizard dialog boxes. This one explains what you are about to do. You can ignore the two check boxes on the bottom because you are already set up to go online — provided you followed the directions earlier in this chapter under the "Telling Money about your modem, browser, and Internet connection" section.

4. Click Next.

5. If necessary, enter the name of your bank or credit card company in the text box and click Next.

6. If necessary, enter your user name and password in the Internet Connection dialog box, and click OK.

Money tells you that it is connecting to the Internet, and then that it is looking for your financial institution. With luck, the institution is found, and you see a dialog box similar to the one in Figure 7-3.

If Money can't find your bank or financial institution, a message box tells you so. You are out of luck, I'm afraid. If you are especially keen on using online services, either change banks or call your bank and ask a representative when the bank will start offering online services.

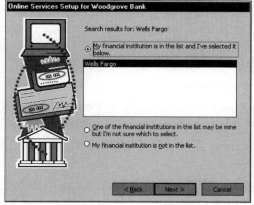

Figure 7-3:
This financial institution was lost, but now it's found.

7. Click Next.

Money downloads information about the bank or credit card company into your computer.

8. Click the Finish button.

Back in the Get Connected! window, button 3, Review Service Details, is now highlighted and ready to be clicked.

9. **Click the Review Service Details button to get the phone number of the bank, jot down the phone number, and click Finish.**

10. **Click the Read Signup Info button, read about the services that your bank or credit card company offers, and click Finish.**

    Among other things, the window tells you how much the service costs and whether you can pay bills directly though your bank or credit card company.

After you download information from your bank or credit card company, click the Contact Information button on the Get Connected! window. On the Contact Information window is the Internet address of your bank. Click the Go To button beside the Internet address to visit the Web site of your bank or credit card company and learn more about the bank's online banking and bill-paying services.

Signing up to bank and pay bills online

If the online banking services tickle your fancy, the next step is to apply to go online. To do that, click the Review Service Details button on the Get Connected! window, take note of the phone number, and call a bank representative.

Be sure to ask the bank or credit card company representative these important questions before you decide whether or not to bank online:

- ✔ How much do the services cost? How much for bill payment and banking online? Do you charge a flat rate or do you charge per account? Is there a trial period for using the services?

- ✔ Can I transfer money between accounts?

- ✔ Which accounts can be online accounts? For example, banks as a rule do not allow IRA accounts to be online accounts.

- ✔ If I decide to cancel the service, what is the quickest way to do that?

- ✔ Will my browser work with the online services that the bank offers?

- ✔ How will I be billed? Will the charges show up on my monthly bank statement, for example? If I bank online with more than one account, which statement will the bill appear on?

If you like the replies and decide to sign up for online banking, the bank or credit card company representative will ask for the following information, so be ready to provide it:

- ✔ Your address, home telephone number, and work telephone number.

- ✔ Your account number(s) and perhaps your ATM card number.

- ✔ Your birthday and birthplace.

- ✔ Your mother's maiden name.

- ✔ Your Social Security number.

- ✔ Your e-mail address.

- ✔ The type of browser you have, including its version number. To find out your browser's version number, go online. While the browser is on-screen, choose Help➪About. A window appears and tells you the name of your browser and its version number.

Ten days or so after you sign up, you receive a startup kit. The kit includes the personal identification number (PIN) you need to access your accounts, as well as instructions for banking online.

If your bank doesn't offer an online bill payment service, you can still pay bills online. Call the On-Line Services Corporation at 630-300-3020 or 800-200-7622 to find out more.

Setting up a money account so it works online

After the startup kit arrives from the bank along with your top-secret PIN number, your next step is to give the account you want to work with online status. In other words, you need to set up the account so you can use it to pay bills or bank online. The following section explains how to do that, and also how to do it all over again if you didn't do it right the first time.

Setting up a bank account for the online services

Follow these steps to set up a bank or credit card account so it works online:

1. **Go to the Get Connected! window if you are not already there.**

   To get to the window, go to the Online Banking & Investments window by clicking Online Banking on the Navigation bar.

2. **Click the arrow in the upper-left corner and select the name of the financial institution where you keep the account.**

3. **Click button 5, Set up Online Services.**

   You see the first of several dialog boxes that ask for information about the bank account or accounts you will go online with.

4. **Click Next, make sure that the Yes option is selected in the dialog box, and click Next again.**

Unless the Yes, I have this information option is selected, you can't go any further.

As shown in Figure 7-4, the next dialog box asks for your name, rank, and serial number.

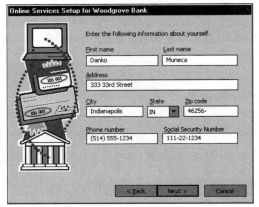

Figure 7-4:
A few
important
details that
you must
give Money
if you want
to bank
online.

5. **Fill in the dialog box and click Next.**

6. **In the next dialog box, enter the ID number of your bank or credit card company and click Next.**

   You will find the number in the startup kit you received in the mail.

7. **In the next dialog box, select the account that you want to make an online account and click Next.**

   If you have more than one account with the bank, click the one that is to be an online account. Don't worry if you want more than one account to have online status. You get the chance to return to this dialog box and select another account.

8. **Click the Online Bill Payment check box, Online Statements check box, or both check boxes, and then click Next.**

   This dialog box is where you tell Money whether you want both services or one of the services. Don't be confused by the name of the Online Statements check box: When you click that check box, you tell Money that you want to bank online, not simply receive bank statements over the Internet.

9. **In the next dialog box, enter the account number (if it isn't listed already), account type, and routing number; and click Next.**

   You find the routing number in the startup kit. The *routing number* is the first nine numbers in the lower-left corner of checks. On either side of the routing number is a colon (:).

10. **In this dialog box, click Next if no other accounts need to be given online status; otherwise, click the Yes button.**

    If you click the Yes button, you land back at the dialog box you visited in Step 6 so you can repeat Steps 6 through 9 and give another account online status.

11. **Click Next to save the setup information in your Money file.**

12. **Click the Finish button on the Congratulations window.**

    You land back at the Ready to Connect! window. You are ready to bank online and pay bills online. Notice that the Set up Online Services button has changed names. Now it's called Change Online Services. And the Get Connected! window has been given a new name — now it's called the Ready to Connect! window.

To find out which bank accounts have been given online status, click the Online Banking button on the Navigation bar or choose Go⇨Online Banking to see the Online Banking & Investments window. From there, click the Accounts button. On the Accounts window, check marks appear in the Online Statements and Online Bill Payment columns of accounts that are geared for cyberspace.

Changing the status of an online bank account

Suppose that you have trouble connecting to your bank over the Internet, or that you want to cancel the online bill payment service but keep the online banking services. In cases like these, you have to revisit the dialog boxes that you used to make your bank or credit card account an online account and change the settings. Follow these steps to do so:

1. **Go to the Ready to Connect! window.**

   To get there, click Online Banking on the Navigation bar and, on the Online Banking & Investments window, click the arrow and select the name of the institution where you keep the account whose status you want to change.

2. **Click the Change Online Services button.**

   The dialog box shown in Figure 7-5 appears. From this dialog box, you can change the way you connect to your bank over the Internet, add new services to an account, remove services from an account, or set up the online services for an account.

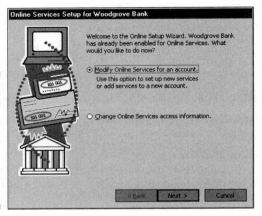

Figure 7-5:
From this
dialog box,
you can
change an
account's
online
particulars.

3. **Click one of the radio buttons:**

   • **Modify Online Services for an account:** Select this option to give
     an account online status, take online status away from an account,
     give or take away the online bill payment or online banking capabil-
     ity, change an account number, change an account type, or change
     a routing number.

   • **Change Online Services access information:** Select this option to
     change your address, phone number, Social Security number, or
     financial institution ID.

4. **Click Next, and answer the questions in the dialog boxes as they are
   presented to you.**

Changing Your Mind about the Online Banking Services

You tried. You tried your best and really put your heart into it, but banking
online was not for you. It just didn't work out. You weren't ready for an
online relationship. Hey, rather than weep about never being able to have
an online relationship again, read on to find out how to disable an online
account and cancel the online banking services.

Disabling an online account

Follow these steps to disable an online account:

1. **Go to the Ready to Connect! window.**

   To get to the Ready to Connect! window, click Online Banking on the Navigation bar and then, from the drop-down list in the upper-left corner of the window, select the name of a financial institution.

2. **Click the Change Online Services button.**

3. **In the Online Services Setup dialog box (refer to Figure 7-5), click the Modify Online Services for an account radio button and click Next.**

4. **Under Account, click the name of the account that you want to disable, and click Next.**

5. **Click to remove the check marks from the Online Bill Payment and Online Statements check boxes; then click Next.**

6. **Click Yes in the warning box that tells you what a drastic measure disabling an online account is.**

7. **Click Next to keep moving ahead.**

8. **Click Next yet again to save the changes to your Money file.**

9. **Not a moment too soon, click the Finish button.**

Canceling the online banking services

To cancel the online services, visit the Get Connected! window (or the Ready to Connect! window), click the Review Service Details button, take note of your bank's phone number, and click Finish. Then call the bank and deliver the bad news. Tell the bank representative, "Hey, it just wasn't working out, but it's not your fault. It's me. I need, like, more space, that's all."

Chapter 8

Banking and Bill-Paying Online

. . . .

. . . .

*B*anking online and paying bills online is a brave new world. If you've made the arrangements with your bank and prepared Money for online banking (see Chapter 7), you're ready to blast off for that world. You're going to do for the first time what will be considered routine by the year 2002. You're about to enter the future. You're about to take your digital cash into cyberspace.

This chapter shows you how to pay bills electronically over the Internet and how to keep tabs on a bank account by banking online. Throughout, I explain how to record online transactions and online payments in account registers. So strap yourself in. Liftoff is approaching.

Connecting to Your Bank

After you record online transactions and online payments, they appear on the Connect window. The Connect window shown in Figure 8-1, for example, lists instructions for downloading bank statements, transferring money, sending e-mail to a bank, and making online payments.

The Connect window is where you tell Money which instructions to send your bank, credit card company, or brokerage firm. After you decide which instructions to send, you click the Connect button to go onto the Internet.

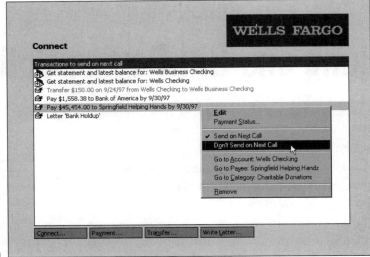

Figure 8-1:
Deciding
which
transactions
to send to
the bank.

Follow these steps to reach the Connect window:

1. **Click Online Banking on the Navigation bar or choose <u>Go</u>⇨<u>O</u>nline Banking.**

   You see the Online Banking & Investments window.

2. **From the Online drop-down list in the upper-left corner of the window, choose the name of the financial institution that you want to connect to.**

3. **Click the <u>C</u>onnect button.**

   Be sure to click the Connect button on the left side of the window, not the one along the bottom of the window. If you click the one along the bottom of the window, you see the Call your Financial Institution dialog box.

The Reminders box tells you when instructions need to be sent over the Internet. You can also click the words *Online Banking* in the Reminders box to go to the Connect window.

Telling Money which transactions to send

Sending all the transactions in the Connect window isn't necessary. No indeed. You can postpone sending a transaction or even cancel it altogether by following these steps:

- ✔ **Postponing:** Right-click the transaction and choose Don't Send on Next Call from the shortcut menu, as shown in Figure 8-1. Postponed transactions are grayed out in the Connect window. If you change your mind about postponing a transaction, right-click it and choose Send on Next Call.

- ✔ **Canceling:** Right-click the transaction and choose Remove from the shortcut menu. If you remove a transaction this way, it is not deleted from the account register where you recorded it. The transaction stays intact but is no longer an online transaction.

Making the connection

After you have told Money which transactions to send, make the connection and send the transactions. Follow these steps:

1. Click the Connect button.

That's the Connect button along the bottom of the window, not the one in the upper-left corner. When you click Connect, you see the Call your Financial Institution dialog box shown in Figure 8-2.

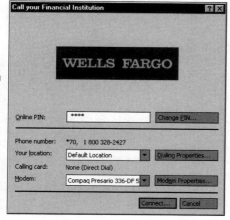

Figure 8-2:
Click the Connect button in this dialog box to blast off into cyberspace.

You can ignore the Dialing Properties and Modem Properties buttons in this dialog box, because you should already have established your modem connections. If you haven't, turn to Chapter 7.

By the way, banks recommend changing your PIN from time to time for security reasons. Just make sure that you don't forget your PIN. Forget it and you may have to wait two weeks for the bank to issue you a new one.

The first time you go online . . .

The first time you click the Connect button to go online, you see the Change PIN dialog box. As a security measure, you have to change the PIN (personal identification number) that the bank sent you to a PIN of your own before you can go online. Enter the bank's PIN in the Current PIN text box and your own PIN twice, once in the New PIN box and once in the Verify new PIN box.

> **Change PIN** ? X
>
> Enter your current Personal Identification Number (PIN) below. This is the one assigned to you in the information kit or the one you've been using.
>
> OK
> Cancel
>
> Current PIN: ****
>
> New PIN: ****
>
> Verify new PIN: ****
>
> You're automatically asked to change your PIN on your first call and any time you upgrade this application.

2. Enter your PIN in the Online PIN text box.

Asterisks appear in case a spy is looking over your shoulder and wants to see your PIN.

3. Click the Connect button.

You hear your phone dialing, and then you see the Connecting dialog box. Then your modem is initialized, you establish a secure connection, and the data is transferred. If all goes well, the Call Summary dialog box appears to tell you that `Your call completed successfully`.

4. Click Close in the Call Summary dialog box.

Banking Online

Remember the old movies and TV shows about Buck Rogers? Not one of them showed Buck banking online. Sure, you got to see Buck battle Ming the Merciless, but you never saw him battle his check book as he tried to balance it. Too bad Buck didn't have Money to download a bank statement and use it to update an account register, transfer money between online accounts, or send e-mail messages to a bank.

If you bank online with more than one institution, be sure to open the Online drop-down list in the upper-left corner of the Connect window and select the name of the right institution before you attempt to download or record online transactions.

Getting accurate, up-to-date account information

With the online banking service, you can find out how much money is in an account and which transactions have cleared the bank. After you get the information, you can compare it to the records in your account register and update the register with the downloaded information. You can even let Money do the work of recording transactions in registers. Instead of entering the transactions yourself, the bank "pours" them into the account register when you download.

Downloading a statement from the bank

Follow these steps to download a statement from the bank:

1. **Click Online Banking on the Navigation bar or choose Go⇨Online Banking.**

   The Online Banking & Investments window appears.

2. **Click the Connect button to see the Connect window.**

   You see the Connect window, where instructions to `Get statement and latest balance` for each online account you have appear. Make sure that these instructions will be sent to the bank when you connect to the Internet (the earlier section, "Telling Money which transactions to send," explains how).

3. **Click the Connect button.**

   The Call your Financial Institution dialog box appears.

4. **Enter your PIN, and click the Connect button in the dialog box.**

   The Call Summary dialog box appears.

5. **Click Close after the bank's records have finished downloading.**

   You see the Statements & Balances window, which lists how many transactions were downloaded and shows you your bank balance.

6. **If necessary, click the name of the account whose records you want to see.**

7. **Click the Read Statement button.**

   You see a Statement dialog box like the one in Figure 8-3. By scrolling in the dialog box, you can find out which transactions have cleared the bank. Your balance appears at the top of the dialog box. By the way, the Statement dialog box balance is probably different from the balance shown in your records. The dialog box balance shows cleared transactions, whereas your account register shows the balance of all transactions.

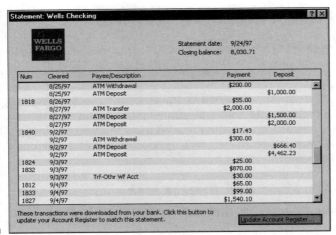

Figure 8-3:
The Statement dialog box shows which transactions have cleared the bank as of 4 p.m. on the previous business day.

Using the downloaded statement to update a register

After you've downloaded the transactions from the bank, you can compare the bank's records to yours for the sake of accuracy. By doing so, you make sure that the amounts in your register match the amounts in the bank's records. If a discrepancy is found, Money gives you the chance to fix it.

Follow these steps to use the bank's records to update an account register:

1. **In the Statement dialog box (refer to Figure 8-3), click the Update Account Register button.**

   Money compares your records to those on the statement. When Money encounters what it thinks is an error, you see either the dialog box in Figure 8-4 or the dialog box in Figure 8-5.

Figure 8-4:
You see this dialog box when the transaction you entered in the register and the transaction in the bank's record are slightly different.

	Num	Date	Payee / Category / Memo	Deposit	Payment
This is in your Account Register...	1792	7/24/97	Big Anthony's Groceries / Food		45.90
This is on your Bank Statement...	1792	7/24/97	Food		49.50

The amounts are different. Are these the same transaction?

⊙ Yes. Correct the amount in my Account Register and mark it as electronically cleared (E).
○ No. These are different transactions.

Next >   Postpone

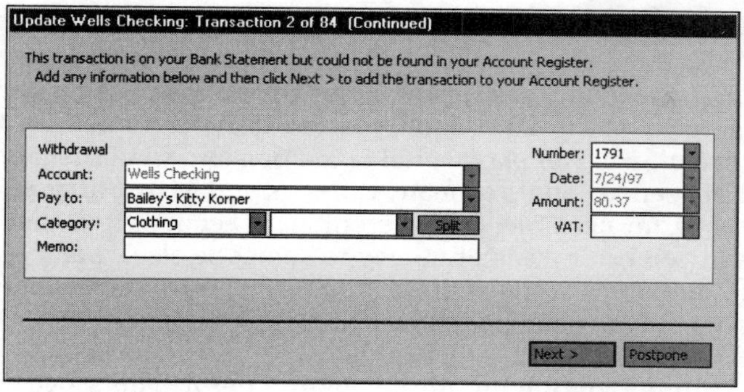

Figure 8-5:
You see this
dialog box
when a
transaction
appears in
the bank's
records but
not in your
records.

Update Wells Checking: Transaction 2 of 84 (Continued)

This transaction is on your Bank Statement but could not be found in your Account Register.
Add any information below and then click Next > to add the transaction to your Account Register.

Withdrawal
Account: Wells Checking
Pay to: Bailey's Kitty Korner
Category: Clothing   Split
Memo:

Number: 1791
Date: 7/24/97
Amount: 80.37
VAT:

Next >   Postpone

2. Correct the error and then click Next.

- **Discrepancy error (refer to Figure 8-4):** Click the Yes radio button to accept the bank's version of the story and enter the bank's record in your account register, or click No to enter the transaction from the bank's records and keep the transaction in your register as well.

- **Absent from account register error (refer to Figure 8-5):** Fill in the transaction form, including the Category boxes.

3. Repeat Step 2, and keep clicking Next, until you have updated your account register.

4. Click the Finish button.

TIP

For clumsy typists — a fast way to record transactions

If you write a lot of checks each month or charge a lot of items on a credit card, or if you are a horrible typist who isn't good at entering numbers correctly, consider letting Money do the work of recording your transactions.

Here's how: Every few days, download a statement from your bank. Then, in the Statement dialog box, click the Update Account Register button. When Money compares your records to the bank's, it finds all the transactions that you, the clumsy typist, didn't enter, and you see the Update dialog box shown in Figure 8-5. The amounts, check numbers, and dates in the dialog box are 100-percent accurate. All you

have to do is enter a payee name, categorize the transaction, and click Next. That task is a little bit easier than entering the transaction yourself. And the information from the bank is sure to be accurate.

However, to make this technique work, you have to download transactions every few days. If you wait a month, you may have a difficult time remembering payee names and categories for the transactions you made a month ago. When the time comes to enter the payee names and categories, you scratch your head a lot and find yourself in a state of bewilderment.

Transferring money between accounts

As long as both accounts are signed up for the online banking service and both accounts are at the same bank, you can transfer money between accounts. In fact, you can play digital Ping-Pong and send the money back and forth between accounts as many times as you wish. Sorry, you can't transfer money, for example, from a credit card account to a checking account. And you can't transfer money to someone else's bank account. Money laundering is not allowed. But you can transfer money between accounts at the same bank by following these steps:

1. **Click Online Banking on the Navigation bar or choose Go⇨Online Banking.**

   That step takes you to the Online Banking & Investments window.

2. **Click the Connect button.**

   You see the Connect window.

3. **Click the Transfer button.**

   You see the Edit Transaction dialog box shown in Figure 8-6. I don't know why they call it the Edit Transaction dialog box when it is actually used to transfer money between accounts.

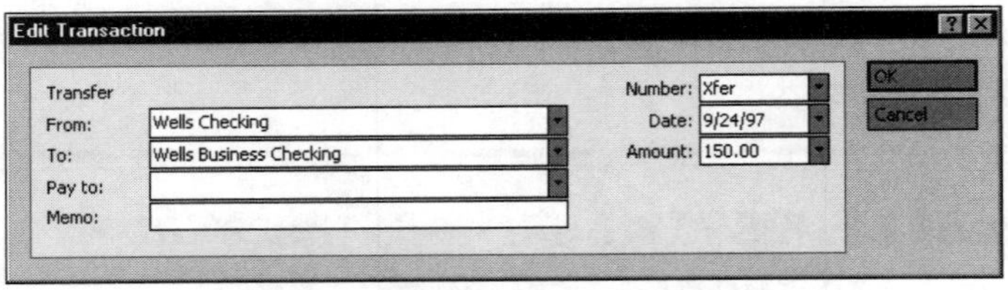

Figure 8-6:
Transferring
money
between
online bank
accounts.

Edit Transaction		? ☒
Transfer	Number: Xfer	OK
From: Wells Checking	Date: 9/24/97	Cancel
To: Wells Business Checking	Amount: 150.00	
Pay to:		
Memo:		

4. **Select the name of the account that the money will be transferred from in the From drop-down list.**

5. **From the To drop-down list, select the account that will receive the money.**

6. **Enter the date that you want the transfer to occur in the Date text box.**

7. **Enter the amount of money to be transferred in the Amount text box.**

8. **Click the OK button.**

   You land in the Connect window, where the instruction to transfer money appears on the list of transactions to send to the bank.

TIP

The speedy way to record an online transfer is to do it the usual way (see Chapter 3), but select Electronic Transfer (Xfer) from the Number drop-down list on the Transaction form.

Sending e-mail to the bank

A fringe benefit of banking online is that you can also send e-mail messages to your bank, credit card company, or brokerage house. You may request a copy of a check, ask for more paper checks, or wish the bankers a glorious good morning, for example.

Follow these steps to send an e-mail message to a bank:

1. **Click Online Banking on the Navigation bar or choose Go⇨Online Banking.**

   You land on the Online Banking & Investments window.

2. **Click the Connect button.**

   The Connect window appears.

3. **Click the Write Letter button.**

   You see the Write Letter dialog box, which asks you to choose the type of letter you want to send.

4. **Click the radio button that best describes why you must correspond with a banker and click the Continue button.**

   Now you're getting somewhere — the Letter dialog box shown in Figure 8-7 appears.

Figure 8-7: Scribble a note to your banker in this dialog box.

5. **From the A̲ccount drop-down list, select the bank account that the message pertains to.**

6. **Enter a descriptive word or two on the S̲ubject line and then compose your message in the D̲ear Online Services box.**

7. **Click OK.**

   Back in the Connect window, your e-mail message appears on the list of transactions to send to the bank.

If you decide not to send an e-mail message to the bank, right-click it on the Connect window and choose Remove from the shortcut menu.

Paying the Bills Online

Sure, paying bills online is disconcerting, at first. That's your hard-earned money flying across cyberspace. Those coins that used to jangle in your pocket have been digitized and turned into bits and bytes — nothing you could feed a jukebox, for example.

On the other hand, you don't have to rummage through desk drawers to find stamps and envelopes when you pay bills online. And as I note in Chapter 7, paying bills online is a little cheaper than paying bills by mail. The following sections explain how to record an online payment, stop a payment, and inquire about a payment.

If you're especially nervous about sending an online payment, send one to yourself.

Recording the online payment

To record an online payment, follow these steps:

1. **Click Online Banking on the Navigation bar or choose G̲o⇨O̲nline Banking to go to the Online Banking & Investments window.**

2. **Open the Online menu in the upper-left corner of the screen and choose the institution you make online payments with.**

3. **Click the C̲onnect button.**

   You land on the Connect window (refer to Figure 8-1).

4. **Click the Pa̲yment button.**

The Payment button is located along the bottom of the window. When you click it, you see the Edit Transaction dialog box shown in Figure 8-8. Except for the Due Date text box and the Number box, which says Epay (for Electronic Payment), this dialog box works exactly like the Check transaction forms described in Chapter 3.

Figure 8-8:
Recording
an online
payment.

5. **From the Account drop-down list, select the account from which you will make the payment.**

6. **In the Due Date text box, enter the date by which you want the payment to be made.**

    Processing and making a payment usually take five days. If you enter tomorrow's date in the Due Date text box and click OK, Money warns you that the payment cannot be delivered that quickly. Select a date no fewer than five days in advance of today's date. Or, to put it another way, be sure to pay your bills online at least five days ahead of their due dates.

7. **In the Pay to box, type the first few letters of the payee's name and press the Tab key.**

    If you have recorded a payment to this payee before, the Category information is filled in automatically. You have to provide Money with information about the payee if you have never made an online payment to this person or party before. If you haven't dealt with this payee before, you see the Online Payee Details dialog box. "Providing the payee information," the next section of this chapter, explains how to handle that dialog box.

8. **Enter the amount of the payment in the Amount text box.**

9. **Click OK.**

    You land back on the Connect window.

The fastest way to record an online payment is to start from an account register and record the payment as you usually would, except select Electronic Payment (Epay) from the Number drop-down list. You can also record a scheduled online payment from the Bill Calendar. To do so, select the payment, click the Edit Bill button, and select Electronic Payment (Epay) from the Number drop-down list.

What about check numbers for online payments?

When you record an online payment and send it across the Internet, Money assigns it a check number that is far, far removed from the numbers on the checks you enter by hand. The check number isn't assigned until the payment has been sent. In fact, Money even puts the online icon — an envelope being struck by lightning — next to the check number in the register so you know that the payment was made online.

Providing the payee information

When you send an online payment, information about the payee is sent, too. The On-Line Services Corporation (the company that handles online payments) needs the addresses, phone numbers, account numbers, and other information about payees in order to relay online payments to the right places.

The first time you record an online payment to a company or person and you click OK in the Edit Transaction dialog box, you see the Online Payee Details dialog box shown in Figure 8-9. This is where you tell Money everything you know about the payee. Be sure to enter the information correctly. The On-Line Services Corporation needs this information in order to administer the payment.

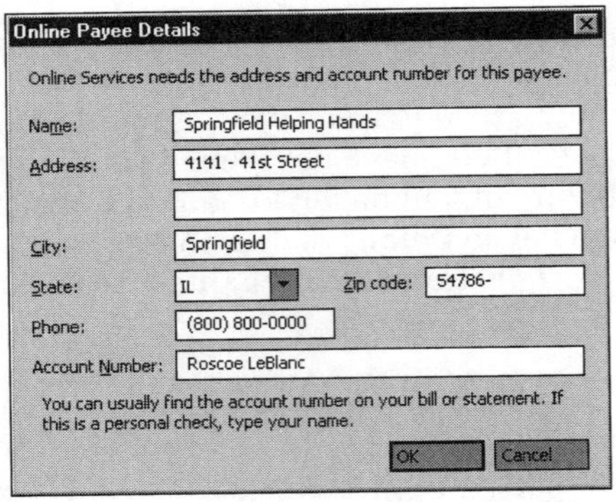

Figure 8-9:
Telling
Money
where the
bill is
supposed to
be sent.

Online Payee Details

Online Services needs the address and account number for this payee.

Name:	Springfield Helping Hands
Address:	4141 - 41st Street
City:	Springfield
State:	IL Zip code: 54786-
Phone:	(800) 800-0000
Account Number:	Roscoe LeBlanc

You can usually find the account number on your bill or statement. If this is a personal check, type your name.

OK   Cancel

You only have to fill out the Online Payee Details dialog box once for each payee. After you make the first online payment, you aren't asked for the payee's address and phone number again. If the payee's address or phone number changes, go to the Payees window and record the changes there (see Chapter 11).

Occasionally, a company requires that a check paid through an online bill payment service be sent to a different address than the return address that appears on the bill. How do you handle this dilemma? One way is to merrily pay the bills online and wait to see if one is returned because it was sent to the wrong address. The other way is to call each company that you will pay online and request the address where online bill payments are to be sent.

Shooting your payment into cyberspace

After you have recorded an online payment, send it into cyberspace by going to the Connect window (refer to Figure 8-1) and clicking the Connect button. The "Connecting to Your Bank" section at the start of this chapter explains how to do it.

Stopping a payment after it's sent

What? You sent a payment over the Internet and now you regret doing so? If the payment was sent in the past four days, you can try to stop it by following these steps:

1. **Open the account register where the online payment is recorded.**

2. **Right-click the online payment transaction and choose <u>M</u>ark As⇨<u>V</u>oid from the shortcut menu.**

   A dialog box asks if you want to create an instruction to cancel the payment.

3. **Click <u>Y</u>es in the dialog box.**

The next time you go to the Connect window, you see a Cancel Payment instruction. Send it right away so the payment can be stopped.

Inquiring about a payment

Money keeps records of online payments for sixty days. During that time, you can inquire about a payment to find out when it was submitted to the On-Line Services Corporation, when it cleared the bank, and when the payee received it. Follow these steps:

1. **Click Online Banking on the Navigation bar or choose <u>G</u>o⇨<u>O</u>nline Banking to go to the Online Banking & Investments window.**

2. **From the Online menu in the upper-left corner of the screen, choose the institution you make online payments with.**

3. **Click the Payments in Progress button.**

You see a list of the payments you sent in the last 60 days.

4. **Find and click the payment you want to inquire about.**

5. **Click the Payment Status button.**

You see the Payment Status dialog box shown in Figure 8-10. From this dialog box, you can learn everything you need to know about the payment's whereabouts.

Figure 8-10:
Finding out
what
happened
to an online
payment.

Click the Ask About this Payment button in the Payment Status dialog box to send an e-mail message that asks about the payment to the On-Line Services Corporation.

6. **Click the Close button.**

Chapter 9

The High-Tech Investor

• •

• •

*F*or investors who dabble in stocks, mutual funds, and bonds, being able to download share prices from the Internet with Money is too good to be true. Instead of updating share prices yourself by entering numbers in text boxes, all you have to do is plug into the Internet, grab the numbers, and be done with it. No fooling, downloading share prices from the Internet with Money takes about two minutes. And it's free, too.

Chapter 7 explains how to tell Money about your modem, browser, and Internet connection so that the program knows how to get around in cyberspace. This chapter explains how to update a portfolio from the Internet. For users of the Money 98 Financial Suite, I also explain how to research investments over the Internet.

Getting Ready to Download Stock and Mutual Fund Quotes

As long as you have access to the Internet through an Internet service provider, a browser is installed on your computer, and you have entered ticker symbols for your investments, you can download stock, mutual fund, and bond prices. When you installed Money 98, you also installed Internet Explorer. Therefore, as far as a browser is concerned, you have everything you need to start downloading stock quotes.

A *ticker symbol* is an abbreviated company name that is used for tracking the performance of stocks, mutual funds, and bonds. You can find these symbols on the pages of *The Wall Street Journal* and in the business sections of most newspapers. Unless its ticker symbol is on file with Money, you can't download the current price of a stock, bond, or mutual fund.

In Chapter 17, I explain how to enter a ticker symbol when you describe the securities in an investment and retirement account, but here are shorthand instructions for entering ticker symbols in case you don't want to wear out your fingertips turning to Chapter 17:

1. **Click the Investments button on the Navigation bar or choose Go⇨Investments to open the Portfolio window.**

2. **Either double-click the investment for which you want to enter a ticker symbol, or click it and then click the Go To button.**

   You see a Details window like the one in Figure 9-1. If a Symbol text box doesn't appear in your window, the investment can't be updated by way of the Internet because it is not a stock, mutual fund, or bond.

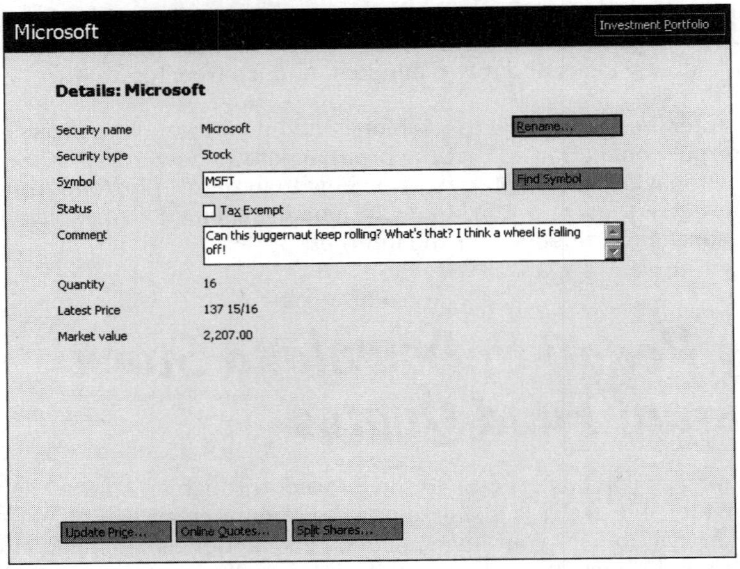

Figure 9-1:
Enter a ticker symbol so you can update stock or mutual fund share prices on the Internet.

Microsoft		Investment Portfolio
Details: Microsoft		
Security name	Microsoft	Rename...
Security type	Stock	
Symbol	MSFT	Find Symbol
Status	☐ Tax Exempt	
Comment	Can this juggernaut keep rolling? What's that? I think a wheel is falling off!	
Quantity	16	
Latest Price	137 15/16	
Market value	2,207.00	

Update Price... Online Quotes... Split Shares...

3. **Enter the ticker symbol in the Symbol text box.**

   If you're running the Money 98 Financial Suite, you can find out a company's ticker symbol by clicking the Find Symbol button on the Details window, connecting to the Microsoft Investor Web site, and looking for it there.

Canadians have to perform one little chore before they can download stock quotes: They have to follow these steps to tell Money that they are Canucks, not Yankees:

1. **Click the Investments button on the Navigation bar or choose** Go⇨Investments **to open the Portfolio window.**

2. **Click the Online Quotes button.**

   The Online Services dialog box appears.

3. **Click the Settings button and click Next twice, until you come to a dialog box that asks for the country from which you will retrieve quotes.**

4. **Select Canada from the drop-down list, click Next twice, and click Finish.**

Tracking stocks and mutual funds that you don't own

Suppose that you want to track a stock or mutual fund that you don't own, perhaps to decide if you want to buy it later. Downloading quotes online is a great way to find out from day to day or from week to week how a stock or mutual fund performs. Follow these steps to tell Money to track a stock or mutual fund that you don't own:

1. **Click the Investments button on the Navigation bar to go to the Portfolio window.**

2. **Click the New button. You see the New dialog box.**

3. **Click the A new investment radio button and then click Next.**

4. **In the Create New Investment dialog box, enter the name of the investment in the text box, click the radio button that describes what kind of investment you want to monitor, and click Next.**

5. **In the New dialog box, enter the ticker symbol of the investment you want to track.**

   Users of the Money 98 Financial Suite can click the Find Symbol button and go on the Internet to look up ticker symbols.

6. **Click the Finish button.**

After you have downloaded quotes from the Internet a few times, you can see how the investment has performed. To do so, follow these steps:

1. **On the Portfolio window, click the Position View button.**

2. **Find the investment you are monitoring on the list and double-click it.**

3. **On the Details window, click the Performance button.**

   You see a Price History chart as well as other information about the investment's performance.

Downloading Stock and Mutual Fund Quotes

I am very happy to report that downloading stock, bond, and mutual fund prices is one of the easiest tasks you can do in Money. As long as your connection to the Internet is running smoothly, all you have to do is click one or two buttons.

Follow these steps to update the prices of stocks, bonds, and mutual funds in your portfolio:

1. **Click Investment on the Navigation bar or choose Go➪Investments to open the Portfolio window.**

2. **Click the Online Quotes button.**

   You can also find the Online Quotes button on the Details window.

   You see the Online Services dialog box shown in Figure 9-2. From this dialog box, you tell Money which security prices you want to download. To keep a security price from being downloaded, click to remove the check mark from its check box, but I see no reason to do that. You are not going to save any time by not downloading a security's price. Downloading even a dozen security prices takes less than a minute.

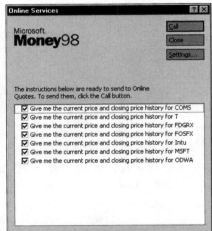

Figure 9-2: Click to uncheck a check box if you don't want to download a security's price from the Internet.

3. **Click the Call button.**

   You see the Internet Connection dialog box.

You also download the security's price history

When you download a security's share price from the Internet, you also update its price history. After you download, click an investment and then click the Update Price button to see its price history. Or try double-clicking an investment on the Portfolio window to open the Details window. From there, you can click the Performance button to see a chart that shows the investment's price history.

4. Enter your user name and password and click OK.

A dialog box shows you that Money is connecting to the Internet. Then a message box tells you that prices are being retrieved from the Internet (users of the Money 98 Financial Suite are also informed about all the other stuff that gets updated).

After a moment, you land back where you started, either on the Portfolio window or the Details window. That's all she wrote. The stock, bond, and mutual fund share prices in your portfolio are up-to-date.

Microsoft Investor: Researching Investments Online

Users of the Money 98 Financial Suite can take advantage of Microsoft Investor to research investments online. Microsoft Investor is a Web site with all sorts of tools for researching investments. You can use Microsoft Investor to keep tabs on investments you already have and to research new investments.

To reach the Microsoft Investor Web site, follow these steps:

1. Click Investment on the Navigation bar or choose Go⇨Investments to open the Portfolio window.

2. Click the investor.msn.com button on the Portfolio window.

You see the Microsoft Investor window.

3. Click a hyperlink.

4. Enter your user name and password in the Internet Connection dialog box, and click OK.

No matter which hyperlink you choose, you go to the Microsoft Investor Web site, whose Home page is shown in Figure 9-3.

Figure 9-3:
From the
Microsoft
Investor
Web site,
you can
investigate
prospective
investments
and ride
herd on the
ones you
already
own.

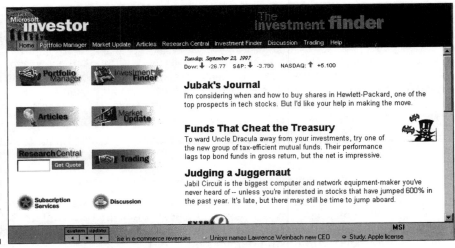

To go to different pages on the Web site, either click hyperlinks or click the buttons along the top of the window.

Obviously, Microsoft wants you to camp out at the Web site, because it offers a lot of different stuff. Table 9-1 explains all that is available.

Table 9-1:	Pages in the Microsoft Investor Web Site
Page	*How It Can Help You*
Portfolio Manager	Lets you keep tabs on the securities you own (see the "Researching securities you already own" section later in this chapter). *Cost:* Free.
Market Update	Offers business articles, late-breaking news about the financial markets, and market statistics. *Cost:* Free.
Articles	Offers articles in six "feature areas": Spotlight (information about stocks and financial trends), Mutual Funds, Strategies (stock-picking strategies), Interviews, TGIF (a "wild-card area" with articles on sundry subjects), and Jubak's Journal (articles by a fellow named Jim Jubak, one of them financial gurus, I suspect). *Cost:* Free.
Research Central	Lets you gather detailed information about stocks and mutual funds (see the "Researching prospective investments" section later in this chapter). *Cost:* Free.

Page	How It Can Help You
Investment Finder	Offers "unlimited access" to a "wealth of stock and mutual fund information," according to the Help window. Click the Investment Finder button or hyperlink, click the Help button, and then wade through the hoopla to see if this service is for you. *Cost:* $9.95 per month, with a free six-month trial period.
Discussion	Offers chat rooms and discussion groups for investors. *Cost:* Free.
Trading	Offers information about brokers. Click a hyperlink to visit a broker's Web site. *Cost:* Free, although you have to pay to trade if you sign up with one of the brokerage houses.

After you are done visiting the Microsoft Investor Web site, don't forget to disconnect from the Internet. If you forget, you will needlessly run up your online services bill. To disconnect, click the Connected to button on the taskbar, and then click Disconnect in the Connected to dialog box.

Researching prospective investments

The Research Central page is where you go to get information about a prospective investment. Follow these steps to research a prospective investment:

1. **After you arrive at the Microsoft Investor Web site, either click the Research Central button or click the Research Central hyperlink.**

   You see the Web page shown in Figure 9-4.

Figure 9-4: Research an investment on the Research Central page.

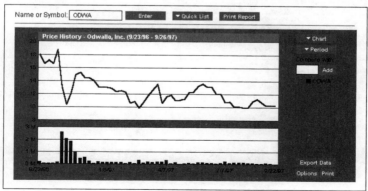

2. **In the Name or Symbol text box, enter the ticker symbol of the company you want to research, and then click the Enter button.**

   If you don't know the ticker symbol, type the company's name and click the Enter button. You see the Find Symbol dialog box. Click the Find button. If Microsoft Investor can find the ticker symbol, it is listed in the dialog box. Click OK. Back on the Research Central page, the symbol is entered in the Name or Symbol text box, and you get information about the company.

3. **Click tabs along the right side of the window to learn more about the company, fund, or whatever.**

Researching securities you already own

To keep on top of investments you own already, *link* those investments to Microsoft Investor. That way, you can get information about your investments each time you visit the Microsoft Investor Web site (actually, you can get information about each investment you own for which there is a ticker symbol). All you have to do is go to the Microsoft Investor Web site and click the Portfolio Manager button.

Click the button and you see a chart like the one in Figure 9-5 with all sorts of interesting data about the securities you own. By clicking the icons in the PR and News columns, you can read press releases and articles about securities. The window also shows the latest price of each investment, how much its value has changed, how many shares you own, those shares' market value, and how much you gained or lost per share.

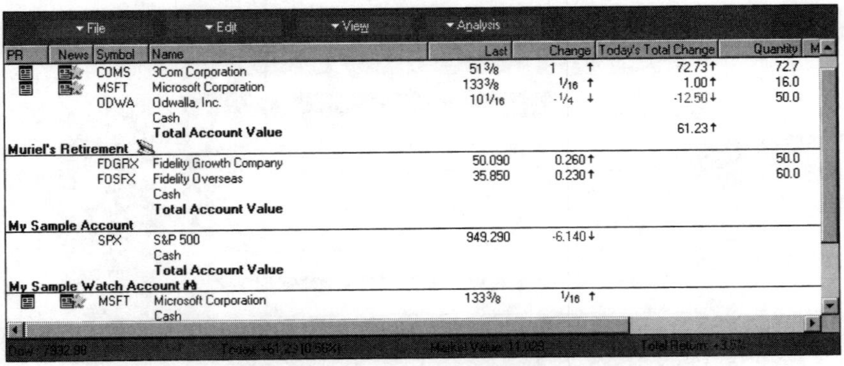

Figure 9-5:
By linking your investments to Microsoft Investor, you can see windows that offer lots of ways to analyze securities.

PR	News	Symbol	Name	Last	Change	Today's Total Change	Quantity	M
		COMS	3Com Corporation	51 3/8	1 ↑	72.73 ↑	72.7	
		MSFT	Microsoft Corporation	133 3/8	1/16 ↑	1.00 ↑	16.0	
		ODWA	Odwalla, Inc.	10 1/16	-1/4 ↓	-12.50 ↓	50.0	
			Cash					
			Total Account Value			61.23 ↑		
Muriel's Retirement								
		FDGRX	Fidelity Growth Company	50.090	0.260 ↑		50.0	
		FOSFX	Fidelity Overseas	35.850	0.230 ↑		60.0	
			Cash					
			Total Account Value					
My Sample Account								
		SPX	S&P 500	949.290	-6.140 ↓			
			Cash					
			Total Account Value					
My Sample Watch Account								
		MSFT	Microsoft Corporation	133 3/8	1/16 ↑			
			Cash					

Follow these steps to link your investments to Microsoft Investor:

1. **After you arrive at the Microsoft Investor Web site, click the Portfolio Manager button or the Portfolio Manager hyperlink.**

   This button is in the upper-left corner of the window, to the right of the Home button. When you click it, you see the first Portfolio Manager Setup Wizard dialog box.

2. **Read the windows and keep clicking Next until you arrive at the window that asks which of your investment and retirement accounts to link to Investor.**

3. **Click the names of the accounts that you *don't* want to link to Investor, and then click Next.**

4. **Click the Finish button.**

 The fastest way to research an investment you already own is to right-click it in the Portfolio window, choose investor.msn.com from the shortcut menu, and choose the submenu option that best describes what you want to know. The options are Company Snapshot, Historical Charts, Company News, Business Profile, Analyst Info, and Financial Results. Not coincidentally, these are the names of tabs on the left side of the Research Central window (refer to Figure 9-4).

Part III
Getting Your Money's Worth

"We were told to put our money into something that got more interest, so we started sticking it in this mason jar that's got some dang thing in it we bought from a traveling freak show."

In this part . . .

The next three chapters show you how to get the most out of Money. They tell you how to draw up a budget and schedule bills so that you can pay them on time. Oh, and you also pick up a handful of housekeeping hints, such as backing up your data files, that make your trip to Moneyland more enjoyable.

Chapter 10

Budgeting with Money

- -

In This Chapter

▶ Formulating a budget with Money

▶ Opening the Budget & Savings Plan window

▶ Declaring your income for budgeting purposes

▶ Declaring how much to set aside for retirement and savings

▶ Deciding what to spend in different categories

▶ Creating a budget graph

- -

*E*xcept for getting a higher-paying job, begging, borrowing, or stealing, the only way to save more money is to put yourself on a budget. A *budget* is a plan by which you decide how much to spend in different areas, the idea being to cut spending so that more money is available for the things you want to do — go to college, go to Greece, pay off a credit card debt.

If you've ever tried to draft a budget on paper, you'll be delighted with Money's budgeting features. As long as you categorize expense transactions when you record them in registers (see Chapter 3), half the work of drafting your budget is already done. You already know how much you spend on groceries, clothing, and dining, for example. Now all you have to do is get Money's help to target the categories where you spend too much. In other words, all you have to do now is set budget goals for yourself.

This chapter explains how to draft a budget with Money, including how to set budget goals and, just as importantly, how to generate a graph that tells you whether you met your budget.

I strongly recommend waiting at least three months before formulating a budget. The reason: Money gathers data about your spending habits from the transactions you enter in registers. You can save a lot of time by using this data for budget projections. To use the data, however, you must have been recording transactions in Money for at least three months.

Some gratuitous budgeting advice

Budgeting is like dieting. It requires discipline. When you are on a diet, your stomach rumbles. You feel hungry all the time. At dinner parties, you have to say "Just a sliver, please" no matter how delicious the cake looks. The only pleasures in going on a diet are noticing how well your clothes fit and seeing the needle on the bathroom scale point to new, uncharted regions.

Similarly, the only pleasure in living with a budget is seeing the balances in your savings and checking accounts rise to new, uncharted heights. Having to compare prices in the supermarket and go without fancy new duds is hard. Postponing a vacation is hard. Eating meat loaf at home when you could be enjoying *oie rôtie aux pruneaux* (roast goose with prune stuffing) in a swanky restaurant is hard.

To make living with a budget easier, try to set realistic goals for yourself. Don't set yourself up for failure by making your budget too strict. Draft a budget that you can live with. Challenge yourself but don't go overboard. That way, disciplining yourself is easier and a lot more rewarding.

Drawing Up the Budget

Formulating a budget in Money is done in the Budget & Savings Plan window, where you tell Money what you expect your income to be in the next several months and how much you prefer to spend in different expense categories. The Budget & Savings Plan window also offers places for telling Money how you want to pay off your debts and how much you want to contribute toward retirement and investment plans.

Before you get to that window, however, I suggest you take two steps:

- ✔ **Prepare your budget estimates.** The mechanics of drawing up a budget with Money 98 are pretty simple, but drawing up a budget is not. No way. You, my friend, should think long and hard about the amount you want to spend in each category. Nobody said it was going to be easy.

   Before you start formulating your budget, create and print a Monthly Cash Flow report, which can help you decide how much to spend each month in different categories. Chapter 13 explains how to create and print reports.

- ✔ **Gather the necessary documents.** Figures from pay check stubs and bills come in handy when budgeting with Money.

Looking at the Budget & Savings Plan window

Figure 10-1 shows the Budget & Savings Plan window. Follow these steps to get there:

- ✔ **In Money 98:** Click the Budget button on the Navigation bar.

- ✔ **In the Money 98 Financial Suite:** Click the Planner button on the Navigation bar to open the Goal Planner window, and then click the Make a Budget and Savings Plan button.

On the Budget & Savings Plan window are ten lines divided into four categories. You can see the category names on the left — Monthly Income, Monthly Debt Payments, Monthly Savings Contributions, and Monthly Expenses.

Explanation of line you clicked on ⌐

| Money Home | Accounts | Bills | Online Banking | Investments | Budget | Reports | Categories | Back | ❓ |

Budget & Savings Plan

The top-level budget below provides a bird's-eye view of your cash flow. You can also click the Details buttons on the right to modify the specifics.

Monthly Income	Your gross salary	+	6,620.00
	Partner's gross salary	+	3,583.34
	Other household income	+	75.00
Monthly Debt Payments	Pay off existing debt	-	0.00
Monthly Savings Contributions	Your retirement	-	426.32
	Partner's retirement	-	166.67
	Long-term investments	-	0.00
	Short-term savings	-	300.00
	Leave in spending accounts	-	450.00
Monthly Expenses	Expenses and taxes	-	6,579.76
Your monthly income exceeds spending by		**=**	**$2,355.59**

To balance your budget, Money recommends that you increase your savings contributions or your payments toward debt. (If you think you'll spend this money, set your expense budget to 8,935.35.) To adjust your top-level budget, click a line item above, then modify its amount on the right.

Your gross salary

Gross salary is the amount you earn before any deductions (such as taxes and retirement contributions). You can find this information on your pay stub.

I earn a total of

| 3,310.00 | Twice a month |

plus an additional | 150.00 |

during the year. (Include any bonuses or other income from your employer.)

[Income Details...]

- Some of your income has not been itemized in Income Details.

Figure 10-1: The Budget & Savings Plan window, where you tell Money how much you expect to earn and spend each month.

Difference between spending and income

To enter the budget data, regardless of the category, follow these steps:

1. **Click a subcategory line.**
2. **Enter the raw numbers in the text boxes on the right side of the screen.**

In Figure 10-1, I clicked the first subcategory line on the window, Your gross salary. The right side of the screen explains what gross salary is and offers text boxes for entering salary information.

As you fill in the Budget & Savings Plan window, keep your eye on the Your monthly income exceeds spending by figure at the bottom of the window. The object of budgeting on the Budget & Savings Plan window is to bring this figure as close as possible to 0. When you draw up your budget, the extra mo-ney that you save by spending less on monthly expenses is allocated toward retirement, long- and short-term investments, and spending accounts — the five lines in the Monthly Savings Contributions part of the window.

Notice the Income Details button on the right side of the screen. Details buttons appear when you click some of the lines on the Budget & Savings Plan window. Click Details buttons and you go to special screens for calculating and entering information for your budget.

Telling Money about your income

The first step in formulating a budget is to tell Money what your income is (and perhaps what your spouse's income is, too). To stay within the budget you create, your spending cannot exceed your income.

Click the Your gross salary, Partner's gross salary, and Other household income lines, respectively, and fill in the text boxes on the right side of the window. Be sure to enter your *gross income* — the amount you earned before taxes and other deductions were taken out.

Unless your income varies from month to month, you don't have to be a rocket scientist to complete this part of the budget. Take note, however, of the drop-down list for describing how often you get paid. If you get paid every other week, for example, enter the amount your get paid and select Every other week from the drop-down list.

If you are self-employed or you use Money to track a business, your income varies from month to month and likely comes from many different sources. The best way to handle this situation is to enter your average gross monthly income from the past several months. You can click the Income Details button, see a list of income sources, and adjust the numbers in the Income Details dialog box, but why bother when entering an average monthly income is so much easier?

Describing monthly debt payments

The second part of the Budget & Savings Plan window is for declaring how much you want to spend each month to pay off outstanding debts, such as credit card debts. In the Monthly payments text box on the right side of the window, enter how much you want to set aside each month to pay down your credit card debt. For example, if you carry $5,000 in credit card debt from month to month on your credit card and you want to pay down the debt by $1,000 a month, enter **1000** in the Monthly payments text box.

Note: The explanation of the Pay off existing debt line on the right side of the Budget & Savings Plan window tells you to include payments on mortgages, loans, and revolving credit card debt. This advice is misleading. You *should not* declare monthly mortgage or loan payments on this line. Those expenses are covered under the Monthly Expenses line at the bottom of the Budget & Savings Plan window. Only enter mortgage and loan payments that you intend to pay above and beyond what the lenders want you to pay. For example, if your mortgage payment is $900 but you want to pay an additional $100 each month in order to pay off the loan faster, enter the $100 in the Monthly payments text box.

Money Financial Suite users can utilize the Debt Planner to figure monthly debt payments into their budgets. See the "Making a plan to get out of debt" section in Chapter 14.

Telling Money about retirement, investment, and savings plans

The next part of the Budget and Savings Plan window is for declaring how much money you want to set aside each month for retirement, investing, and savings accounts:

✔ Your retirement: Enter the amount of money you want to set aside each month for retirement.

If you are a lucky soul whose employer matches your contributions toward retirement, or if your employer offers a profit sharing plan, click the Employer Contributions button. You see the Employer Contributions dialog box shown in Figure 10-2. In the Employer matches text box, enter the percentage of your contribution that your employer matches. In the Up to text box, enter the percentage of your salary beyond which your employer stops matching your contribution. In the Employer contributes text box, enter the percentage of your salary that your employer contributes toward your retirement.

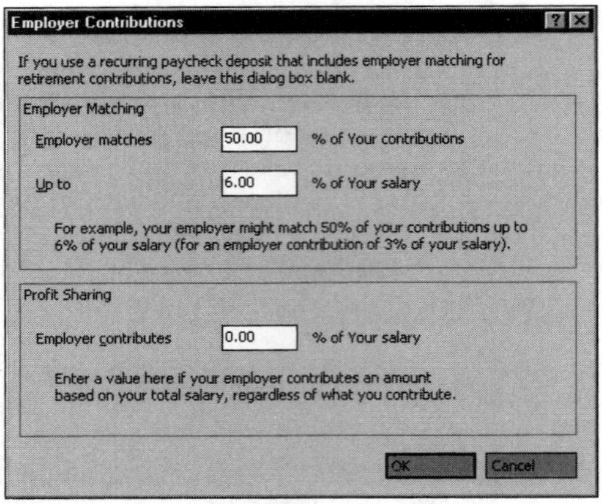

Figure 10-2:
Telling
Money
about
employer-
matching
and profit-
sharing
retirement
plans.

✔ Partner's retirement: If you have a spouse, enter the amount of money he or she sets aside each month for the golden years that you will share together. Again, you may click the Employer Contributions button if your spouse's employer offers a profit-sharing or employer-matching retirement plan.

✔ Long-term investments: In the Monthly contribution text box, enter the amount you want to set aside each month for long-term investments, such as a child's college education or the down payment on a house.

✔ Short-term savings: In the Monthly contribution text box, enter the amount you want to save each month for the unexpected, the abrupt, and the unforeseen. Nobody knows when the car's transmission will blow or when a molar will need removing. Enter the amount you want to save each month for emergencies like these and for short-term savings goals such as vacations.

✔ Leave in spending accounts: Enter an amount, if any, that you want to leave behind in savings and checking accounts just to be on the safe side.

Budgeting your monthly expenses

Now comes the hard but interesting part. When you click the Expenses and taxes line, Money tells you in the Monthly expenses and taxes text box how much on average you spent in the last six months to pay your expenses. (If you have used Money for less than six months, the program gathers the data from months in which you entered transactions.)

Your task now, if you choose to accept it, is to enter category-by-category budget goals and tell Money how much you will pay in taxes and how often you pay taxes.

Entering the category-by-category budget goals

Expense Details...

The object of budgeting is to look long and hard at the numbers to find out where you spend and how you can keep your spending low. To look at the numbers and decide how much to spend in each category, click the Expense Details button. You see the Expense Details dialog box shown in Figure 10-3.

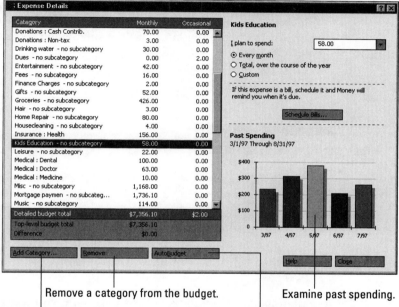

Figure 10-3:
The
Expense
Details
dialog box
is where
you
hammer out
your budget
goals.

Remove a category from the budget.

Add a category to the budget.   Get Money's help in setting budget goals.

Examine past spending.

To get the numbers in this dialog box, Money has averaged out your monthly spending in each category and subcategory. The numbers you see now are too high. Your next step is to enter new numbers that are lower than the ones that are in the dialog box.

Follow these steps to enter your budget goals:

1. **Click a category or subcategory name.**

2. **Click one of the radio buttons under I plan to spend to tell Money the time frequency you want to budget for the category.**

   You have three options:

   • **Every month:** Click this radio button for categories (such as Food and Automobile: Gasoline) in which you spend every month.

- **Total, over the course of the year:** Click for expenses that occur occasionally, such as annual membership dues and vacation expenses.

- **Custom:** Click to enter expenses that fall at different times throughout the year, but not monthly or occasionally. When you click the Custom radio button, you see the Custom Budget dialog box shown in Figure 10-4. Enter figures in the month text boxes to describe when payments are due. For example, if you are self-employed and you pay taxes on a quarterly basis, enter your quarterly tax bill in the Jan, Apr, Jun, and Sep boxes, as shown in Figure 10-4.

Figure 10-4:
Describe
budget
expenses
that occur
periodically
but not
monthly in
the Custom
Budget
dialog box.

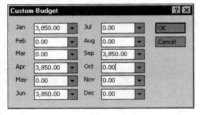

3. **In the I plan to spend text box, enter the amount you want to spend each month or each year.**

   Total yearly spending is entered in the box automatically if you entered the numbers by way of the Custom Budget dialog box.

   Entering the numbers in each category is the difficult part. You must decide what you can do without, what you can do with less of, and what you absolutely require for your health and well-being. Good luck.

4. **Click the next category or subcategory in the dialog box and repeat Steps 2 and 3.**

   As you set budget goals, notice how the Detailed budget total at the bottom of the dialog box changes. Money also lists the Top-level budget total, the total of expenses you started with before you began setting budget goals, and the difference between the amount you started with and the amount you intend to save each month by budgeting. Watch the Difference number grow. It lists the amount you save each month by budgeting.

The Expense Details dialog box offers the Remove button for removing a category or subcategory from the budget, and the Add Category button for adding a category. When you remove a category, it isn't removed from the Categories list, so you can still assign transactions in registers to the category. But when you add a category, it is added to the Category list and can be used to categorize transactions that you enter in the future.

By the way, the amounts you spend in categories to which you have assigned scheduled transactions are already entered in the Expense Details dialog box. To budget for spending above and beyond what you are scheduled to spend, enter a figure in the Addition Spending text box. You can also click the Edit button and fill in the Edit Scheduled dialog box. Chapter 11 describes scheduling payments.

5. **Click the Close button after you are done setting budget goals.**

   A dialog box asks if you want to change the top-level budget to the amount that your new budget goals call for you to spend each month. The top-level budget is the budget that is shown on the Expenses and taxes line of the Budget & Savings Plan window (refer to Figure 10-1).

6. **Click Yes to return to the Budget & Savings Plan window.**

AutoBudgeting with Money

One way to take some of the tedium out of setting budget goals is to click the AutoBudget button on the Expense Details dialog box. An AutoBudget is a bit like the 1040EZ tax form: It does the job if your finances are not particularly complicated.

When you click the AutoBudget button, you see the AutoBudget dialog box. The dialog box analyzes your past spending (yeah, right) and lists the amounts it thinks that you should spend in most of your categories. The figures in the AutoBudget dialog box are lower than the ones in the Expense Details dialog box.

To enter new budget goals quickly, enter numbers from the AutoBudget dialog box into the Expense Details dialog box. To do that, click the check box next to each category and subcategory that you want to enter in your budget and then click OK. The numbers from the AutoBudget dialog box are transferred to the Expense Details dialog box.

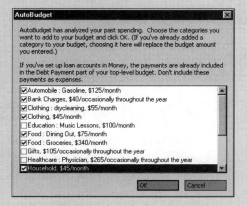

Entering tax-deduction information

When you enter income figures on the salary lines at the top of the Budget & Savings Plan window, you enter your gross salary (refer to Figure 10-1). In other words, you enter the amount you make before taxes and other deductions are struck from your income. To complete the budget, you have to click Expenses and taxes and tell Money how much money is taken out of your pay for tax deductions. That is where the Tax Tracking button on the Budget & Savings Plan window comes in.

Tax Tracking...

Click the Tax Tracking button and you see the Tax Tracking Options dialog box shown in Figure 10-5. If you know how much you pay in taxes each month, click the Track taxes as a single, lump-sum monthly amount radio button and enter the amount you pay. The other radio button is for people and businesses that itemize their monthly pay checks. If you itemize your pay check, click the first radio button.

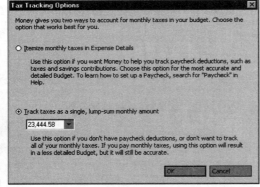

Figure 10-5:
Telling
Money how
you want to
track tax
payments
and other
paycheck
deductions.

If you pay taxes quarterly, don't bother with the Tax Tracking button. Your tax expenses are already covered on the Expenses and taxes line, the last line on the Budget & Savings Plan window.

Reporting on yourself

Now that you've filled in the Budget & Savings Plan window, start living. Enter transactions in the registers when you receive income and make purchases. After a month has passed, you will be able to see whether or not you met your budget.

Oh, that reminds me. Before you set aside this budgeting business, you may want to create and print a My Budget report. That way, you can easily study the numbers and make sure that your budget is just-so. You can read more about how to create and print reports in Chapter 13, but here are shorthand instructions for creating a My Budget report:

1. **Click the Reports button on the Navigation bar or choose Go⇨Reports.**

   The Reports & Charts window appears.

2. **Click My Budget.**

3. **Click the Go to Report/Chart button.**

   You see the My Budget report, which lists expense and income categories and shows how much you expect to spend or earn in each one.

4. **Choose File⇨Print (or press Ctrl+P) to open the Print Report dialog box.**

5. **Click OK.**

Creating a Budget Graph to See How Well You Did

You drew up a budget, you carefully recorded your income and expenses for a month or more, and now the moment of truth has arrived. It's time to see whether you met your budget. The envelope, please. . . .

Follow these steps to create a budget graph and find out how well you did:

1. **Click the Reports button on the Navigation bar.**

   The Reports & Charts window appears.

2. **Click How I'm Doing on My Budget.**

3. **Click the Go to Report/Chart button at the bottom of the window.**

   That's all there is to it. You see a How I'm Doing on My Budget graph like the one in Figure 10-6.

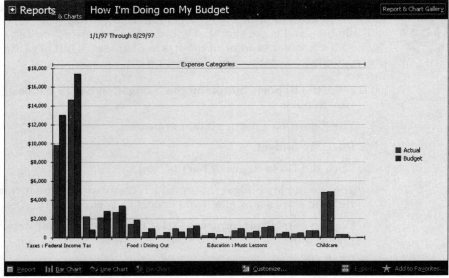

Figure 10-6:
For each category in the chart, the Actual bar shows how much you spent and the Budget bar shows the budget projection.

A pair of bars corresponds to each category and subcategory in your budget. The Actual bar on the left shows what you spent, and the Budget bar on the right shows how much the budget called for you to spend. If the bar on the right is taller than the one on the left, you met your budget.

Gently slide the mouse pointer over the bars to read the category names and spending amounts. As Figure 10-7 shows, a box appears and lays out budget statistics for your reading pleasure.

If you want to see more clearly where you did or did not meet your budget, follow these steps:

1. **Click the Customize button on the Reports & Charts window.**

   The Customize Chart dialog box appears.

2. **Click the Difference check box in the lower-right corner of the Customize Chart dialog box.**

3. **Click the View button.**

Yellow Difference bars appear on the chart to show precisely how over budget or under budget you are in the different categories, as shown in Figure 10-7.

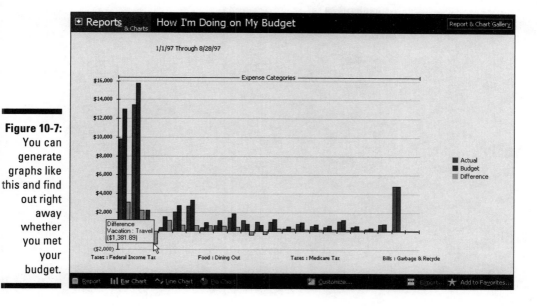

Figure 10-7:
You can
generate
graphs like
this and find
out right
away
whether
you met
your
budget.

In Figure 10-7, the Difference bar dips below zero only two or three times. Whoever generated this graph was only able to stick to the budget in two or three categories. This person overspent significantly in only one category, Vacation: Travel, where he or she overspent by $1,381.89. Couldn't help it, I guess.

Note: For more on customizing graphs, see Chapter 13.

Chapter 11

Paying the Bills on Time

• •

• •

*E*verybody forgets to pay a bill now and then. Usually an envelope with an ominous red warning appears in the mail, you pay the bill, and that's the end of it. But sometimes you have to pay a fee for being late. Credit card issuers, for example, are notorious for charging late fees. Mortgage lenders also do not tolerate tardiness. And if you forget to pay the IRS on time . . . well, I shudder to think what happens if you forget to pay the IRS.

To make sure that you pay bills on time, schedule them in the Money 98 Bill Calendar. Bills that have been scheduled appear very prominently on the Money Home screen under the word Bills. On the Home screen in Figure 11-1, for example, you can plainly see that one bill is overdue and four are "upcoming." What's more, as Chapter 10 explains, scheduling bills makes formulating budgets easier, because scheduled bills are automatically calculated in budget projections.

Which bills are candidates for the Bill Calendar? Any bill for which you have to pay a late fee. Go ahead and schedule the mortgage payment or rent, vehicle registration fees, credit card payments, alimony payments, and the like. But don't crowd the Bill Calendar with every bill you receive. The purpose of the Bill Calendar is to help pay the bills on time. A crowded Bill Calendar is very discouraging, for one thing. And facing all those bills is hard, because it's difficult to identify in a long list of bills which ones are most important and need to be paid first.

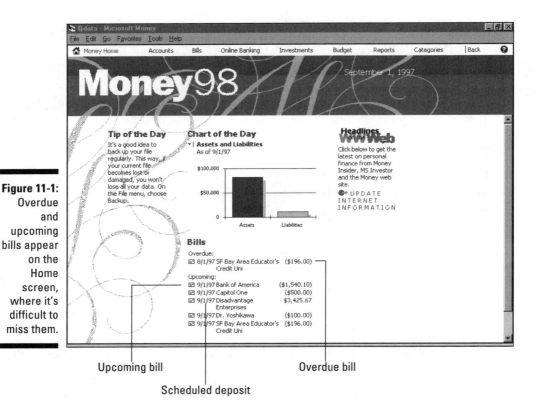

Figure 11-1:
Overdue
and
upcoming
bills appear
on the
Home
screen,
where it's
difficult to
miss them.

Upcoming bill   Overdue bill

Scheduled deposit

By the way, bills aren't the only things you can schedule on the Bill Calendar. You can also schedule deposits and account transfers (I'll show you how later in this chapter). If your employer deposits your pay directly into a bank account, you can schedule the deposit in the Bill Calendar. By doing so, you save yourself the trouble of recording the deposit twice a month or every other week, as the case may be.

Scheduling a Payment in the Bill Calendar

Follow these steps to schedule a bill in the Bill Calendar:

1. Click the Bills button on the Navigation bar or choose Go⇨Bills.

You see the Bill Calendar window shown in Figure 11-2. The window lists bills and deposits that have been scheduled as of the date clicked in the small calendar on the left side — in this case, September 1.

Calendar

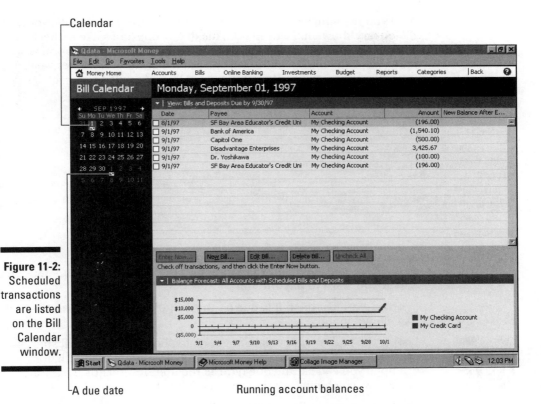

Figure 11-2:
Scheduled
transactions
are listed
on the Bill
Calendar
window.

A due date   Running account balances

Notice the small calendar on the left side of the window. Click a date on the calendar to see which bills are due and which deposits are scheduled to be made as of the date you clicked. Due dates for all bills are marked on the calendar with a tiny envelope.

The bottom of the window forecasts account balances for the month. To draw the graph, Money takes into account the bills that are scheduled to be paid and the deposits that are supposed to be made during the month.

2. **Click the New Bill button.**

   You see the Create New Recurring Payment dialog box, which offers radio buttons for scheduling recurring deposits, transfers, and investment purchases.

3. **The Bill radio button is already selected, so click the Next button, glance at the long-winded explanation of what you are going to do next, and then click the Next button again.**

Now you're getting somewhere. You see the Edit Scheduled Withdrawal dialog box shown in Figure 11-3. This dialog box looks like a Check transaction tab, does it not? Except for the date, the information you enter will be recorded in the register each month, every other week, or however often you tell Money to record the scheduled payment.

Figure 11-3:
Use this
dialog box to
describe bill
payments
you intend
to make.

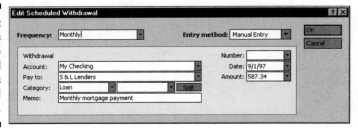

4. **In the Date text box, enter the date that the bill is due or the date on which you want to pay the bill.**

   In other words, if the bill is due on the first of the month, enter the first day of next month.

   Listing the bill's real due date in the dialog box isn't absolutely necessary. If you pay the bills on the first and fifteenth of the month, for example, you can list the due date as the first or fifteenth. That way, you know which bills are due on bill-paying day.

5. **Click the arrow in the Frequency box and select an option that describes how often the bill falls due from the drop-down list.**

   Options range from Daily (yikes!) to Only once. Very likely, the bill is due monthly, so you should select Monthly, but select Every three months if the bill is due quarterly, or Yearly if the bill is for annual fees such as a credit card or membership fee.

6. **Make sure that Manual Entry appears in the Entry method text box.**

   The Automatic Entry option is for recurring transactions that are recorded automatically by the bank. Bills don't fall into this category, but direct paycheck deposits do, for example.

7. **From the Account drop-down list, select the account from which you will pay the bill.**

8. **In the Pay to text box, either enter the person or party who is to receive the bill, or select a name from the drop-down list.**

9. **If necessary, categorize the transaction by using the Category and Subcategory drop-down lists.**

   Categorizing the transaction may not be necessary. If this is a payment you have made before, categories are entered automatically, just as they are when you record a check on a Check form.

   While you're at it, you can enter a few descriptive words in the Memo box if you want to.

10. **Enter the amount of the transaction in the Amount text box.**

   Credit card bills change from month to month. If you don't know exactly how much the billing amount will be each time, enter a ballpark figure. When the time comes to pay the bill, you will get the opportunity to enter the amount that is due.

11. **Click the OK button.**

   The due date, payee, account from which the bill will be paid, and the amount of the bill appear on the Bill Calendar window.

Telling Money When to List Bills on the Home Screen

After a bill is scheduled, a notice appears on Money's Home screen to tell you about it ten days before the bill is due (refer to Figure 11-1). In other words, Money gives you ten days' warning to get out of Dodge. If you don't heed the warning, if you stick around and gamble at the saloon, Wyatt Earp and Doc Holiday ride you out of town on a rail (whatever that means).

If ten days isn't enough time, follow these steps to tell Money how many days in advance you want to be warned that bills are due:

1. **Choose Tools⇨Options.**

   The Options dialog box appears.

2. **Click the Bills tab.**

3. **In the Remind me text box, enter how many days ahead of their due dates you want to be reminded that bills are due.**

   While you're here, notice the other options on the Bills tab. Click the Count only business days check box to exclude weekends and holidays from the countdown, or select an option from the Week starts on drop-down list if your calendar week doesn't start on Sunday.

4. **Click the OK button.**

Recording a Scheduled Payment in the Register

Terrible, isn't it, when a bunch of bills raise their ugly heads on the Home screen? How can you remove all those notices from under the word Bills and start from a clean slate? I'm afraid you have to pay the bills (or else skip or cancel them, the subject of the next section in this chapter).

Many a Money user has recorded a bill that is due in the Bill Calendar but then forgotten to actually pay the bill. I don't know why that is. Having gone to the trouble of recording a bill payment that is due on the Bill Calendar, it seems that many people think that the bill is really paid. It's not paid. No, you still have to get out the old checkbook and mail the check.

Before you start paying bills from the Bill Calendar window, glance at your checking account register or check book to find out either the next check number or the check numbers you used to pay the bills. Unless you print the checks (see Chapter 6), you need check numbers when you record bill payments from the Bill Calendar window.

Follow these steps to pay the bills that you have scheduled in the Bill Calendar:

1. On the Home screen, move the pointer over a bill, and then click when the pointer changes into a gloved hand.

You see the Bill Calendar window. You can also get to the window by clicking the Bills button on the Navigation bar or choosing Go⇨Bills.

To begin with, the Bill Calendar window lists all bills that are due today. However, you can see the bills that are due as of a particular date by clicking that date on the calendar on the left side of the window.

2. Select the bills you want to pay.

Money offers you two ways to do this. If you want to select the bills individually, click the check box beside each bill you want to pay. As you click, the New Balance After Entering column tells you how much money is left in the account after you pay each bill.

If, however, you want to pay all the bills due by a certain date, right-click that date on the calendar. A little pop-up menu appears, as shown in Figure 11-4. On the menu, choose Check All Bills and Deposits Due up to.

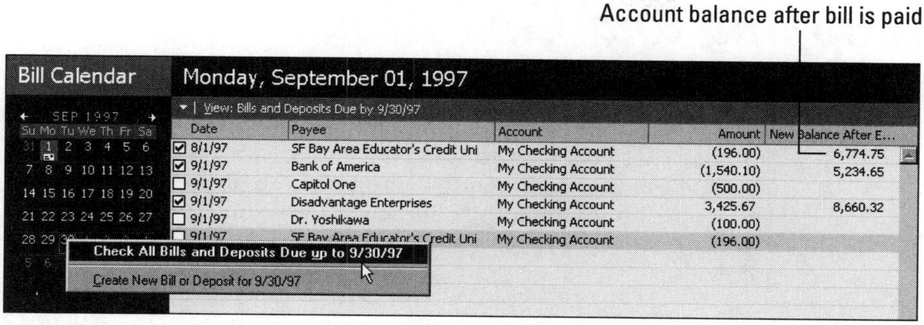

Account balance after bill is paid

Figure 11-4:
Telling
Money
which bills
to pay.

Bill Calendar	Monday, September 01, 1997

View: Bills and Deposits Due by 9/30/97

	Date	Payee	Account	Amount	New Balance After E...
☑	8/1/97	SF Bay Area Educator's Credit Uni	My Checking Account	(196.00)	6,774.75
☑	9/1/97	Bank of America	My Checking Account	(1,540.10)	5,234.65
☐	9/1/97	Capitol One	My Checking Account	(500.00)	
☑	9/1/97	Disadvantage Enterprises	My Checking Account	3,425.67	8,660.32
☐	9/1/97	Dr. Yoshikawa	My Checking Account	(100.00)	
☐	9/1/97	SF Bay Area Educator's Credit Uni	My Checking Account	(196.00)	

Check All Bills and Deposits Due up to 9/30/97

Create New Bill or Deposit for 9/30/97

3. Click the Enter Now button.

You see the Enter Recurring Withdrawal dialog box shown in Figure
11-5. If this dialog box looks familiar, that's because it has the same
information you enter in the Edit Scheduled Withdrawal dialog box
(refer to Figure 11-3).

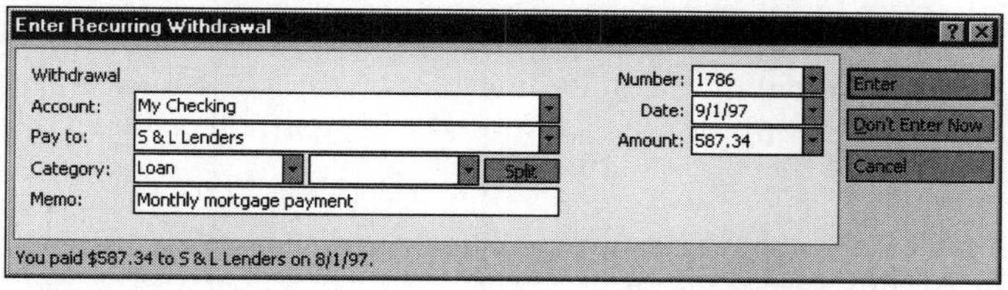

Figure 11-5:
Enter the
scheduled
payment in
the register.

Enter Recurring Withdrawal		? ☒
Withdrawal		
Account: My Checking	Number: 1786	Enter
Pay to: S & L Lenders	Date: 9/1/97	Don't Enter Now
Category: Loan	Amount: 587.34	Cancel
Memo: Monthly mortgage payment	Split	

You paid $587.34 to S & L Lenders on 8/1/97.

4. Fill in the Number box.

You can either enter a check number or click on the arrow for a drop-
down list of options. Select Print this transaction to print the check on
your printer. The Electronic Payment and Electronic Transfer options
are for banking online (see Chapter 8).

5. If you are paying a credit card bill or other bill that changes from month to month, enter the correct amount of the bill in the Amount text box.

6. Click the Enter button or press the Enter key.

Either you return to the Bill Calendar window or you see the Enter
Recurring Withdrawal dialog box again so you can record the next bill
that needs paying.

Skipping and Canceling Scheduled Payments

Suppose that you want to skip a scheduled payment this month or remove it from the Bill Calendar window altogether so it doesn't bother you anymore. The by-mail body-building course isn't working, for example, and you're as scrawny as ever, so you decide to quit making the monthly payments. Better follow these steps:

1. **Click the Bills button or choose Go⇨Bills to go to the Bill Calendar window.**

2. **Find the bill you want to skip or cancel and click it.**

   To display the bill on-screen, you may need to click the triangle on the View menu and choose one of the All Bills and Deposits options.

3. **Click the Delete Bill button.**

   You see the Delete Recurring Payment dialog box.

4. **Select one of the options in the dialog box.**

   If you are canceling the scheduled payment, click Delete All Instances. If you are just skipping the scheduled payment, click Just This Instance.

Paying a Bill Early

Suppose that you are about to embark on a fabulous vacation to Greece. You will be gone for three months and you want to pay your bills in advance so you don't come home to a mountain of debt.

To pay a bill early from the Bill Calendar window, follow these steps:

1. **On the calendar, click the arrow to the right of the month name and advance through time to the month by which you want to pay your bills.**

2. **Click the date by which you want to pay your bills.**

   All the bills that are due by the date you clicked appear on the Bill Calendar window.

3. **Start paying the bills.**

   See the "Recording a Scheduled Payment in the Register" section earlier in this chapter if you need help. When you send the bills, be sure to explain to your creditors that you are paying these bills in advance.

Scheduling Automatic Deposits and Transfers

Besides bill payments, you can schedule deposits and transfers on the Bill Calendar window. If your pay check arrives at regular intervals and is deposited automatically, or if you want to be reminded when to record a pay check deposit, by all means schedule it. Schedule a transaction if, for example, you always transfer part of your pay check to a savings account.

Follow these steps to schedule a deposit or money transfer:

1. **Click the Bills button or choose Go⇨Bills to open the Bill Calendar window.**

2. **Click the New Bill button.**

   You see the Create New Recurring Payment dialog box.

3. **Either click the Deposit or Transfer radio button and then click Next twice.**

   You see the Edit Scheduled Deposit or Edit Scheduled Transfer dialog box.

4. **Fill in the dialog box as if you were recording a transaction in a register.**

   See the "Scheduling a Payment in the Bill Calendar" section earlier in this chapter if you need help.

5. **If you are recording a direct deposit, select Automatic Entry from the Entry method drop-down list.**

   In other words, if your employer deposits your pay check directly into your savings or checking account, select Automatic Entry.

6. **Click OK.**

Keeping Detailed Records on Payees

As you surely know, Money "remembers" the names of people and businesses that you enter in account registers. When you enter a payee name the second time, you only have to type the first two or three letters. Money enters the full name for you. And if you are the sort of person who would rather click than type, you can enter a payee name in an account register by selecting it from the Payee drop-down list.

What you probably didn't know is that you can store all sorts of information about a payee. In most cases, knowing more than the name of the person or business isn't necessary, but if you have to address an envelope to a business you pay regularly or you have to know an account number when you write a check, having the address and account number at hand is mighty convenient.

The following pages explain how to keep information about a payee in Money, how to change a payee name, and how to delete names from the Payees list. Believe it or not, you also find out how to dial a payee on the phone without — literally — lifting a finger.

Entering payee names and data

Information about payees is kept in the Categories & Payees list. Follow these steps to see the list and enter information about a payee:

1. **Click the Categories button on the Navigation bar or choose Go⇨Categories.**

   You land on the Categories & Payees window.

   Payees

2. **Click the Payees button.**

   You can find the button in the upper-left corner of the Categories & Payees window. When you click it, you see the Payees list.

3. **Select the payee about whom you want to store information.**

   To find a payee on the list, either type the first letter in the payee's name or use the scroll bar to find it.

   If you want to store information about a payee and the payee isn't on the list yet, click the New button. In the Create New Payee dialog box, enter a name and click OK.

4. **Either double-click the payee's name or click the Go to Payee button.**

   You see a Payees window similar to the one in Figure 11-6. The chart and mini-register on the window offer a brief summary of your dealings with the payee.

5. **Enter information about the payee by typing it in the text boxes.**

   If there isn't a place for a vital piece of information in one of the text boxes, squeeze it into the Comment box.

6. **Click the Back button or the Categories & Payees button to return to the Categories & Payees window.**

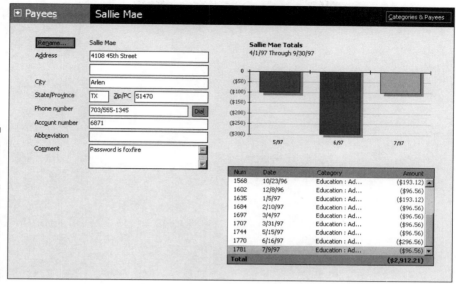

Figure 11-6:
You can
store all
sorts of
information
about a
payee on
the Payees
window.

You can edit information about a payee anytime. Simply follow Steps 1-4 above to get to the appropriate Payees window and then make your changes. Click the Back button after you're done.

Pruning the Payees list

The Payees list has a habit of getting very long. You can, however, prune the list to cut it down to size by following these steps:

1. **To get to the Payees list, click the Categories button on the Navigation bar or choose Go⇨Categories.**

   The Categories & Payees window appears.

2. **Click the Payees button in the upper-left corner of the window.**

   The Payees list appears.

3. **Select a payee name on the list and click the Delete button.**

   A dialog box asks if you really want to go through with it.

4. **Click the Yes button.**

When you delete a payee on the list, nothing happens to his, her, or its name in the account registers. The payee's name remains intact for future generations to see and behold.

Chapter 12

Some Important Housekeeping Chores

*T*his short chapter explains a handful of housekeeping chores that you must do from time to time. Sorry. Nobody likes do to these chores, but they have to get done.

In this chapter, you find out how to back up your data file so that you have a spare copy if your computer fails. You also discover how to restore a file — that is, load a backup copy of a file onto your computer. This chapter explains how to delete old bank accounts, delete a file, and rename a file. You also find out how to archive a file to keep records of past transactions.

Backing Up and Restoring Money Files

Computers are wonderful machines until they break down. If a computer breaks down entirely, it is worse than useless because the data on its hard disk drive can't be recovered. It can't be recovered, I should say, unless someone had the foresight to back up the data.

In computerese, *backing up* means to make a second copy of a file so that the data can be recovered if something evil happens to the hard drive where the original file is stored. As long as you have a backup copy of your Money file, it doesn't matter whether your computer is run over by a bulldozer or struck by lightening. It doesn't matter because you can always restore your data from the backup file. *Restoring* means to load the backup copy of a file onto a computer and use it instead of the parent file from which the backup was made.

Backing up your financial data

Backing up is so important that Money gives you the opportunity to do it whenever you close the program or close a data file. By now you must have noticed the Back Up dialog box shown in Figure 12-1. By clicking the Back Up button in this dialog box each time you close Money, you can make a backup copy of your data file.

Figure 12-1:
The Back Up dialog box appears whenever you close Money, and offers you the opportunity to make a backup copy of your data file.

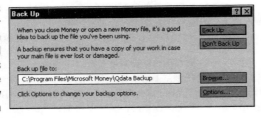

Unfortunately, Money stores the backup copy on the hard drive. Instead of copying the data file to a floppy disk that can be dropped in a drawer or filing cabinet, the backup copy is stored on the same computer that stores the original file. If something wicked happens to that computer — if it crashes or is stolen — you lose the Money data you so carefully assembled. You can't restore the file from a backup copy, because the backup copy is also on your computer.

To remedy this problem, make backup copies to a floppy disk, not to the hard drive. The next sections explain how to tell Money to make backup copies to a floppy disk, not the hard drive, and how to make backup copies of Money files.

If Money doesn't warn you to back up the data file when you close the program, follow these steps to get this all-important warning message:

1. **Choose Tools⇨Options.**

   The Options dialog box appears.

2. **Click the General tab.**

3. **Click the Backup drop-down list and select Remind me to back up.**

4. **Click OK.**

Telling Money to back up to a floppy drive

Computers are good at taking orders. You only have to tell Money that you want to make backup copies to a floppy disk once. After that, the program keeps making backups to the floppy disk. Follow these steps to back up a Money file to a floppy disk for the first time:

1. **Put a floppy disk in the floppy drive of your computer.**

   Before you insert the disk into the drive, label the floppy disk. Give it a descriptive name, such as "Money stuff" or "Yo, Money!"

   By the way, *floppy disks* are the 3¹/₂-inch disks that people are always shoving into their computers. They don't really "flop." They do, however, make excellent coasters for putting drinks on (just kidding).

2. **Click Money's Close button (the X in the upper-right corner of the screen) or choose File⇨Exit.**

   You see the Back Up dialog box (refer to Figure 12-1). You don't have to exit Money to back up a data file. You can also choose File⇨Backup.

   This being the first time you have backed up your data file, the Back Up dialog box is all set to back up your data file to the Microsoft Money folder. You change that in the next three steps.

3. **Click the Browse button in the Back Up dialog box.**

   You see the Backup dialog box, which lists all the Money files in the Microsoft Money folder on your hard drive. Notice that Money has named the backup file after its parent and attached the word Backup to the parent's filename.

4. **Click the arrow in the Save in drop-down box and select 3¹/₂ Floppy (A): from the list, as shown in Figure 12-2.**

   Now 3¹/₂ Floppy (A): appears in the Save in box.

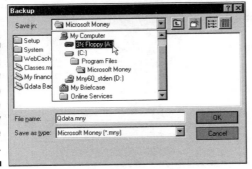

Figure 12-2:
Tell Money
to back up
the data file
to a floppy
disk on the
A drive.

5. **Click the OK button.**

   You return to the Back Up dialog box, but now the dialog box says that it will back up the file to the A drive instead of the Microsoft Money folder on the C drive.

6. **Click the Back Up button.**

   The drive grinds away, the `Money is compressing your backup file` message appears, and then the deed is done.

Be sure to put the floppy disk in a safe place. A "safe place" is one where nothing can be spilled on it, and no one is tempted to use it for a drink coaster.

Backing up a data file

After you have backed up the data file to a floppy disk the first time, you don't have to give instructions for backing up to a floppy disk. Now all you have to do is put your floppy disk in the A drive and follow these instructions to back up the data file:

1. **Click the Close button (the X in the upper-right corner).**

2. **Choose File⇨Exit or choose File⇨Backup.**

   The Back Up dialog box appears.

   The dialog box says that the backup copy will be stored on the A drive where the floppy disk is.

3. Click the Back Up button.

You get the standard `Money is compressing your backup file` message and then you're done.

Restoring a file from its backup copy

Suppose that doomsday arrives, and you have to restore a data file from its backup copy. Perhaps you botched a search-and-replace operation or your computer went momentarily haywire. If that happens, follow these steps to start working with the backup copy of a file instead of the original copy:

1. Put the floppy disk with the backup copy of your data file in the A drive.

2. Choose File➪Restore Backup.

You see the Restore Backup dialog box. Chances are, the Restore file from list includes the file in the A drive that is to be restored. However, if the backup file in the A drive isn't listed, click the Browse button. Then, in the Restore dialog box, click the arrow in the Look in drop-down list and select 3¹/₂ Floppy (A:). Then click the name of the backup file in the dialog box and click OK.

3. Click the Restore button.

You see the Restore dialog box shown in Figure 12-3. The dialog box lists the names of all your Money files. As a precaution, the dialog box instructs you to choose a new name for the restored file so that you don't erase its original.

4. In the File name text box, enter a new name for the file you are about to restore.

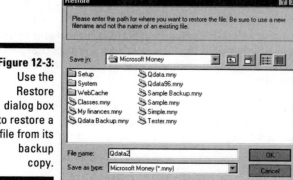

Figure 12-3:
Use the
Restore
dialog box
to restore a
file from its
backup
copy.

5. Click the OK button.

In a moment, the new data file appears on-screen. Now, all you have to do is enter the financial transactions that you entered between the time you last backed up the file and the time you restored it. I hope there aren't many transactions to enter.

If you are satisfied with the backup copy, you can delete the original and perhaps change the name of the backup copy to the name of the original. See the "Renaming and Deleting Files" section later in this chapter.

Deleting and Closing Bank Accounts

When you close a bank account, you may as well either delete it or close it on the Account Manager window. If the transactions in the account no longer matter for your financial history — and if the IRS wouldn't care whether a history of the account remains in your records — delete the account. But if you want to keep a record of the transactions you entered in the account, close it. You can still view the records in a closed account.

Follow these steps to delete or close an account:

1. Click the Accounts button on the Navigation bar and, if necessary, click the Account Manager button in the upper-right corner of the window.

You see the Account Manager window.

2. Click the account you want to delete or close.

3. Either close or delete the account:

- **To close:** Either right-click and choose Account is Closed or choose Edit⇨Account is Closed. An X appears on the account icon to let you know that the account is closed.

- **To delete:** Either right-click and choose Delete from the shortcut menu or choose Edit⇨Delete. Click Yes in the dialog box that asks if you really want to delete the account. The account disappears from the Account Manager window.

To see the transactions in a closed account, double-click its icon on the Account Manager window. To reopen an account that you closed, right-click the account on the Account Manager window and choose Account is Open from the shortcut menu.

Creating an Archive File for Past Transactions

An *archive file* stores all the previous transactions to a certain date for safekeeping. Archive your Money file at tax time, copy it to a floppy disk, and put it away with all your receipts and records from the previous year. That way, you have an electronic record of your financial transactions from the past.

Don't create an archive file on January 1. Wait until you have cleared all transactions from the previous year and filed your income tax returns.

Follow these steps to create an archive file:

1. **Make sure that the file you want to archive is open.**

2. **Choose File⇨Archive.**

   You see the Archive dialog box. Never mind all that verbiage; just glance at the text box in the lower-right corner to make sure that it shows January 1. All transactions in your registers previous to that day are copied to the archive file.

3. **If the date box doesn't show January 1, enter January 1 of this year.**

4. **Click OK.**

   You see the Archive dialog box. Money suggests a name for the archive file — it wants to name the file after last year.

5. **In the File name text box, either enter your own name for the archive file or let Money's name stand.**

6. **Click OK.**

   You see several dialog boxes (one for each account in your data file) that ask which transactions to remove for storage in the archive file. Figure 12-4 shows one of the dialog boxes. Notice that the name of the account is indicated both in the title bar and in the dialog box.

7. **Click the Don't remove any transactions radio button.**

   If you remove transactions from account registers, you won't be able to compare the previous years' income and expense figures to this year's figures. Removing transactions is a mistake.

8. **Click OK.**

9. **Repeat Step 7 until the business is done and finished.**

   To view an archive file, open it as you would any other Money file. Chapter 18 explains how.

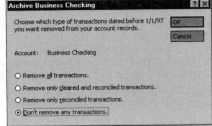

Figure 12-4:
This dialog
box asks
which
transactions
to remove
from your
account
records.

Renaming and Deleting Files

Follow these steps to rename a file or delete one that you no longer need:

1. Choose File➪Open or press Ctrl+O.

You see the Open dialog box.

2. Right-click the file you want to rename or delete.

A shortcut menu appears, as shown in Figure 12-5.

3. Either rename or delete the file:

- **To rename:** Click Rename and type the new name over the old one.

- **To delete:** Click Delete and then click Yes when Money asks if you are brave enough to really do it.

4. Click Cancel or press the Esc key to close the Open dialog box.

Figure 12-5:
Right-click
and choose
Delete or
Rename to
delete or
rename
a file.

Part IV
Improving Your
Financial Picture

"I just don't know where the money's going."

In this part . . .

*I*s your financial picture out of focus? Can't tell how much you're earning or where you're spending all that money? Can't see what your financial future looks like?

Start reading. This part of the book explains how to use Money to generate reports and graphs, plan for your retirement, and do other tasks to bring your financial picture into sharp focus.

Chapter 13

Reports and Charts for Seeing Where You Stand Financially

. . . .

In This Chapter

▶ Figuring out how the Reports & Charts window works

▶ Investigating the different kinds of reports and charts

▶ Creating a report or chart

▶ Seeing the figures with which a report or chart was constructed

▶ Changing the content and appearance of reports and charts

▶ Printing reports and charts

▶ Exporting a report for use in another program

. . . .

*R*eports and charts are two of my favorite things in Money 98. Reports and charts determine right away what your financial standing is. Until I discovered the Money Tax-related Transactions report, I used to spend hours and hours on April 14 tabulating tax-deductible expenses for my income tax report. Until I discovered the Where the Money Goes chart, I had no idea where I spent all that money. Until I spent a night in the Sierra Mountains, I didn't know that there are so many stars in the sky, but that's another story.

Maybe you want to create a report or chart to prove to a loan officer how creditworthy you are. Maybe you want to find out how much you paid in utility bills last year. Maybe you want to see how a stock price fluctuated to find out whether the price fluctuation really resembled a roller coaster ride. Whatever your need, Money can help.

This chapter tells you about the 31 kinds of reports and the 22 kinds of charts that you can create with Money; how to customize a report or chart so it yields precisely the information that you want it to yield; how to print reports and charts; and how to export them to other computer programs.

Strolling through the Gallery of Reports and Charts

To create a report or chart, start by strolling through the Gallery of Reports and Charts shown in Figure 13-1. Don't forget to sample the Brie cheese and the wine that is being served at the gallery opening. Click the Reports button on the Navigation bar or choose Go⇨Reports to get to the Money program's art gallery.

On the left side of the gallery are the five categories (six if you are running the Money 98 Financial Suite) of reports and charts. By clicking a category name, you can see the reports and charts that are available in the category. In Figure 13-1, for example, the Spending Habits category has been clicked, so the window lists the reports and charts in the Spending Habits category.

Chart and report category   Charts and reports available in the category

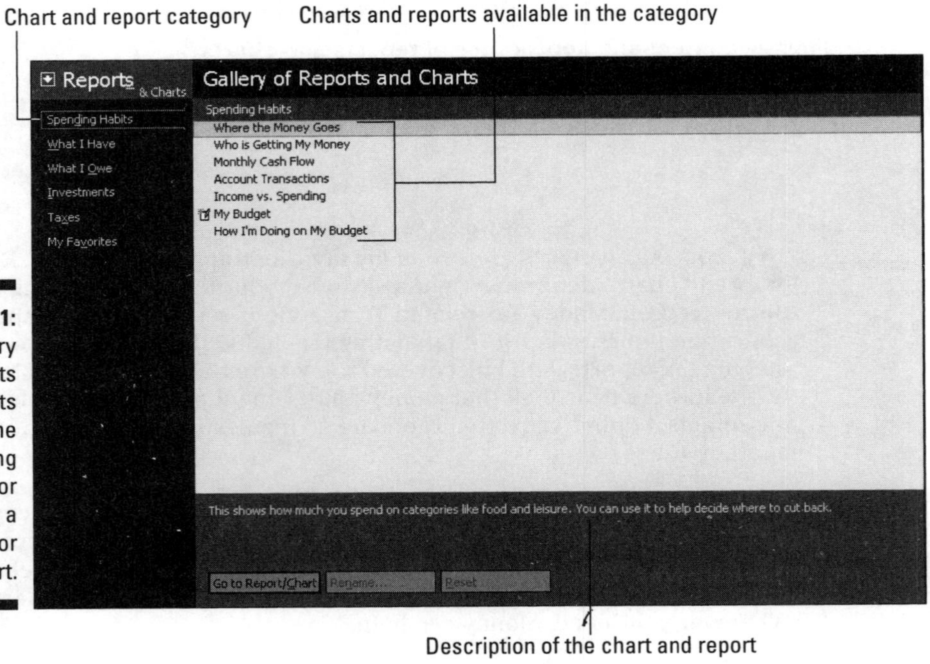

Figure 13-1:
The Gallery of Reports and Charts is the starting point for creating a report or chart.

Description of the chart and report

By now you must be wondering, "But how can I tell which of these names are reports and which are charts?" Good question. The answer is that you can make a report or a chart from almost every name in the Gallery of Reports and Charts. For example, Figure 13-2 shows both the report and the chart that you can create with the Where the Money Goes option in the Spending Habits category. On the top of Figure 13-2 is a Where the Money Goes report; on the bottom is a Where the Money Goes pie chart.

When you are curious about what a report or chart is for, click its name in the Gallery of Reports and Charts and read the description along the bottom of the screen.

8/5/97 Through 9/3/97

Subcategory	Total
Expense Categories	
Vacation : Travel	456.22
Clothing - Unassigned	187.65
Healthcare : Physician	134.29
Gifts	85.19
Household - Unassigned	65.10
Leisure : Toys & Games	65.10
All Others	123.66
Total Expense Categories	1,117.21
Grand Total	(1,117.21)

Figure 13-2:
You can create a report (above) or a chart (below) with almost any option in the Gallery of Reports and Charts.

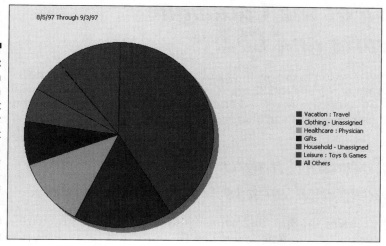

8/5/97 Through 9/3/97

- Vacation : Travel
- Clothing - Unassigned
- Healthcare : Physician
- Gifts
- Household - Unassigned
- Leisure : Toys & Games
- All Others

Money's miscellaneous charts

The Gallery of Reports and Charts isn't the only place where you can get a chart that describes your financial picture. You can also get reports and charts from the following places:

✔ **Home screen:** Each time you open Money, the Chart of the Day on the Home screen sheds light on a different part of your finances. (*Remember:* You can click the triangle beside the Chart of the Day title and select a chart name from the drop-down list to see a new Chart of the Day.)

✔ **A register:** While you are staring at a register, click the History button to see a chart that depicts its account balance in the past month.

✔ **Bill Calendar window:** A chart along the bottom of the Bill Calendar window shows how the bills you have scheduled affect account balances.

✔ **Categories & Payees window:** Click a category name on the Categories & Payees window and click the Go to Category button to see a chart that shows how much you spent in the category in each of the past six months. Click a Payee name and click the Go to Payee button to see how much you paid the payee in the past six months.

Looking at the Catalogue of Reports and Charts

As I mention at the beginning of this chapter, Money offers no less than 31 types of reports and 22 types of charts. As fast as I can — because I know that you're in a hurry — I briefly tell you in the following sections what the different reports and charts are.

Spending habits: Where the money goes and comes from

By clicking the Spending Habits button on the Reports & Charts window, you can create these reports and charts.

Report/Chart	*What It Tells You*
Where the Money Goes	How much you spend by category, ranked from largest expense to smallest (refer to Figure 13-2). *Use:* To find out your biggest expenses.
Who is Getting My Money	The names of payees to whom you paid money, and the amounts you paid. *Use:* To find out where you shop most often and perhaps where you should stop shopping so often.
Monthly Cash Flow	How much you spent and how much you earned last month by category in your bank and credit card accounts. *Use:* To find out what your expenses and sources of income were last month.
Account Transactions	A report that lists all the transactions in an account, or a line chart that shows a running account balance for the history of the account (click the Customize button to select the account). *Use:* To find transactions in an account or to list and print part of an account register.
Income vs. Spending	Your expenses by category and your income by category. *Use:* To compare your income to your expenses and find out how much you are saving or going into the red.
My Budget	Your monthly and annual budget goals (this one is a report, not a chart). *Use:* To help review your budget goals.
How I'm Doing on My Budget	How your budget goals compare to your actual spending and income. *Use:* To find out if you met your budget goals.

What I have: A look at assets and liabilities

These reports and charts fall under the What I Have category on the Reports & Charts window.

Report/Chart	What It Tells You
Net Worth	How the value of your assets and liabilities compare to one another. *Use:* To find out what your net worth is.
Net Worth over Time	How the value of your assets and liabilities compare over a certain time period (click the Customize button to select a time period). *Use:* To examine your net worth over time.
Account Balances	How much money is in your bank and other kinds of accounts at present. *Use:* To find out how much money is on hand.
Account Balance History	How the balance and value of all your accounts has changed over time (click the Customize button if you want to select a single account). Figure 13-3 shows an Account Balance History chart. *Use:* To see how fickle time, fate, and one's spending habits are.
Account Details	The information about your accounts that is kept on the Account Details window — the account number, opening balance, and so on (this one is only available as a report). *Use:* To quickly look up account numbers and other information.

What I owe: A look at debts and upcoming bills

Look to the What I Owe category on the Reports & Charts window to generate these reports and charts.

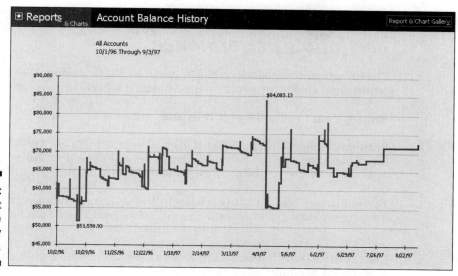

All Accounts
10/1/96 Through 9/3/97

$84,083.13

$51,598.93

Figure 13-3:
An Account
Balance
History
chart.

Report/Chart	What It Tells You
Upcoming Bills	Which bills in the Bill Calendar are supposed to be paid in the coming month (this is a report, not a chart). *Use:* To find out which bills are due 31 days in advance.
Upcoming Bills and Deposits This Month	Which bills and deposits in the Bill Calendar are due between today and the last day of the month (this is a report, not a chart). *Use:* To compare your income to your expenses so you can decide which bills to pay.
Credit Card Debt	Your credit card debt and, if you have more than one card, what percentage of the total debt is owed on each credit card. *Use:* To suffer despair over credit card debt and see which one you owe the most on.
Loan Terms	The information about your loans that is kept on the Account Details screen — the loan number, loan amount, interest rate, and so on (only available as a report). *Use:* Print this report if you apply for a new loan so that you can give the lender details about your other loans.
Loan Amortization	How much of each loan payment goes toward servicing interest, how much goes toward reducing the principal, and a running balance of how much is owed (available as a report only). *Use:* To see how principal and interest payments on a loan break down.

Investments: Examining your portfolio's performance

The Investments category on the Reports & Charts window offers these reports and charts for finding out how skilled an investor you are.

Report/Chart	*What It Tells You*
Portfolio Value by Investment Account	The value of each of your investment accounts, as well as each security in the accounts. *Use:* For seeing how the monetary value of your securities has changed.
Portfolio Value by Investment Type	What percentage of your investments are in mutual funds, stocks, and so on. *Use:* To find out how diversified your investments are.
Performance by Investment Account	The gain or loss in monetary terms and the gain or loss as a percentage of the security's total value in the past year of each security you own. *Use:* For comparing investments to determine which is performing the best.
Performance by Investment Type	The gain or loss in monetary terms and by percentage for each of your securities, with securities grouped by investment type. *Use:* For comparing types of investments — stocks, mutual funds, and so on — to see which type performs best.
Price History	The up-and-down performance of individual stocks and other securities in the past year, as shown in Figure 13-4. *Use:* To exercise your eyeballs and make them move up and down.
Investment Transactions	The investment transactions you entered in investment registers (a report, not a chart). *Use:* For reviewing activity in investment accounts.

Taxes: A look at tax-related transactions and capital gains

As tax time draws nigh, click the Taxes button on the Reports & Charts window and create a handful of these reports and charts.

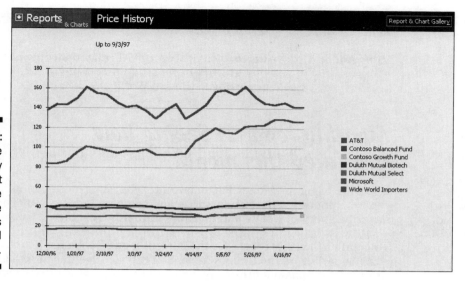

Figure 13-4:
The Price
History
line chart
traces the
performance
of stocks
and
securities.

Report/Chart	What It Tells You
Tax-related Transactions	Category by category, your total income and expenses in tax-related categories. *Use:* For calculating income and tax-deductible expenses on tax returns.
Capital Gains	Capital gains and losses for each security you own or owned. *Use:* For calculating capital gains and losses.
Loan Interest	How much of your loan payments went toward paying interest and how much went toward reducing principal. *Use:* For determining what your loan interest payments were. Some loan interest payments are tax-deductible.
Tax Software Report	Your total income and expenses as can be reported on the tax lines on various tax forms. *Use:* For gathering data so you can plug it into tax software programs.
Value Added Tax by VAT Rate	Value-added-tax expenses arranged by decreasing rate (a report only). Our friends in Europe suffer from the VAT tax. *Use:* For Europeans, who struggle under this particular tax.

(continued)

(continued)

Report/Chart	What It Tells You
Value Added Tax by Category	Category by category VAT-related income and expenses (a report only). *Use:* For tax reporting in the Old World.

Monthly reports: Seeing how you fared this month

If you are using the Money Financial Suite, you can generate Monthly reports. Monthly reports summarize and compare income and expenses, describe your net worth, and do a lot of other busy things.

To create a Monthly report for the current month, click the `Monthly report` hyperlink on the Home screen. You can also see this month's report — or reports for past months — by going to the Reports & Charts window, clicking the Monthly Reports button, and selecting a report. Money keeps reports from past months in the Gallery of Reports and Charts.

My Favorites

The Favorites category on the Reports & Charts window is for you and you alone. The "Adding a customized report or chart to the Favorites category" section later in this chapter explains how you can keep your own customized reports in the Favorites category and draw upon them whenever you please.

Creating a Report or Chart

So far in this chapter, you have been viewing previews of coming attractions, but now that you know your way around the Reports & Charts window, you are ready to create a report or chart. You may be interested to know that you can turn a report into a chart and a chart into a report. Too bad life isn't always that easy.

Generating the report or chart

Follow these steps to create a report or chart:

1. **Click the Reports button on the Navigation bar or choose Go⇨Reports.**

   The Reports & Charts window appears (refer to Figure 13-1).

2. **Click a category name on the left side of the window.**

   The first category is Spending Habits; the last is My Favorites. The "Adding a customized report or chart to the Favorites category" section later in this chapter explains how to put customized reports and charts in the Favorites category or on the Favorites menu so you can generate them faster.

3. **Click a report or chart name in the Gallery of Reports and Charts.**

4. **Either double-click the name or click the Go to Report/Chart button.**

What you see next depends on which report or chart you created. Sometimes you get a chart and sometimes you get a report. Sometimes the report or chart covers the right time period and sometimes it doesn't. Read on to find out how to turn a report into a chart or a chart into a report. Later in this chapter, the "Customizing Reports and Charts" section explains how to change the appearance and parameters of a report or chart.

In the meantime, click the Report & Chart Gallery button or the Back button to return to the Gallery of Reports and Charts.

To create a report or chart in one mighty stroke, click the arrow that points down next to the word *Reports* in the upper-left corner of the Reports & Charts window, select a category from the drop-down list, and then select a report/chart name, as shown in Figure 13-5.

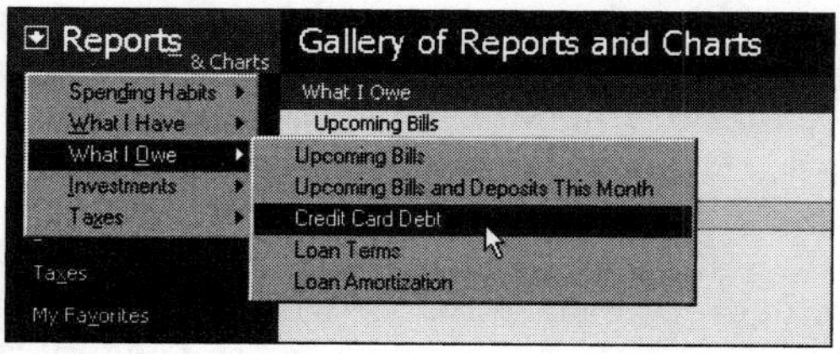

Figure 13-5:
The fast
way to
create a
report or
chart.

Reports &Charts	Gallery of Reports and Charts
Spending Habits ▶	What I Owe
What I Have ▶	Upcoming Bills
What I Owe ▶	Upcoming Bills
Investments ▶	Upcoming Bills and Deposits This Month
Taxes ▶	Credit Card Debt
Taxes	Loan Terms
My Favorites	Loan Amortization

Turning reports into charts and charts into reports

When you create a report or chart from the Gallery of Reports and Charts, Money does its best to give you the report or chart you want, but often it makes the wrong choice. Frequently, the program gives you a chart when you wanted a report or a report when you wanted a chart. You can fix that dilemma by following these steps:

- ✔ **Chart to report:** To turn a chart into a report, click the Report button in the lower-left corner of the window. Some charts can't be turned into reports, and when that's the case, the Report button is dimmed and nothing happens when you click it.

- ✔ **Report to chart:** To turn a report into a chart, click one of the chart buttons in the lower-left corner of the screen or right-click the chart and choose a chart option from the shortcut menu. You can turn a report into a bar chart, line chart, or pie chart. Some reports can't be turned into charts or into certain kinds of charts.

Investigating the figures from which a chart or report was constructed

The figures on reports and the lines on charts are constructed from numbers that you entered in your account registers. Suppose that you get curious about a number on a report or pie slice in a pie chart. Maybe you want to know why the number is so high or the pie slice is so fat. Maybe you can't believe that you spent so much or profited so little. You can move the mouse pointer over the number or pie slice and do some investigating.

In Figure 13-6, the bar on the right side of the Monthly Cash Flow chart is awfully large. Suppose that you want to know why it's so large. As the figure shows, you can move the pointer over part of a chart and see a box with a figure that shows you what the chart segment represents in monetary terms. In the figure, you can see that this person spent a whopping $456.22 on travel expenses in August.

In reports and charts, the pointer turns into a magnifying glass when you move it over a summary figure, pie slice, bar, or whatnot. By double-clicking when the pointer is a magnifying glass, you can see the account transactions from which the part of the chart or report was constructed.

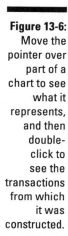

Figure 13-6:
Move the
pointer over
part of a
chart to see
what it
represents,
and then
double-
click to
see the
transactions
from which
it was
constructed.

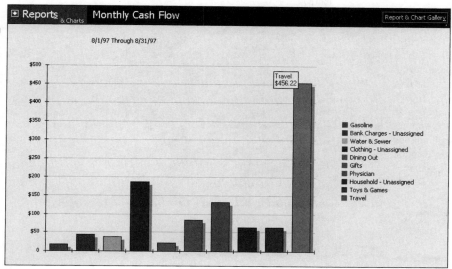

Customizing Reports and Charts

Chances are, the report or chart you created doesn't meet your high expec-
tations. Perhaps it doesn't look right or it covers the wrong time period.
Perhaps you want to remove data from one or two accounts in a report to
keep the report's figures from being skewed. Maybe you want to change a
chart's title.

When you want to change anything about a report or chart, click the Customize button. Depending on whether a report or a chart is open, you see
the Customize Report dialog box shown in Figure 13-7 or the Customize
Chart dialog box shown in Figure 13-8.

Both dialog boxes offer a bunch of different ways to tinker with the contents
of a report or chart. Experiment freely, but don't forget the rules of engage-
ment that apply to the four buttons on the right side of both dialog boxes:

  ✔ **View:** Closes the Customize Report dialog box so you can view your
    report or chart in all its glory. Click this button after you are done
    making the changes you want to make.

  ✔ **Apply:** Applies the changes you've made but does not close the dialog
    box. Click the Apply button after you make a change but you aren't sure
    whether you want it to be permanent. After your improvements have
    been applied, drag the Customize Report dialog box to a corner of the
    screen and look at the damage you did. If you don't like what you see,
    select different options in the dialog box.

Figure 13-7:
Whether
you
customize a
chart or a
report,
change its
content
with options
in the
Customize
Report
dialog box.

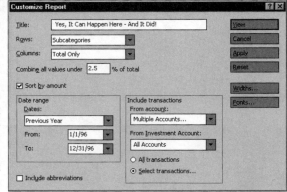

Figure 13-8:
To change
the
appearance
of a chart,
select
options
in the
Customize
Chart
dialog box.

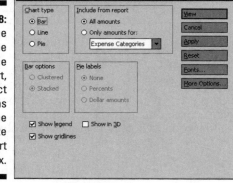

✔ **Reset:** Unravels all the work you did to the report or chart and applies the default settings that you had to begin with. When you click this button, a message box tells you that you will `erase all your customizations`. Click Yes if you really want to do that.

✔ **Cancel:** Closes the dialog box. Click this button if you decide not to customize.

Read on to find out what to do to change the content and appearance of reports and charts.

Changing the content of reports and charts

Whether you are customizing a report or chart, the options for changing the content of your little masterpiece are the same. By content, I mean the title, time period that the report or chart covers, and accounts from which it draws its data.

Changing the title, rows, columns, labels, and legend

The top of the Customize Report dialog box is for changing the title, rows (legend items if you are customizing a chart), and columns (labels if you are dealing with a chart):

- ✔ **Title:** If you want to, enter a new title in the Title box. The title you enter appears across the top of the report or chart.

- ✔ **Rows:** The Rows drop-down list is for selecting how items on the report or chart are grouped. In the case of reports, you specify which items appear as row headings along the left side. In the case of charts, you decide which items comprise the bars, pie slices, or Y-axis values in a line chart.

- ✔ **Columns:** The Columns drop-down list offers a number of different choices. For reports, select the items that are to appear along the top of the report as column headings. For charts, select the X-axis values.

- ✔ **Combine all values under %:** Rather than include every scrap of data in a report or chart, you can bundle the smaller amounts into a single row, pie slice, or whatever. Enter a percentage in this box to tell Money where to draw the line between amounts that get bundled and items that don't get bundled.

- ✔ **Sort by amount:** Usually, items are sorted by amount from highest to lowest, but click to remove the check mark if you want to arrange items in alphabetical order.

Changing the date range

To change the time period that the report or chart covers, either select an option from the Dates drop-down list or enter a beginning and ending date of your own in the From and To text boxes.

Choosing accounts for the report or chart

To start with, your report or chart gathers data from all your accounts, but perhaps you want it to focus on two, three, or four. To decide which accounts get covered, select an option from the From account drop-down list in the Customize Report dialog box. If you select Multiple Accounts, the Select Accounts dialog box shown in Figure 13-9 appears. In this dialog box, click the names of accounts whose data you want to include in the report or chart, and then click OK.

Figure 13-9:
Select the names of accounts that you want to include in the report or chart in this dialog box.

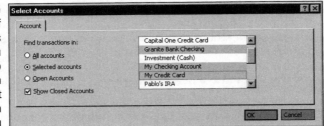

Investment accounts are a class unto themselves in the Customize Report dialog box. To exclude or include investment accounts, select an option from the From Investment Account drop-down list. If you select Multiple Accounts, you'll land in a dialog box like the one in Figure 13-9 for choosing individual accounts.

Excluding transactions from reports and charts

If you want to get really picky, you can even exclude certain transactions from reports and charts. To do that, click the Select transactions radio button in the Customize Report dialog box (refer to Figure 13-7). You see the Select Transactions dialog box, where you can click to exclude certain categories, payees, and classifications.

To make a chart show data exclusively from expense or income categories, click the More Options button and select Expense Categories or Income Categories from the Only amounts for drop-down list in the Customize Chart dialog box.

Changing the look of reports and charts

Now that you've changed the content of your report or chart, you can dress it in its Sunday best. Read on to find out how to change the look of the letters, change the width of columns in reports, and choose chart types and chart options.

Changing the look of the letters

To change the way the letters look on reports and graphs, follow these steps:

1. **Click the Fonts button in the Customize dialog box.**

   This step takes you to the Select Font dialog box shown in Figure 13-10.

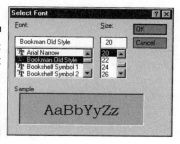

Figure 13-10: Select a font for the letters in reports and charts.

2. **Select a font, or typeface, from the Font box and select a type size from the Size box as well, if you want to.**

   Experiment to your heart's content, but be sure to select a font that is easy to read. The Sample box shows you what your choices look like.

3. **After you're satisfied, click OK.**

Changing the width of columns in reports

Are the columns in your report too narrow to handle all the 000s in your bank account? No problem. You can change the width of report columns by following these steps:

1. **Click the Widths button in the Customize Report dialog box.**

   This step brings up the Set Report Column Widths dialog box with its five options: Automatic, Narrow, Standard, Wide, and Extra wide. These options apply to all the columns in the report. The options are a bit like the Small, Medium, Large, and Extra Large options at an Italian restaurant; it's impossible to tell what they really mean until the pizza arrives.

2. **Select an option.**

3. **Click OK.**

   The Set Report Column Widths dialog box disappears — sort of like the restaurant waiter does after he delivers the pizza.

4. **Click the Apply button in the Customize Report dialog box.**

Money immediately adjusts the report with the new column width. If you don't like the new column setting, experiment until you belch or find a column width that pleases you.

Choosing chart types and chart options

The options in the Customize Chart dialog box (refer to Figure 13-8) for changing the look of a chart are self-explanatory, I think. True, it's difficult to figure out what the bar chart's Clustered and Stacked options are, but all you have to do to find out is click one of the options, click the Apply button, and peek at your bar chart.

On the other hand, if you really need an explanation, here are descriptions of the options for changing the look of a chart:

- **Chart type:** Click the appropriate radio button to change the chart to a bar chart, a line chart, or a pie chart.

- **Bar options:** When you are working with a bar chart, click Clustered to line up the bars in a row or Stacked to put the bars one on top of the other and show total amounts.

- **Pie labels:** Select None to keep labels off the chart, percents to display a percentage figure that shows how fat each pie slice is, or Dollar amounts to list dollar figures rather than percentage figures next to each pie slice.

Don't forget the check boxes at the bottom of the dialog box, either. Pie charts, for example, look especially good in three-dimensions, so you can click the Show in 3D check box if you are dealing with a pie chart.

Adding a customized report or chart to the Favorites category

After you have gone to the trouble to customize a report or chart, you may as well put it in the My Favorites category of the Reports & Charts window. That way, you can generate it again without having to tinker with the settings in the Customize Report or Customize Chart dialog box.

Follow these steps to add a report or chart to the My Favorites category:

1. **Create and customize the report or chart.**

2. **Either click the Add to Favorites button in the lower-right corner of the screen or right-click the report or chart and choose Add to Favorites from the shortcut menu.**

   You see the Add to Favorites dialog box.

3. Enter a descriptive name in the Report name text box.

4. Click OK.

Besides landing in the My Favorites category of the Reports & Charts window, the name of your customized report or chart also appears on the Favorites menu along the top of the screen. You can select it there, too.

To remove a customized report from the Gallery of Reports and Charts, click its name and then click the Delete button along the bottom of the window.

Printing Reports and Charts

Before you can print a report or chart, I strongly recommend visiting the Report and Chart Setup dialog box, where you tell Money what kind of printer you use and whether you want to print in portrait or landscape style. The following pages reveal intimate secrets that I got from a tabloid about the Report and Chart Setup dialog box. They also tell you how to print a report or chart.

Getting ready to print a report or chart

Follow these steps to tell Money how you want to print your report or chart:

1. Choose File⇨Print Setup⇨Report and Chart Setup.

You see the Report and Chart Setup dialog box shown in Figure 13-11.

Figure 13-11: Getting ready to print the report or graph.

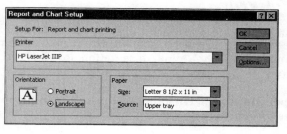

2. From the Printer drop-down list, select the name of the printer you will print on, if you print on more than one printer.

3. **Under Orientation, select the** **L**andscape **option if you want to print lengthwise on the paper.**

Wide reports and charts fit on the page better when they are printed in landscape fashion. With the Landscape option, the page is turned on its side and it is longer on the top and bottom, like a landscape painting.

4. **Click OK.**

If you are printing a detailed chart and you want it to look especially good, click the Options button in the Report and Chart Setup dialog box. That opens the Printer Properties dialog box. Click the Graphics tab, click the Fine option button, and click OK.

Printing the report or chart

To make a hard copy of your report or chart so that you can send it to the hard-hitting *Hard Copy* television show, follow these steps:

1. **Put the report or chart on your computer screen.**

2. **Press Ctrl+P or choose** **F**ile➪**P**rint.

You see the Print Report or Print Chart dialog box.

3. **In the Copies box, enter the number of copies you want, if you want more than one copy.**

4. **Click OK.**

Exporting a Report

The wonderful report that you created is not trapped inside the Money program. No indeed. You can export it to other programs so that you can include it in an annual report or a slide presentation, for example. Follow these steps to export a report and help improve the trade deficit:

1. **With the report on-screen, click the** **E**xport **button in the lower-right corner of the screen.**

The Export Report dialog box shown in Figure 13-12 appears.

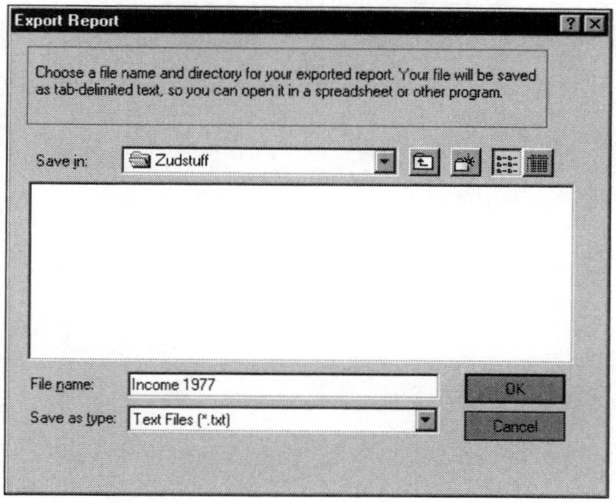

Figure 13-12:
Export a
report so
others can
make use of
it in a word-
processing
or spread-
sheet
program.

2. In the File name text box, enter a descriptive name for your report.

3. Select the folder in which to save your report.

4. Click OK.

The report is saved as a *tab-delimited text file*. That's no big deal, however, because most spreadsheet and word-processing programs can open tab-delimited text files. The only thing you have to worry about is reformatting your report after it lands in the other program.

To open your report in Microsoft Word, press Ctrl+O and, in the Open dialog box, select All Files from the Files of type drop-down list. Then find your file, click on it, and click Open.

To format the report in Word, remove all empty rows from the report and then select the table part of the file — that is, select everything except the title, date, and so on. To do that, click to the left of the first row in the report (the row with the column headings), hold down the mouse button, and drag down the screen until the last row is selected. Then choose Table⇨Convert Text to Table and click OK in the Convert Text to Table dialog box. If you need help formatting the table, get a good book on Word. May I suggest *Word 97 For Windows For Dummies Quick Reference,* by Peter Weverka (published by IDG Books Worldwide, Inc.)? It's a classic.

Chapter 14

Planning for the Years Ahead

· ·

In This Chapter

▶ Describing yourself to the Goal Planner

▶ Stating how your accounts will increase in value

▶ Describing your financial goals in the Goal Planner

▶ Devising a plan to get out of debt

▶ Generating forecast charts to see how well you planned your future

▶ Estimating your tax bill

· ·

*M*ost people don't like focusing on the future, and you can't blame them. Retirement, childrens' college expenses, next year's taxes — who wants to think about that? It's better to live fast, die young, and leave a beautiful memory.

Actually, you would do well to plan ahead for, or at least give a moment's consideration, to your financial future. This chapter explains how to enlist Money's help in planning for retirement and other long-term objectives. I also show you how to gaze into the future with Money and predict what next year's income tax bill will be.

I don't know why Microsoft decided that users of the Money 98 standard edition are reckless and never give a thought to the future, but they did. All the tools for planning ahead are available to users of the Money 98 Financial Suite, but not to the plebes who use the standard edition. That means that you can't use any of the features I describe in this chapter unless you run the Money 98 Financial Suite.

Introducing the Goal Planner

Click the Planner button on the Navigation bar or choose Go⇨Planner, and you land on a monster of a window called the Goal Planner window. Figure 14-1 shows the window.

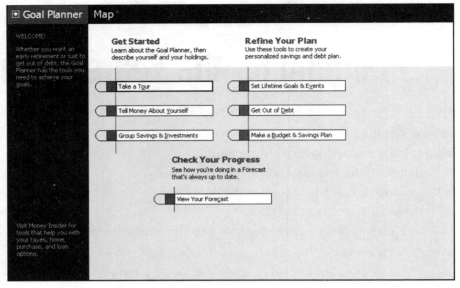

Figure 14-1:
The Goal
Planner
window,
where you
measure
the cost
of your
dreams and
aspirations.

I call the Goal Planner window a "monster" because if you want to, and if you have a lot of spare time on your hands, you can use it to map out your hopes and dreams for the future and find out whether your income will support your hopes and dreams. However, you do need a lot of time to use the Goal Planner.

After you tell Money how long you expect to live, you establish "lifetime goals" for yourself. For example, you can tell Money how much you want to put away for retirement, how much you want to set aside for a vacation, or how much you want to set aside to make the down payment on a house.

Besides "lifetime goals," you tell Money about the "lifetime events" that you expect to encounter. For example, if you expect to receive an inheritance or pay raise, you tell Money when you anticipate the extra income to arrive and how much you plan to receive. There is even an event called "Have a child" in which you tell Money how much you expect your living expenses to increase when you have an extra mouth to feed.

After you are done mapping out the goals and events in your life that affect your pocketbook, you see a Lifetime Forecast chart like the one in Figure 14-2. To generate the chart, Money looks at the balances in your accounts, makes projections about your future income, and compares your future income to how much you expect your lifetime goals and events to cost.

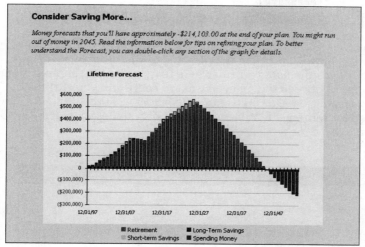

Figure 14-2:
The Lifetime
Forecast
chart shows
whether
your income
will support
your goals
and
aspirations
in the
long-term.

The fellow whose chart is shown in Figure 14-2 will retire in the year 2024, start drawing on his savings and retirement income, run out of money in 2045, and live in dire poverty until his death in 2053. The message `Consider Saving More` appears at the top of the chart. Thanks for the advice, Bub.

Besides a Lifetime Forecast chart, you can generate a Short-term Forecast chart like the one in Figure 14-3. This chart looks one year in advance to find out whether you are saving enough to pay day-to-day bills and other expenses.

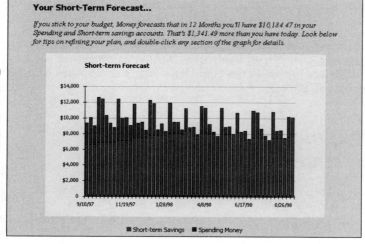

Figure 14-3:
The Short-
term
Forecast
chart shows
whether you
are meeting
your
day-to-day
expenses.

Telling Money about yourself

The first step in using the Goal Planner is to click the Tell Money About Yourself button and fill in the About You window shown in Figure 14-4. Money uses the data you enter here to make long-term projections. For example, between the Age you want to retire and your Estimated life expectancy (read: "the age you want to die"), you will draw from the money you saved for retirement. Money uses that data to determine how much you need to save for retirement.

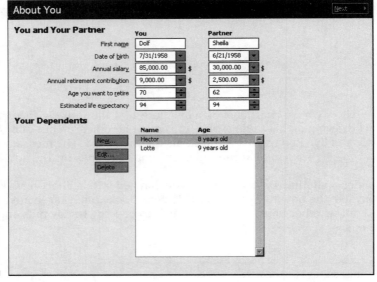

Figure 14-4:
The data you enter on this window is used for making long-term projections.

If you have dependents or a spouse, enter that data in the You and Your Partner and Your Dependents areas. Kind of strange that you can click the Edit or Delete button in the Your Dependents area to edit or delete a child or aging parent, isn't it?

Grouping your savings and investment accounts

The next step is to click the Group Savings & Investments button on the Goal Planner window and tell Money how you expect your accounts to grow over the years. When you click the button, you see the Savings & Investments window shown in Figure 14-5. The amounts in the `Value` column on this window come directly from your account registers. Money uses these numbers to project your future income, but to do so, it needs to know the rate at which you expect the accounts to grow in value.

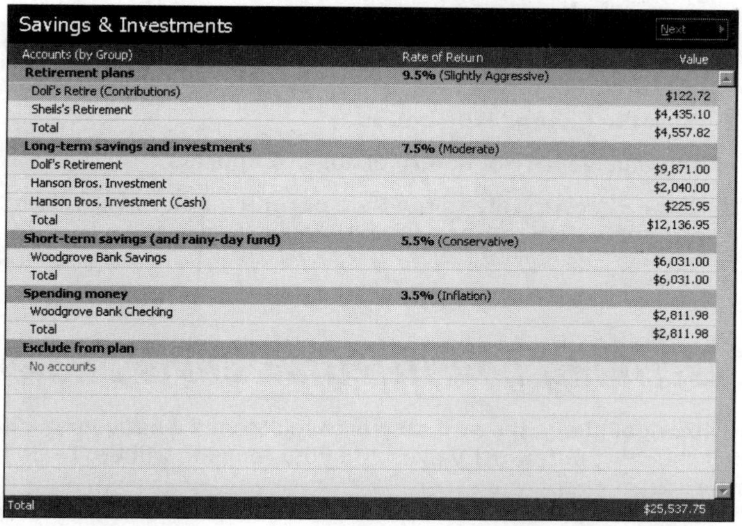

Figure 14-5:
On the
Savings &
Investments
window, tell
Money
how each
of your
accounts
will grow in
value over
the years.

Money offers four categories by which to describe how accounts grow in value:

- **Retirement plans:** For accounts you will keep over the long haul that yield a high rate of interest. Investment accounts can fall in this category, despite the category name.

- **Long-term savings and investments:** For long-term accounts that will grow at a moderate rate of interest.

- **Short-term savings:** For accounts such as savings accounts that you draw upon on a regular basis.

- **Spending money:** For checking accounts that are used for day-to-day bill paying.

Chances are some of your accounts are not in the right category. To move an account into a different category, follow these steps:

1. **Click on the account name and then click the Move Account button.**

2. **In the Move Account to a Different Group dialog box, click the radio button beside the name of the category that the account belongs in.**

3. **Click OK.**

To keep an account from being calculated in future income projections, move it to the Exclude from plan category.

If you don't like the rates of return that Money has established for the account categories, you can change them. Follow these steps:

1. **Click the name of the category whose return rate you want to change.**

2. **Click the Change Rate button.**

   The Change Rate of Return dialog box appears.

3. **Enter a growth rate in the Rate of return before retirement and Rate of return after retirement text boxes.**

4. **Click OK.**

Describing your lifetime goals and events

Moving right along, the next step is to tell Money what your goals are and what the most noteworthy events in your long life will be. To do that, follow these steps:

1. **Click the Set Lifetime Goals & Events button in the Goal Planner window.**

2. **Click the New Goal button.**

   The New Goal Wizard dialog box appears.

3. **Select a goal or event in the New Goal Wizard dialog box and click Next.**

   You see the first of several dialog boxes that ask about the goal or event in question.

4. **Answer all the questions that the interrogator asks you, and click the Finish button after the interrogation is over.**

As I mention earlier in this chapter, Money tabulates how much the goals and events you describe cost. Then Money compares that cost to your present and future income to see if you will meet your financial goals.

The Money Insider offers lots of good advice about how to plan for retirement, college, and other long-term objectives. Click the Money Insider button on the Navigation bar or choose Go⇨Money Insider to get the advice of experts and money gurus.

Making a plan to get out of debt

To meet your financial goals, you have to rid yourself of outstanding debts. To devise a plan for doing that, follow these steps:

1. **Click the Get Out of Debt button on the Goal Planner window.**

   This step brings up the Debt Reduction Planner window, which explains the three steps you must complete to devise your plan.

2. **Click Next (the button in the upper-right corner).**

   You see the Include debt amounts on your plan window, which lists all the loan accounts you set up with Money (Chapter 11 explains loan accounts), the amount you must pay monthly, and the interest rate of each loan. On this window, you tell Money which accounts to include in your plan by selecting an account and clicking a button:

   - **Move out of Plan:** Removes the loan account from the plan.

   - **Edit Debt Info:** Opens the Details dialog box, where you can change the interest rate, payment frequency, and other particulars of the plan.

Except for boosting the amount you pay each month by a few dollars, loan and mortgage payments do not change substantially. You may as well click the Move out of Plan button to remove those accounts from the plan. Credit card debt is another matter. If you carry credit card debt, click the Edit Debt Info button and enter a higher-than-usual amount in the Estimated spending text box. Credit card debt is expensive. To reduce this kind of debt, pay more each month until you pay down the amount that you owe.

3. **Click the Next button to move to the Define your payment plan window.**

   Under Status in the lower-left corner of the window, you see how much you owe, how much you spend to service your debts, and when you will be out of debt, according to your plan.

   If you would like to climb out of debt sooner, you can include this noble aspiration in your plan for reducing debt by entering a date in the Enter the date you want to be out of debt text box (you can also drag the slider to change the date).

4. **Enter a new target date for getting out of debt, and then click the Next button.**

   You see the View your debt plan graph, which shows how your debt is reduced over time.

5. **Click the Next button.**

You see the Take action & reduce your debt window. It offers some gratuitous advice about reducing debt. Read the advice.

6. **Click the Finish button.**

You land back on the Goal Planner window.

Generating a Lifetime Forecast or Short-term Forecast chart

If you've come this far, you either have a lot of stamina or you are a firm believer in Money's Goal Planner gizmo. Now you are ready to see what your income, goals and events, plans for getting out of debt, and budget aspirations add up to. Money can generate charts outlining both short-term and lifetime forecasts for your financial future.

(However, to help generate these projections, you may want to first create a budget as I describe in Chapter 10. Money can use the income and expense figures from the budget to create the forecast charts.)

For a look at your financial future, click the View Your Forecast button on the Goal Planner window and then do one of the following:

✔ Click the Short-term Forecast button to see a chart that reveals whether you have enough scratch to pay your bills and cover your expenses in the coming year (refer to Figure 14-3).

✔ Click the Lifetime Forecast button to see if you are saving enough to meet your lifetime goals (refer to Figure 14-2).

Estimating Your Tax Bill

Knowing what you will owe in taxes next year never hurts, especially if you don't like surprises, so Money offers the Tax Estimator to help you estimate what you owe for last year or what you will owe for this year. Notice, however, that the thing is called the Tax Estimator, not the Tax Accountant. The Tax Estimator can give you a rough idea of what you owe or will owe the IRS, but it can't take the place of a tax accountant and do your income taxes for you.

Finding out what the tax rates are

Built into the Money 98 Tax Estimator are accurate tax rates for the year 1997. But suppose that you are trying to estimate your income taxes for 1998 or 1999. How can you obtain the correct tax rates for those years?

If you connect to the Internet through Money, perhaps to pay bills or update an investment portfolio, the tax rates in the Tax Estimator are up-to-date. Money updates them when it connects to the Internet. Follow these steps to make sure that the tax rates are being automatically updated:

1. **Choose Tools⇨Options.**

   The Options dialog box appears.

2. **Click the Online Services tab.**

3. **Make sure that the Mortgage and tax rates from Money Insider check box is checked.**

4. **Click OK.**

If you don't have a modem, you can still update the tax rates manually, but to do it you have to know more about the tax rates than you may know or care to know. Follow these steps:

1. **Choose Tools⇨Options.**

   The Options dialog box appears.

2. **Click the Tax tab.**

3. **In the Show rates for filing status drop-down list, select Custom.**

4. **Fill in the boxes to describe the current tax rates.**

   Not very easy, is it? You have to know more than the average Joe about tax rates to make it work.

5. **Click OK.**

Follow these steps to use the Tax Estimator to find out what your tax bill is for last year or may be for the coming year:

1. **Click the Money Insider button on the Navigation bar or choose Go⇨Money Insider.**

   You land on the Insider window.

2. **Click Tax Worksheet in the lower-right corner of the window.**

   You see the Tax Estimator window, as shown in Figure 14-6. To estimate your tax bill, you fill in each page of the worksheet — Overview, Income, Adjustments, and Deductions.

Worksheet explanation

Worksheet buttons

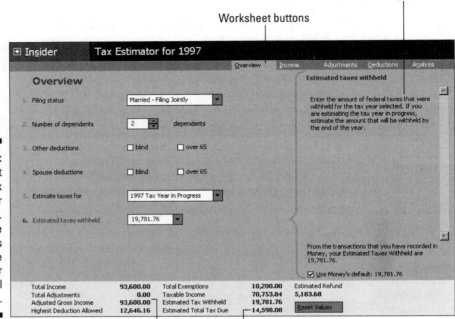

Ongoing totals   What you owe the IRS

Figure 14-6: The first Tax Estimator worksheet. Fill out the worksheets to estimate what your tax bill will be.

As you enter the numbers, Money updates the figures along the bottom of the screen. Keep your eye on the Estimated Total Tax Due figure. It shows the amount you owe the IRS.

On each worksheet page is a Reset Values button. If you get yourself in a tangle and enter the wrong numbers, click the Reset Values button to begin anew with the numbers you started with.

3. Fill in the Overview worksheet.

Overview, the first worksheet, asks for your filing status and number of dependents, as well as other information. Be sure to select the right option from the Estimate taxes for drop-down list in box number 5. That is where you tell Money whether you want estimates for last year or this year.

4. Click the Income button and fill in the Your Income worksheet.

As Chapter 4 explains, you can tag income and expense categories to tax form line-items. If you did that, some numbers may already be entered in the Your Income worksheet and the other worksheets. If not, enter the numbers. You can either make a best guess as to what to enter or generate reports to find out precisely what the numbers are.

5. **Click the Adjustments button and fill in the Your Adjustments worksheet.**

   If you have trouble figuring out what an adjustment is, click its box and then read the explanation on the right side of the window.

6. **Click the Deductions button and fill in the Your Deductions worksheet.**

   After you finish filling out this worksheet, you'll know what your estimated tax bill is. Check out the figure beside Estimated Total Tax Due on the bottom of the screen.

7. **Click the Analysis button to move to the Your Tax Analysis window.**

   What's the verdict? The window may have some useful advice about how to save on your income taxes.

Chapter 15

Making Loan and Mortgage Decisions with Money

*I*f you are shopping for a home loan, I'll bet my bottom dollar that you are confused by terms such as "points" and "closing costs." With the Money 98 Financial Suite, you can analyze different kinds of mortgages or loans and cut through the mumbo-jumbo. You can find out exactly how much borrowing costs — that is, you can find out exactly what the monthly mortgage payments on a loan will be.

I hate to be like one of those thuggish individuals who bars the door of a nightclub and only allows the chic and well-dressed to enter, but I'm afraid that this chapter is strictly for users of the Money 98 Financial Suite. You can't compare loans and mortgages with the standard edition of Money.

The Money 98 Financial Suite includes a gizmo called the Loan Worksheet that you can use to compare loans or mortgages or find out what a loan or mortgage costs. The Loan Worksheet cannot come to your aid as fast as the Lone Ranger, but it can help with the following difficult tasks:

✔ Finding out how much money you can afford to borrow

✔ Finding out how high the payments on a loan are

✔ Finding out how long it takes to pay off a loan

✔ Finding out how interest rates affect loan payments

> ✔ Comparing one loan or mortgage to another to see which is the better deal
>
> ✔ Comparing a mortgage that you are paying now to another mortgage to see if refinancing is worthwhile

Read on if you are in the market for a loan or mortgage or you simply need more information about financing.

The Loan Worksheet: Calculating the Costs of Borrowing

When you are shopping for a loan or mortgage, the two most important questions to ask yourself are "How large a loan can I afford?" and "How much will my monthly payments be?" The Loan Worksheet can help answer these questions, as well as show how interest rates affect loans and how long paying off a loan will take.

Follow these steps to use the Loan Worksheet as you agonize over whether you should buy a house, new car, or other expensive commodity that requires taking out a loan:

1. **Click the Money Insider button on the Navigation bar or choose <u>G</u>o⇨Money<u>I</u>nsider.**

   You land on the Insider window.

2. **Click the Loan Worksheet button.**

   You see the introductory page of the Loan Planner Worksheet. To calculate the cost of a loan or mortgage that you want to analyze, you fill out one, two, or three pages, depending on what you want to know: Initial Costs, Loan Terms, and Variable Rate. After you fill out one page, click a button in the upper-right corner of the window to move to the next one.

3. **Click the <u>L</u>oan Terms button.**

   You see the Loan Terms page shown in Figure 15-1. On this page, you tell Money what you want to know about the loan and provide all the particulars that you do know.

   You can ignore the boxes under Loan B. Those boxes are for comparing one loan or mortgage to another, as you can read about in the "Comparing One Loan or Mortgage to Another" section later in this chapter.

Advice for home and car buyers on the Insider window

The Insider window offers advice for car buyers and home buyers:

✔ Click the Car Buying link to access articles about buying and leasing cars, obtaining car insurance, and determining how much you should spend for a car.

✔ Click the Home Buying link to access articles about shopping for homes and mortgages, dealing with real estate agents, and preparing a deed of title.

4. **Click box 1, I want Money to calculate, and select the option from the drop-down list that describes what you want to know about the loan or mortgage in question.**

Choose what you want to know about the loan or mortgage

Explanation of box

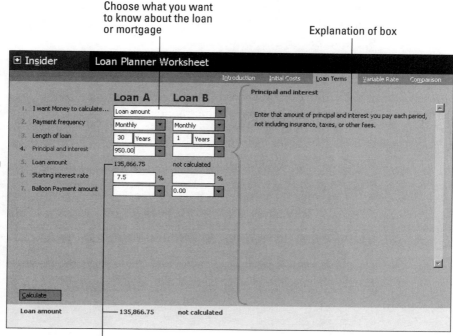

Figure 15-1: On the Loan Terms page, tell Money what you want to know about the loan or mortgage.

Money's calculation

This table explains the options in the I want Money to calculate box:

Option	Question That You Want Money to Answer
Length of loan	How long will it take to pay off this loan?
Principal and interest	How much can I afford to pay each month (or other time period)?
Loan amount	How much can I afford to borrow altogether?
Starting interest rate	How will the interest rates change if I pay points up front or pay some of the closing costs out of my own pocket?
Balloon Payment amount	If I make a lump-sum payment at the end of the loan, how will the principal, interest, and other loan particulars be affected?

You can't fill in one of the boxes. One box says "not calculated" because it names the thing that you want Money to calculate — the thing you chose in Step 4. The answer to your question about your loan or mortgage appears where "not calculated" is now when you are done filling in the Loan Terms page.

5. **Fill in boxes 2 through 7.**

In the figure, I asked Money how much I can afford to borrow on a 30-year mortgage, given that $950 per month is the amount I can pay comfortably and the interest rate on the loan is 7.5 percent.

If you can't understand what Money wants you to enter in one of the boxes in the Loan Planner worksheet, click in the box and then read the explanation on the right side of the window.

6. **Click the Calculate button.**

The answer to the question that you put to Money in Step 4 is listed next to the appropriate category and at the bottom of the window. In Figure 15-1, Money tells me that I can afford to borrow $135,866.75.

You're done — unless you intend to pay initial costs for the loan or mortgage you are wrestling with, or the loan or mortgage charges a variable interest rate, not a fixed interest rate (see the following sections).

Investigating how initial costs alter the costs of a mortgage

By "initial costs," Money refers to a down payment you make at the start of the loan, closing costs, discount points, and other such fees. *Closing costs* are appraisal fees, sales commissions, and other fees that you are charged when you take out a loan. Closing costs are expressed as a percentage of the purchase price of the item you want to buy with the loan.

When you take out a mortgage to buy a house, you are charged *discount points,* also known simply as *points.* Like closing costs, points are expressed as a percentage of the amount you borrow.

To tell Money about the closing costs, points, and down payment you intend to make on a loan, follow these steps after you have filled out the Loan Terms page of the Loan Planner worksheet (see the preceding section of this chapter):

1. Click the Initial Costs button.

You see the Initial Costs page, shown in Figure 15-2.

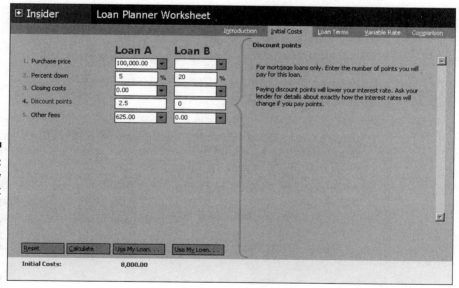

Figure 15-2:
Tell Money the amount of the up-front fees and down payment for the loan.

2. **Fill in the blanks on the Initial Costs page.**

   Again, unless you are comparing two loans (which I discuss later in this chapter), just fill out the Loan A column.

3. **After you are done, click the Calculate button.**

   Money produces the Initial Costs total at the bottom of the window.

4. **Click the Loan Terms button to return to the Loan Terms page, where you see how the particulars of the loan are affected by initial costs.**

   For example, if you entered a number in the Percent down text box because you plan to make a down payment on the loan or mortgage, the amount you borrow is lowered, as are the monthly payments.

Entering the variable-rate data

Your loan or mortgage may not have a fixed rate. Adjustable-rate mortgages (ARMs) have variable rates, and many lenders offer a low introductory rate for the first few months or years to entice you, after which they raise the rate.

Determining the cost of a variable-rate loan, also known as an adjustable-rate loan, is tricky. To figure out the costs, follow these steps after you have filled out the Loan Terms page of the Loan Planner worksheet:

1. **Click the Variable Rate button.**

   You see the Variable Rate page shown in Figure 15-3.

2. **In box 1, select Variable from the drop-down list.**

3. **Fill in the other boxes.**

   The other boxes ask when the first adjustment occurs, how much time passes between adjustments, the highest interest rate you can be charged for the loan, and how much you expect the interest rate to rise each year.

4. **After you are done filling in the Variable Rate page, click the Loan Terms button to return to the Loan Terms page and see what the particulars of the loan look like now.**

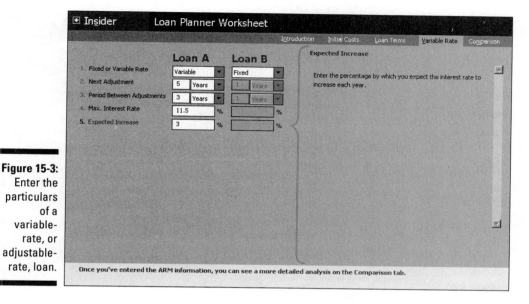

Figure 15-3:
Enter the
particulars
of a
variable-
rate, or
adjustable-
rate, loan.

Comparing One Loan or Mortgage to Another

As you must have noticed by now, the Loan Planner worksheet includes boxes for Loan A and Loan B. Those boxes are for comparing one loan or mortgage to another to find out which is least expensive or which meets your needs better.

To enter the particulars of Loan B, fill in the boxes as the last handful of pages told you to do. Each worksheet page clearly compares the two loans, and you can also click the Comparison button to see a summary comparison on the Comparison page. In Figure 15-4, I compared a 30-year mortgage at 7.5 percent interest (Loan A) to a 15-year mortgage at 6.25 percent (Loan B). The Comparison page tells me that I will pay $92,817 more in interest payments on the 30-year mortgage.

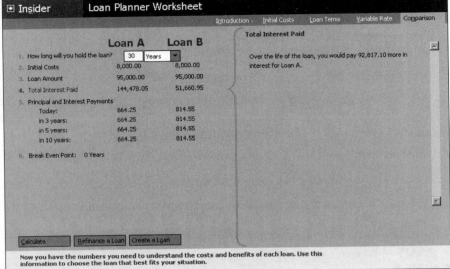

Figure 15-4:
The
Comparison
page
outlines the
differences
between
the loans or
mortgages
you are
comparing.

Finding out if refinancing is worthwhile

When interest rates start to drop, homeowners get itchy. They ask themselves whether refinancing is worthwhile. *Refinancing* means to trade in one mortgage for another, less expensive mortgage.

One way to find out if refinancing is worthwhile is to enter the mortgage you are currently paying for in the Loan Planner worksheet and compare it to a lower-interest mortgage.

Follow these steps to compare a mortgage you are paying for to another mortgage:

1. **Open the Loan Planner Worksheet and click the Initial Costs tab.**

2. **Click the Use My Loan button and enter the particulars of the mortgage you currently have in the Loan A boxes.**

If you set up a loan account for tracking the mortgage (see Chapter 16), you can enter the particulars of the mortgage by clicking the Use My Loan button, selecting the mortgage from the drop-down list in the Loan Selection dialog box, and clicking OK. Money enters the data from your present mortgage in the worksheet in the Loan A boxes.

3. **Enter the particulars of the second, less expensive mortgage in the Loan B boxes.**

4. **Click the Comparison button to see a comparison of the two mortgages.**

Line 6, Break Even Point, tells you whether the savings you get from lower monthly payments covers the costs of refinancing and how long it will take to recoup refinancing costs. If line 6 shows "Never," don't refinance.

The Home Worksheet: Finding Out How Much You Can Pay

A lot of factors go into figuring out how expensive a house you can afford. You have to determine the monthly mortgage payment that you can make comfortably. You have to find out how much points, mortgage insurance, and closing costs add to the cost of the house. You have to drive around strange neighborhoods with real estate agents and imagine yourself living in houses that would be okay if not for the threadbare carpets and all that cottage cheese on the ceilings.

Money can't help you locate a dream house, but the Home Ownership worksheet can help you do the numbers and find out how expensive a house you can buy. Follow these steps to use the Home Ownership worksheet:

1. **Click the Money Insider button on the Navigation bar or choose Go⇨MoneyInsider.**

   You see the Insider window.

2. **Click the Home Worksheet button.**

   You see a Welcome window that explains what the Home Ownership worksheet is all about.

3. **Click the Information button.**

   The How much can I afford? window shown in Figure 15-5 appears. If you have scheduled paycheck deposits (see Chapter 11) or have given Money information about your debt (see Chapter 13), some of the boxes on this window are already filled in.

4. **If necessary, click the Reset button to empty the boxes and enter accurate information.**

5. **In box 1, Calculate, select an option from the drop-down list to tell Money what you want to calculate.**

   The options are monthly payment, purchase price, cash, and various combinations of the three:

   • **Monthly payment:** The monthly house payment, or maximum payment that you can afford, given your debt and other monthly expenses.

   • **Purchase price:** The cost of the most expensive house that you can realistically afford.

   • **Cash:** The expenses that you must pay initially, including the down payment, points, and closing costs. The down payment represents most of the cash you will spend.

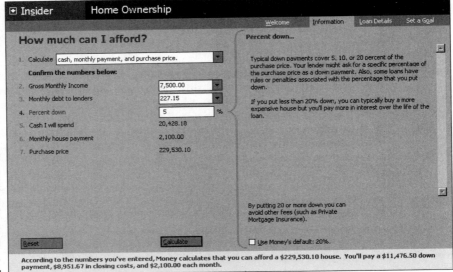

Figure 15-5:
Finding out
how
expensive a
house you
can afford
to buy.

6. **Fill in boxes 2 through 7 on the worksheet.**

Depending on which option you select in Step 5, you may not be able to fill in some of the boxes, because they represent the data that you are trying to calculate.

Be sure to enter your gross monthly income — the amount you earn *before* taxes — in box 2. When you enter your debt in box 3, enter the sum of your average monthly credit card payments and other debt payments. Money needs this data to help determine how much is left over for a mortgage payment.

7. **Click the Loan Details button.**

The Confirm the details of the loan window appears, as shown in Figure 15-6.

8. **Fill in boxes 1 through 8 to tell Money the specific information about the loan.**

If you don't understand what a box is for, click it and then read its explanation on the right side of the window. You may have to call lenders to get some of the information that this window requires.

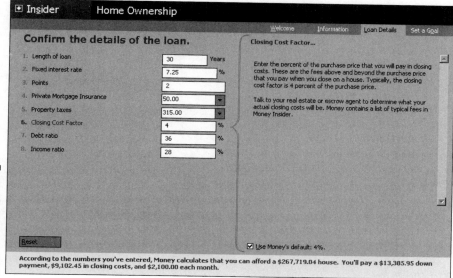

Figure 15-6:
Enter the
particulars
of the loan
you want to
apply for.

9. Click the <u>I</u>nformation button to return to the How much can I afford window.

10. Click the <u>C</u>alculate button.

Money produces the amounts you asked for in Step 5.

Chapter 16

Tracking Assets, Liabilities, Loans, and Mortgages

. . . .

In This Chapter

▶ Deciding when to create asset, house, liability, and loan accounts

▶ Defining assets and liabilities

▶ Setting up an asset and house account

▶ Associating an asset or house account with a loan account

▶ Recording changes in the value of an asset or equity in a house

▶ Setting up and recording transactions in a liability account

▶ Setting up an account for tracking loans and mortgages

▶ Recording loan and mortgage payments

▶ Paying extra on a loan or mortgage payment

. . . .

*A*nything of value that you own or that adds to your net worth can be counted as an *asset* — jewelry, stock, the equity in a house, a vintage baseball card autographed by the great Willie Mays. The money in your checking and savings account is an asset. So is money that is owed to you.

A *liability,* on the other hand, counts against net worth. A debt that you owe is considered a liability. Credit card debt is a liability, as is tax owed to the IRS, a mortgage, a student loan, and a car loan.

So if you want a clear picture of your net worth or the net worth of your business, you need to identify your assets and liabilities. Fortunately, Money offers account types to track not only assets and liabilities, but also track loans and mortgages, two other critical elements in the net-worth equation. In this chapter, you discover how and why to set up and use these kinds of accounts. You also find out how to fine-tune them so they track exactly what you want them to track.

Understanding How to Track Assets, Liabilities, Loans, and Mortgages with Money

If you think about it, all the accounts that you can set up in Money fall either into the asset or liability category. The money in savings and checking accounts is an asset. Debt that you track in a credit card account is a liability. However, Money offers these special account types for keeping a close tab on assets and liabilities:

✔ **Asset account:** For tracking the value of personal property, such as art collections, coin collections, and cars. If you use Money to track a business, you can create asset accounts for office equipment, trucks and cars, machinery, or anything else that adds to the worth of the business or can be used as collateral.

✔ **House account:** For tracking how much equity is in a house. *Equity* is a house's market value, less the amount that is owed on the house. For example, if $100,000 is owed on the house and its market value is $150,000, the owner has $50,000 equity in the house. Each time you make a mortgage payment, you can transfer the principal part of the payment to a House account and thereby track how much equity is in the house. A House account is a specific type of asset account.

✔ **Liability account:** For tracking no-interest debt, such as quarterly tax payments that you owe the IRS, property taxes, insurance premiums, or money you owe a friend.

✔ **Loan account:** For tracking loans for which you have to pay interest, such as mortgages, student loans, and car loans. Loans for which you pay interest are called *amortized loans*. With an amortized loan, part of each payment goes toward paying interest on the debt and part goes toward reducing the principal (the amount you borrowed). A Loan account is a type of liability account.

What's your most valuable asset?

Did you know that your most valuable asset is not your car or truck, your most profitable investment, or even your house? No, your most valuable assets are your abilities and talents. They are the qualities employers value you for. And they can't be measured by any computer program.

Tracking the Value of a House or Other Asset

Ask most homeowners what their most valuable asset is, and they'll say their house. But ask them how much equity they have in that house, and you usually get a much less definitive answer — if you get an answer at all. And you would probably get the same response if you ask about other tangible assets, such as art collections, baseball cards, or office equipment. Money can help you peg the value of your assets.

This part of the chapter explains how to track the value of an asset or the equity in a house. Read on to find out how to track the equity in a house or the value of tangible assets, such as art collections, baseball cards, office equipment, and other property that you could sell.

Setting up an asset or house account

A Money house account and a Money asset account work exactly the same way. They're also easy to set up. You can find more specific instructions for setting up accounts in Chapter 2 (where I show you how to set up checking and savings accounts), but for now, follow these steps to set up a house or asset account:

1. **Go to the Account Manager window and click the New Account button.**

2. **When Money asks for the bank or financial institution where the account is held, click Next without entering anything.**

   The next dialog box asks what kind of account you want to set up.

3. **Select Asset or House and click Next.**

   You see the first of several dialog boxes that ask questions about the new account.

4. **Keep answering questions and clicking Next.**

   Only two questions may give you trouble:

   - **The asset's (or house's) value:** When Money asks for the asset's value, enter its value as of today if you just acquired it or you don't want to track its growth since the time you acquired it. If you want to track how the asset (or house) grew or shrunk in value since you acquired it, enter **0**; also be sure to enter an appropriate date when Money asks when you acquired the asset.

- **Associate a loan with the asset (or house):** As the "Tracking Loans and Mortgages" section explains later in this chapter, you can transfer the principal portion of a loan or mortgage payment to an asset or house account. By doing so, you can track how much the value of the asset or the equity in the house increases each time you make a payment.

  To track value or equity increases this way, click the Yes radio button when Money asks which loan account to associate the asset or house with, as shown in Figure 16-1. When you click Next, you see a dialog box for selecting loan accounts. From the drop-down list, select the loan account from which you will transfer the principal portion of the loan payments.

  As the dialog box in Figure 16-1 explains, home equity loans should be associated with a house. When you took out the home equity loan, you used your house as collateral. Even if you used the money from the loan to buy a car or boat, for example, associate the home equity loan with your house, not with the asset you purchased with money from the loan.

5. **Click Finish after you are done answering the questions.**

Figure 16-1:
By "associating" the asset or house with a loan account, you can track how the value of the asset or house changes each time you make a loan or mortgage payment.

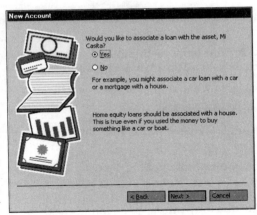

Another way to associate an asset account with a loan account

Suppose that you set up an asset or house account but you forgot to associate it with a loan account, and now you want to do that. Here's how:

1. **Open the asset account or house account register.**

2. **Click the Details button.**

3. **Click the Add Association button on the Account Details window.**

4. **In the Associate Loans dialog box, select the name of the loan that you took out in order to pay for the asset or house.**

In the figure, Arlette is choosing Arlette's car loan so that payments made on that loan contribute to the value of the car whose value she tracks in an asset account called, not surprisingly, Arlette's Car.

5. **Click OK.**

The Details window also has a Remove Association button. Click it to sever the link between a loan account and an asset or house account.

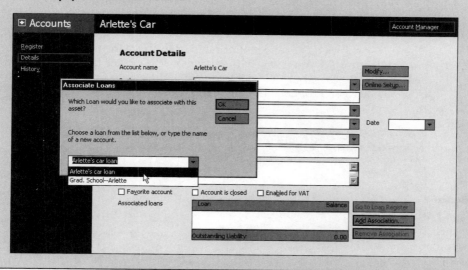

Recording changes in the value of an asset or house

Now that you have set up the asset or house account, all you have to do to record changes in its value is open the account register and enter amounts in the Decrease or Increase column. Follow these steps:

1. **Open the register of the house or asset account.**

2. **Click the Decrease tab to record a decrease in value; click the Increase tab to record an increase in value.**

3. **Enter the date of the change in value in the Date text box.**

4. **Enter the amount of the change in the Amount text box.**

5. **Categorize the change in value.**

   For example, you may use a category called Increase Mkt Value (Increase Market Value) to record an increase in value, or Decrease Mkt Value (Decrease Market Value) to record a decrease in value.

6. **Click the Enter button.**

Figure 16-2 shows an asset account register for tracking the value of a Ming vase collection. As you can see, the value of Ming vases has fluctuated in the last couple of years, but the collection nevertheless has increased in value from $5,000 to $5,725. Let's hope none of the vases get broken.

Figure 16-2: To track the value of an asset, use the transaction tabs to enter amounts in the Decrease and Increase columns.

Tracking Your Liabilities

Set up a liability account to track loans on which you don't have to pay interest, income tax payments, and other debts that don't fall in the credit card, line of credit, or loan category, or anything else that counts against your net worth.

It's hard to imagine anything easier than creating a liability account in Money. Follow these steps:

1. **Go to the Account Manager window and click the New Account button.**

2. **When Money asks for the bank or financial institution where the account is held, click Next without entering anything.**

   The next dialog box asks what kind of account you want to set up.

3. **Select Liability and click Next.**

4. **Keep answering questions and clicking Next.**

   The only place where you may trip is when Money asks how much you owe on the account. Enter what you owe as of today if you just started owing or you don't care to track how your liability has shrunk or grown since the time you started owing. If you want to track how the liability has grown or shrunk since the time you acquired it, enter **0**.

5. **Click Finish after you are done answering the questions.**

Figure 16-3 shows a liability account register that tracks gambling debts from weekly poker parties. To record transactions in a liability account like this one, simply enter numbers on the Increase or Decrease transaction form, as was done in the figure.

Tracking Loans and Mortgages

The following sections explain how to set up a loan account for tracking amortized loan payments and mortgage payments. An *amortized loan* is a loan for which you make regular payments of the same amount. Part of each payment goes toward paying interest on the loan and part goes toward reducing the principal (the amount you borrowed).

After you find out how to set up a loan account, I will show you how to stand on your head and sing *Dixie*. Actually, I will do no such thing. I will show you how to record loan payments in loan account registers, handle irregular loan payments that involve escrow accounts, and record a payment above and beyond the amount you are expected to pay.

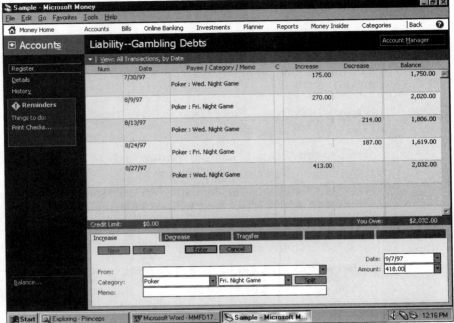

Figure 16-3:
Using a
liability
account
to track
gambling
debt.

Is creating a loan account worthwhile?

Before you go to the considerable trouble of creating a loan account, you should know that you may not have to create one to track mortgage or loan payments. As long as the lender tells you how much you owe after each payment and how much you are paying in interest, you really don't need to track the loan. You can simply get the numbers from the lender and record the interest portion of the payment as a decrease in a liability account and the principal part of the payment under Loan: Loan Interest or a similar category.

In the case of mortgages, business loans, and investment loans, the lender should send you a 1098 tax form at the end of the year that explains how much of your payments went toward interest. That is the amount you need to know for income tax purposes. To save time and heartache, you may as well let the lender do the work and get the numbers from the lender rather than track the loan yourself.

Setting up a loan account

When you set up a loan account, Money asks you all kinds of questions and uses the information to break down the loan payments into interest charges and principal reductions. With each payment you make on the loan or mortgage, Money reduces the amount you owe and records how much of the payment did not lower the debt but only went toward servicing the interest.

Gather all the papers that pertain to the loan or mortgage and then follow these steps to set up a loan account for tracking the payments:

1. **Go the Account Manager window and click the New Account button.**

   You see the first of many New Account dialog boxes.

2. **Enter or select from the drop-down list the name of the financial institution that tendered you the loan and click Next.**

3. **In the next dialog box, which asks what kind of account you want to set up, click Loan and then click Next.**

4. **Speed-read the "You are about to enter the Twilight Zone" message box and click Next.**

   No, it doesn't really say that you are about to enter the Twilight Zone. It just tells you what the dialog boxes in the New Loan Account wizard are about to ask you.

5. **Speed-read the next message, which explains the three types of general information that will be needed, and click Next.**

6. **You're borrowing money, and the Borrowing money radio button is already selected, so click Next.**

7. **Enter a name in the Loan name text box and choose to whom the payments will be made by entering a name in the Make payments to box or selecting a name from the drop-down list; then click Next.**

   The name you enter appears on the Account Manager window.

8. **Select Adjustable Rate Loan (ARM) or Fixed Rate Loan, and click Next.**

   The interest rate remains the same in a fixed-rate loan. In an adjustable-rate loan, the rate of interest is subject to change.

   Which dialog box you see next depends on the option you chose in this step.

9. **If you selected Fixed Rate Loan in Step 8, click the Yes or No radio button to say whether payments have been made on the loan; if you selected Adjustable Rate Loan, enter the date that the first interest rate adjustment is to be made and enter the number of years or months between adjustments.**

If you are setting up a fixed rate loan and you select the Yes, payments have been made option in this dialog box, you see an additional dialog box that asks whether to schedule all the payments made on the loan or mortgage since you began paying it. Money needs this information to create a loan payment schedule. Money can gather information for scheduling no matter how you answer this question. May as well click Yes. Clicking Yes saves you a little time in Step 14.

Click Next, of course, after you're done.

10. **Enter the date when the first payment on the loan or mortgage was due.**

    Be sure to enter the due date of the first payment, not the next payment. Money needs the first due date to create the amortization schedule.

11. **Speed-read the next dialog box, which tells you how far you've come, and click Next.**

12. **From the Paid how often drop-down list, select the option that describes how often payments are due (probably Monthly) and click Next.**

13. **Select the option that describes how the loan is calculated and click Next.**

    Home mortgages are usually calculated based on the date that the payment is due, and consumer loans (such as car loans) are based on the date the lender receives payment. However, you may have to dig into the papers that came with your loan or call the lender to find out how interest is calculated.

14. **In the following five dialog boxes, enter the amount of the loan, the interest rate, the loan length, the principal and interest, and the balloon payment, if there is one.**

    If you clicked Yes back in Step 9, the Interest Rate dialog box is already filled out. Keep clicking Next after you make each entry. After you are done, your dialog box looks something like Figure 16-4. Click the Back button if you need to go back and change an entry.

    The Principal + interest entry is a little confusing. What Money is really asking for is the amount of your monthly payment (or weekly payment or whatever). If you don't know the amount offhand, leave the box blank. Money can calculate payment amounts for you as long as you can provide information in the other four boxes.

    When you enter the interest rate, be sure to enter the loan interest rate, not the annual percentage rate (APR). The two are different.

15. **Speed-read the dialog box, which tells you how far you have come, and click Next.**

    It's not as though you have any choice in the matter, is it?

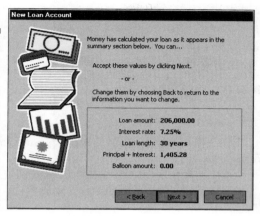

Figure 16-4: Calculating the particulars of the loan. If you leave one of the entries blank, Money calculates it for you.

16. **Enter category and subcategory names or select the names from the drop-down lists, and click Next.**

    When you make a loan or mortgage payment, the portion of the payment that goes toward interest is categorized under the category and subcategory choices you make in this step. The portion that goes toward reducing the debt is recorded in the loan account register as a decrease in the amount you owe.

17. **Click Yes or No to tell Money whether or not the account you are setting up tracks a mortgage, and click Next.**

18. **Click Yes or No to tell Money whether or not interest on the loan is tax-deductible, and click Next.**

    Mortgages and home-equity loans are usually tax-deductible. This is an important matter. If you aren't sure whether your loan or mortgage is tax-deductible, ask an accountant.

19. **If part of your payment goes toward fees such as escrow accounts, click the Other Fees button; otherwise, click Next.**

    This dialog box asks whether you must pay fees on top of the principal and interest payments that are due. Chiefly, this dialog box is for people who pay into escrow accounts. An *escrow account* is an account that a mortgage company takes out on behalf of a borrower to make sure that property taxes and property insurance get paid.

    If you click the Other Fees button, you see the Other Fees dialog box shown in Figure 16-5. This box works exactly like the Split Transaction dialog box I describe in Chapter 3. Use the Other Fees dialog box to categorize the fees you have to pay, and then click Done.

Figure 16-5:
If you have
to pay fees
as part of
loan or
mortgage
payments,
categorize
the fees
in this
dialog box.

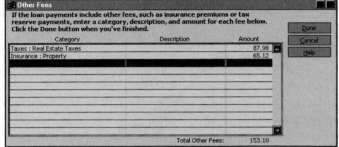

20. **If you want to schedule a payment in the Bill Calendar so that you are reminded when payments are due, click Yes, remind me and fill in the dialog box; otherwise, click No, do not remind me and click Next.**

Chapter 11 explains how the Bill Calendar works. I strongly recommend scheduling the loan payment. Lenders charge hefty fees for late payments. By scheduling your loan or mortgage payment, you increase your chances of paying it on time.

21. **Study the next dialog box, and then click Next.**

As shown in Figure 16-6, the next dialog box you see provides a rundown of all the information you gave Money in the last *(whew!)* 20 steps. Study this dialog box for a moment, and if anything is wrong, start clicking the Back button like a madman until you reach the dialog box where you can correct the error.

Figure 16-6:
The Grand
Total line of
the Loan
Amortization
report tells
you how
much in
interest you
have to pay
over the life
of a loan.

Reports & Charts   **Loan Amortization**

Big Mortgage

Date	Payment Number	Payment Amount	Principal	Interest	Other Fees	Principal Balance
6/1/25	342	1,558.38	1,253.29	151.99	153.10	23,903.41
7/1/25	343	1,558.38	1,260.86	144.42	153.10	22,642.55
8/1/25	344	1,558.38	1,268.48	136.80	153.10	21,374.07
9/1/25	345	1,558.38	1,276.14	129.14	153.10	20,097.93
10/1/25	346	1,558.38	1,283.86	121.42	153.10	18,814.07
11/1/25	347	1,558.38	1,291.61	113.67	153.10	17,522.46
12/1/25	348	1,558.38	1,299.42	105.86	153.10	16,223.04
1/1/26	349	1,558.38	1,307.27	98.01	153.10	14,915.77
2/1/26	350	1,558.38	1,315.16	90.12	153.10	13,600.61
3/1/26	351	1,558.38	1,323.11	82.17	153.10	12,277.50
4/1/26	352	1,558.38	1,331.10	74.18	153.10	10,946.40
5/1/26	353	1,558.38	1,339.15	66.13	153.10	9,607.25
6/1/26	354	1,558.38	1,347.24	58.04	153.10	8,260.01
7/1/26	355	1,558.38	1,355.38	49.90	153.10	6,904.63
8/1/26	356	1,558.38	1,363.56	41.72	153.10	5,541.07
9/1/26	357	1,558.38	1,371.80	33.48	153.10	4,169.27
10/1/26	358	1,558.38	1,380.09	25.19	153.10	2,789.18
11/1/26	359	1,558.38	1,388.43	16.85	153.10	1,400.75
12/1/26	360	1,562.31	1,400.75	8.46	153.10	0.00
Grand Total		548,553.69	204,686.90	289,975.59	53,891.20	0.00

Seeing a loan amortization schedule

Are you curious about how much you spend on interest payments over the life of a loan? Want to know how much the total payments on a loan are?

To find out, go to the Reports & Charts window, click the What I Owe button, and double-click Loan Amortization. You see a Loan Amortization report (refer to Figure 16-6). Scroll to the bottom of the report, and you see the total payments and total interest payments. The report in the figure shows that, on a $204,686.90 mortgage, $289,975.59 — let's call it $290,000 — is devoted to servicing interest, and that the total payments equal $548,553.69.

---

22. **If you want to associate your new loan account with a house or asset account, click Yes, click Next, and select the asset or house account from the dialog box; otherwise, click the Finish button.**

    The dialog box you see if you click Yes asks if you want to associate an asset account with this loan account. Earlier in this chapter, the sidebar, "Another way to associate an asset account with a loan account," explains how to associate an asset account with a loan account that you already set up.

    If you have already created a house account for tracking the equity in a house, or if you have already created an asset account for tracking the value of a car or other asset, you can associate your house or asset account with the loan account you are almost finished setting up.

    You can always go back later and associate your asset or house account with your new loan account.

23. **Make sure that the I have no other accounts radio button is selected; then click Next.**

    Even if you had another loan account to set up, you wouldn't set it up now, would you? Who wants to suffer through this ordeal all over again?

24. **Click Finish in the dialog box that advertises Money's online banking features.**

    Big Mortgage

    Not a moment too soon, you land on the Account Manager window, where a new loan account icon appears above the name of your new loan account.

Fixing loan account errors

Suppose that you make an error when you set up a loan account. One little mistake — an incorrect due date, for example — can throw everything out of whack. To fix mistakes you made when you set up a loan account, open the loan account register, click the Details button, and then click the Change Loan Info button. Money opens the Change Loan wizard. Answer the wizard's question and keep clicking Next until you have corrected the error you made.

Recording loan and mortgage payments

Follow these steps to record a loan or mortgage payment:

1. **Open the checking account register from which you will make the payment.**

2. **Enter the payee (the lender's name), check number, date, and amount of the payment.**

3. **From the Category drop-down list, select Loan Payment.**

4. **From the Subcategory drop-down list, select the name of the loan account that tracks the loan or mortgage for which you are about to record a payment.**

5. **Click the Enter button.**

   In the loan account register, the balance is reduced by the amount of the payment that is devoted to reducing the principal of the loan.

When you record a mortgage or loan payment, the payment is split:

✔ The portion that goes toward reducing the debt is recorded as a transfer to the loan account. In the loan account register, the balance is reduced accordingly.

✔ The portion that goes toward paying the interest is categorized as mortgage interest (or another category, depending on which category you selected when you set up the account).

✔ If you have to pay fees, the payment is split even further.

Paying early and often

The faster you pay off an amortized loan, the less you have to pay altogether, because much of the cost of an amortized loan goes toward paying interest. Suppose that you want to pay more than you are required to pay so that you can pay off the loan quicker. How do you record a payment you've made above and beyond what the lender expects of you?

Take note of the next check number in the account from which you will make the payment and then follow these steps to record a larger than usual loan or mortgage payment:

1. **Open the loan account register.**

2. **Click the Make Extra Payment button.**

   You see the Edit Transaction dialog box.

3. **From the Account drop-down list, select the account from which you will make or have made the payment.**

4. **Enter the payee (the lender's name), check number, date, and total amount of the payment.**

5. **Click the Split button.**

   You see a Loan Payment dialog box similar to the one in Figure 16-7.

Figure 16-7:
To record a payment beyond the one you are supposed to make, add the extra amount you want to pay to the amount you are scheduled to pay.

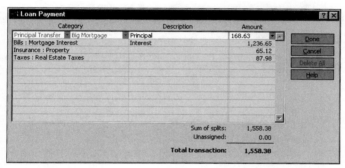

6. **Add the extra amount you want to pay to the amount that is already shown on the Principal Transfer line, and enter the total amount on the Amount line.**

   Amounts you pay above and beyond what the lender expects go toward reducing the principal of the loan — they go directly toward reducing the total amount that you owe. Therefore, you have to add the extra amount to the amount that is already shown on the Principal Transfer line.

   For example, if the amount of principal you are scheduled to pay is $68.63 and you want to pay an extra $100 this time around, enter $168.63 on the Principal Transfer line.

7. **Click Done to leave the Loan Payment dialog box.**

   You return to the loan account register.

8. **Click Enter on the Check transaction tab to record the payment.**

   In the loan account register, the amount entered in Step 6 appears in the Principal column and the amount you owe is reduced by the amount you entered. Not only that, but Money recalculates how many payments you have to make and the amounts of the payments that are devoted to paying interest and principal.

Adjusting loan account balances

Money does its best to calculate interest and principal payments, but computers are only human and sometimes they make mistakes. When you receive a statement from a lender, compare the balance on the statement to the balance in your loan account, and if the balances are out of line with each other, follow these steps:

1. **Open the loan account register.**

2. **Click the Balance Account button.**

   You see the Adjust Loan Balances dialog box shown in Figure 16-8.

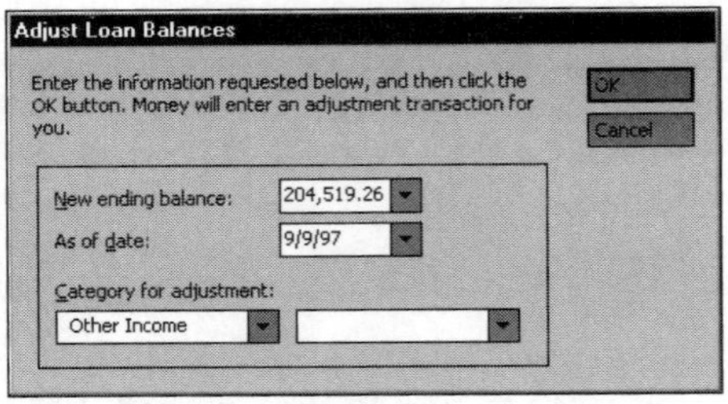

Figure 16-8:
When your records and the lender's are out of whack, make adjustments in this dialog box.

3. **Enter the date shown on the statement in the As of date text box.**

4. **Enter the ending balance shown on the statement in the New ending balance text box.**

5. **Use the Category for adjustment boxes to describe the few cents' or few dollars' difference between your records and the lender's.**

   Select an expense category like Miscellaneous if the lender's records show a higher amount than what your records show; select an income category like Other Income if the lender's records show a lower amount.

6. Click OK.

Money makes an account adjustment entry in the register and all's well that ends well, as Shakespeare used to say when he used Money.

Updating the interest rate on a loan

Suppose that the interest rate on your loan changes. If yours is an adjustable rate loan (ARM), it's bound to happen sooner or later. When the interest rate changes, you have to burrow into your loan account and record the change.

To adjust the interest rate, open the loan account register and click the Update Interest Rate button. Money presents you with a series of dialog boxes for changing the interest rate. Keep answering the questions and clicking Next until, gratefully, you are finished.

Chapter 17

Money for Investors

- -

- -

The title of this chapter is "Money for Investors." I hope you didn't come to this part of the book expecting to find 10-, 20-, and 50-dollar bills folded between the pages. No, you have to get money for your investments elsewhere. After you do, though, you can use Microsoft Money to track your investments.

In this chapter, you discover how to record the sale and purchase of mutual fund shares, stock shares, and bonds. You find out how to set up an electronic investment portfolio and examine the investments in the portfolio in different ways. You find out a lot of things, truth be told. But beware: Tracking investments with Money is not for the faint of heart.

Your Own Electronic Portfolio

A *portfolio* is a collection of investments. This section shows you how to create an electronic portfolio for your investments like the one in Figure 17-1. Looking at the figure, you can see the following:

✓ **The names of the investment or retirement accounts.** Create one investment or retirement account for each statement you receive from a brokerage house, each financial institution you buy CDs or other investments from, and each retirement plan that you participate in. Doing so makes keeping the records easier, because you can enter data in the account straight from the brokerage or bank statement and even reconcile your account from the statements that you receive in the mail.

✓ **The names of the individual investments.** After you set up the accounts, you list the names of the securities — the stocks, bonds, mutual funds, CDs, and so on — that belong in the account. You can then record purchases, sales, share reinvestments, capital gains, dividends, stock splits, and so on in the register.

✓ **The total value of your investments.** This sum appears in the lower-right corner of the page.

When your portfolio is complete, you can see at a glance the market value and price of each investment. By clicking the buttons on the left side of the Portfolio window, you can see how your investments perform, how they have changed in value, and how you have allocated them, among other things.

Who needs to track their investments

Not everyone needs to track their investments or retirement plans with Money. To find out how well your investments perform or to track investment earnings and losses for the IRS, by all means track your investments. But if your investments are tax-deferred — if you invest in IRAs, SEPs, 401(k) plans, or tax-deferred mutual funds — I suggest letting the managers do the work for you. If the managers are worth anything, they send statements that spell out your profits and losses.

Instead of going to the significant trouble of recording those profits and losses in an investment account, simply create an asset account and record profits and losses as increases or decreases (Chapter 16 explains asset accounts). When you cash in part of your tax-deferred investment, record it as a transfer from your asset account to a savings or checking account.

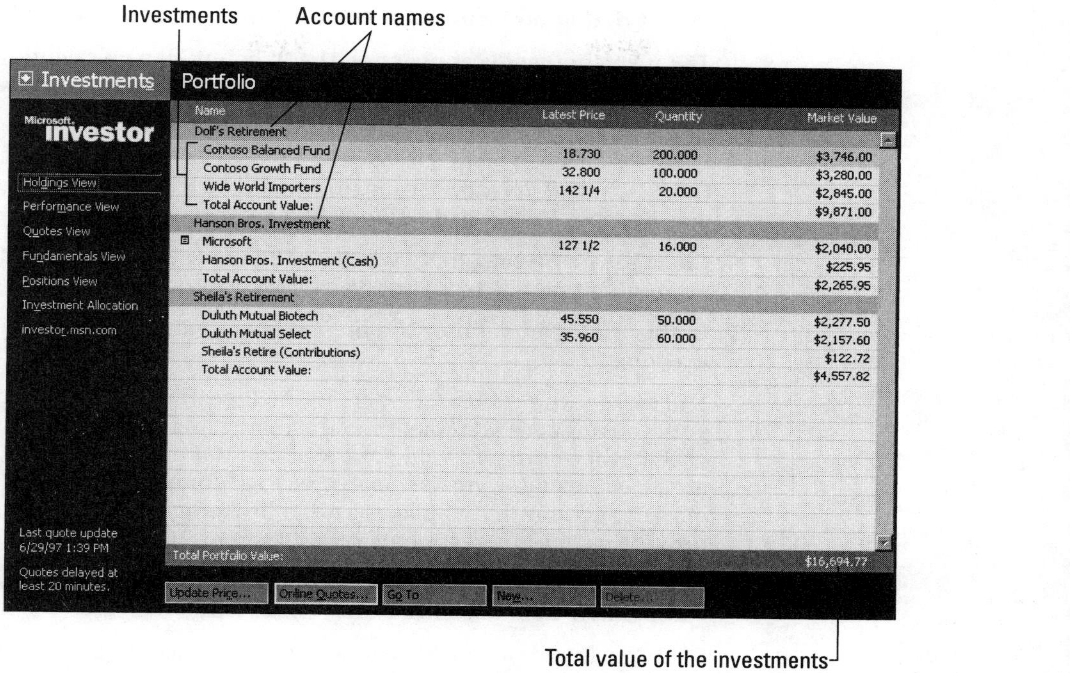

Investments   Account names

Figure 17-1:
The
Portfolio
window
offers many
different
ways of
examining
your
investments.

Total value of the investments

Setting up an investment or retirement account

Spread the last statement from the bank or brokerage house across your desk and follow these steps to set up an investment or retirement account:

1. Go to the Account Manager window.

To get there, choose Go⇨Accounts or click the Account Manager button while you are viewing a register.

2. Click the New Account button.

The first New Account dialog box appears.

3. Enter the name of the brokerage house or bank (where you keep the account) in the text box or select a name from the drop-down list; then click Next.

Another dialog box appears.

4. Select the account type, Investment or Retirement, and click Next.

5. In this dialog box, enter a name for the account and click Next.

The name you enter appears on the Account Manager window after you finish setting up the account. For convenience' sake, you may want to enter the name of the brokerage house or mutual fund where you keep the account.

Guess what? If you are setting up a retirement account, your work is nearly done. Skip ahead to Step 11. Investors, read on.

6. Click Y̲es or N̲o to specify whether the money you track in this account is tax-deferred, and then click Next.

7. In this dialog box, enter the approximate value of the account in the text box.

You can get the estimated value of the investments in the account from your most recent statement. As the dialog box shows, don't include cash in the estimated value of the account if the account has an associated cash account. An associated cash account is a checking or money-market account that you keep with a brokerage house. Its purpose is to provide cash for investments or hold the profits from investments.

8. Click Y̲es or N̲o to tell Money whether the account includes an "associated cash account"; then click Next.

Click Yes if your account includes an associated cash account; click No and skip to Step 10 if it doesn't.

9. If you clicked Yes in Step 8, enter the amount of money in the cash account in the text box and click Next.

As the dialog box shows, you can handle associated cash accounts in three different ways:

- Enter the ending balance from your last statement if you don't care to track the history of the account.

- Enter the ending balance from a previous statement if you want to track the value of the account beginning in the past.

- Enter **0** if you want to track the value of the account from the day you opened it.

10. In this dialog box, make sure that L̲ong-term Savings and Investments is selected; and click Next.

Know the tax status of your investment

Don't confuse tax-deferred income with tax-exempt income. Income from a tax-deferred account is not taxed until you start withdrawing money from the account. You don't have to pay any tax on tax-exempt income. Most retirement accounts are tax-deferred, not tax-exempt.

11. **Glance at the next window, which briefly explains how to track a retirement or investment account with Money, and click Next.**

12. **Either click I <u>h</u>ave other accounts, click Next, and repeat Steps 4 through 11; or click I have <u>n</u>o other accounts, click Next, and click Finish in the next dialog box.**

    Back on the Account Manager window, you see new icons for your new investment or retirement account, as shown in Figure 17-2. If your investment account is tied to an associated cash account, the associated cash account appears on the window as well. The account gets its name from the investment account. Money sets up an associated cash account for all retirement accounts. For example, the associated cash account for the Dean Witter retirement account in Figure 17-2 is called Dean Witter (Contributions).

Figure 17-2:
An investment account, a retirement account, and their associated cash accounts.

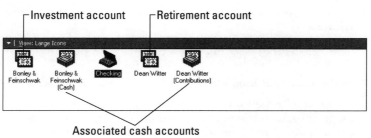

Investment account   Retirement account

View: Large Icons

Bonley & Feinschwak — Bonley & Feinschwak (Cash) — Checking — Dean Witter — Dean Witter (Contributions)

Associated cash accounts

How associated cash accounts work

When you create an investment account, Money gives you the opportunity to create an associated cash account for storing cash for investments and storing the profits from investments. And when you create a retirement account, Money creates an associated account for holding contributions to the account.

Associated cash accounts work the same way as bank accounts. With the transaction tabs, you can record deposits, transfers, and withdrawals. To reconcile a cash account, click the Balance button.

Describing the securities in investment and retirement accounts

After you set up an investment or retirement account, you must describe each security in the account. *Securities* are the stocks, certificates, bonds, or other financial instruments that the account tracks. Gather the paperwork and follow these steps to describe each security that you own:

1. **Open the register of the investment or retirement account in which you hold your investment.**

   To open an account register, click Accounts on the Navigation bar, open the Accounts drop-down list, and select the name of the account whose register you want to see.

2. **Click the New button in the transaction form at the bottom of the window.**

   If no transaction form appears on your window, click the arrow to open the View menu and choose Transaction Forms.

3. **In the Date text box, enter the date that you purchased the security.**

   If you have owned this security for a long time and you intend to track its performance from the day you purchased it, enter the date of the original purchase. You can, however, start tracking the value of the security as of today by entering today's date.

4. **In the Investment text box, enter the name of the security.**

   The name you enter will appear in the Investment column of the register.

5. **Press Tab or click the Activity box.**

   You see the Create New Investment dialog box shown in Figure 17-3.

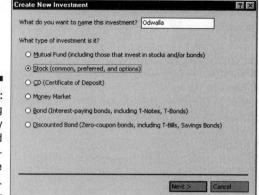

Figure 17-3:
Telling
Money
what kind
of invest-
ment the
security is.

6. **Select an option and click Next.**

In this dialog box, you tell Money what kind of investment the security is. The investment types are pretty self-explanatory; if you need more information on them, check out the glossary in Appendix C.

7. **Enter a ticker symbol if you know it or can find it on the Internet, click the Tax exempt check box if the investment is tax-exempt, and enter a comment if you want.**

In this dialog box, you can enter a ticker symbol for the security, specify whether the security is tax-exempt, and enter a note or two in the Comment box.

The *ticker symbol* is the abbreviated name of a company that is used for tracking investment performance. As long as you know the ticker symbol of a stock, bond, or mutual fund, you can track its value by downloading prices from the Internet. Downloading prices is by far the easiest way to keep a portfolio up-to-date. I highly recommend this method. See Chapter 9 to find out how downloading security prices works.

If you're running the Money 98 Financial Suite, you can find out a company's ticker symbol by clicking the Find Symbol button, connecting to the Microsoft Investor Web site, and looking for it there.

8. **Click the Finish button.**

Back on the transaction tab, the Activity drop-down list is open.

9. Select the Buy option from the Activity drop-down list.

As soon as you do that, a bunch of new boxes appear on the tab, as shown in Figure 17-4.

			Date:	9/14/97
New	Edit	Enter	Cancel	
Investment:	Odwalla		Activity:	Buy
Quantity:	15		Price:	32.50
Commission:	45.00		Total:	532.50
Transfer from:	Larkspur Investment (Cash)		Memo:	

10. In the Quantity text box, enter how many shares of the security you own.

For stocks, enter the number of shares. If you are describing the purchase of a single CD or bond, enter **1**. For investments such as precious metals, enter the number of ounces or other unit of measurement.

If you are tracking the value of this security from the day you bought it, be sure to enter data about your original purchase. You may have bought more shares in the security or sold shares in the past. The value may have gone up or down. You need to enter purchase data as of the date you entered back in Step 3.

11. In the Price text box, enter the cost per unit that you paid for the security.

When you enter share prices of stock, you can enter fractions. For example, you can enter $50^1/_8$ or $10^1/_4$.

For bonds, you have two options. One is to follow the standard convention and enter the price of a bond as a percentage of the bond's par value (its face value). For example, if the bond's par value is $1,000 and its price is $950, enter **95** in the Price text box. If entering bond prices this way is not to your liking, choose Tools⇨Options, click the Investments tab in the Options dialog box, and click to remove the check mark from the Treat bond prices as a percentage of par value check box. Then, to enter the price of the bond, enter **950**.

12. **If necessary, enter the sales commission you paid when you bought the security in the Commission text box.**

    Money enters the total price of the security and the sales commission in the Total box. If the Total figure is wrong, you entered wrong figures in the Quantity or Price text box. Go back and fix your error.

13. **If a bank account is not associated with your retirement or investment account, select the account from which you paid for this security from the Transfer from drop-down list.**

14. **Click the Enter button.**

    The transaction is entered in the investment or retirement account register.

Completing the 14-step program for describing a security in an account isn't such a hassle after you get used to it. Repeat the 14 steps for each security that the account tracks, and then read on to find out how to update the prices of the securities.

Updating the price of a security

By tracking changes in the value of a security, you can analyze the performance of your investments and the change in the value of your portfolio over time.

The fastest and most accurate way to update the price of a security is to download the information from the Internet. Chapter 9 explains how.

Follow these steps to update the price of a security in your portfolio:

1. **Open either the Portfolio window or the investment or retirement account register that holds the security whose price you want to update.**

    Click Investments on the Navigation bar or choose Go⟶Investments to open the Portfolio window; go to the Account Manager window and double-click the icon of an investment or retirement account to open its register.

2. **Click the Update Price button.**

    You see the Update Price dialog box, as shown in Figure 17-5.

3. **Click the arrow to open the Investment drop-down list and select the investment whose price you want to update.**

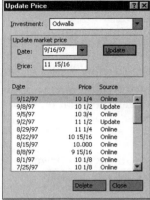

Figure 17-5:
Report
changes in
the price of
a security
in the
Update
Price
dialog box.

4. **In the Date box, enter the date on which you want to report a price change.**

5. **Enter the new price in the Price text box.**

6. **Click the Update button.**

   The new price is entered in the price history list. Notice in Figure 17-5 that the Source column sometimes says `Online` and sometimes says `Update`. After you click the Update button and enter a price yourself, the column says `Update`. Many of the prices in the figure were updated online.

7. **If you want to record the price history of a security, keep entering new dates and new security prices; otherwise, select a new security from the Investment drop-down list and update its price.**

8. **Click the Close button after you are done.**

Examining the Investments in a Portfolio

The fun begins after you enter the securities and list their prices. Now, starting from the Portfolio window, you can examine your investments in different ways. Like peering into the different windows of a house (with the occupants' permission, of course), you can stare into your investments from different angles and see if you gain any insights that way.

Click the Investment button on the Navigation bar or choose Go⇨Investments to open the Portfolio window. On the left side of the window are six buttons that you can click to change views. Table 17-1 describes the six buttons. Figure 17-6 shows five of the six views.

Table 17-1	Ways of Examining Investments on the Portfolio Window
Button	*What You See*
Holdings View	The latest price, number of units you own, and market value of your investment holdings.
Performance View	Performance data, including how much you have profited or lost on each investment, the gain or loss by percentage, and the annual return by percentage.
Quotes View	Market data on each investment, including its latest price and latest change in price.
Fundamentals View	Historical price information, including 52-week high and low prices, P/E ratios, and volatility ratings.
Positions View	Comparison data, with the market value of investments in all the accounts ranked from highest value to lowest value.
Investment Allocation	An Investment Allocation pie chart showing how much of your portfolio is devoted to different types of investments. Choose this view to see whether you incorrectly laid all your investment eggs in the same basket.

If you want to press your nose to the glass and get a very, very close look at an investment, double-click it on the Portfolio window. That action takes you to the Details window, where you can click the Performance button to see the Performance window. As shown in Figure 17-7, the Performance window displays a graph as well as information that is also available in Fundamentals View, Quotes View, and Performance View.

Handling Stocks and Bonds

Keeping track of stocks and bonds — especially stocks — is probably the most problematic task you will ever undertake with Money. Merely figuring out what a "short sell" is, not to mention a "margin buy" and a "stock split," is hard enough to begin with. How can you record these strange events in an investment or retirement account register?

Read on, friend, and you can discover how to record everything from stock sales and purchases to short sells and margin buys.

Holdings View

Name	Latest Price	Quantity	Market Value
Larkspur Investment			
3Com	50 1/8	75.000	$3,759.38
Microsoft	137 15/16	16.000	$2,207.00
Odwalla	10 1/4	50.000	$512.50
Larkspur Investment (Cash)			$709.07
Total Account Value:			$7,187.95

Performance View

Name	Latest Price	Gain	% Gain	Annual % Return
Larkspur Investment				
3Com	50 1/8	($100.00)	(2.59)	(65.52)
Microsoft	137 15/16	$198.95	9.91	56.49
Odwalla	10 1/4	($45.00)	(8.07)	
Larkspur Investment (Cash)				
Total Account Value:		$53.95	0.84	10.85

Quotes View

Name	Latest Price	Change	High	Low	Volume
Larkspur Investment					
3Com	50 1/8	1.06	50.50	48.50	5,073,700
Microsoft	137 15/16	1.13	138.38	135.63	6,072,000
Odwalla	10 1/4	10.25	11.00	10.00	915
Larkspur Investment (Cash)					
Total Account Value:					

Fundamentals View

Name	Latest Price	52 Wk. High	52 Wk. Low	P/E	Volatility
Larkspur Investment					
3Com	50 1/8	81.38	24.00	24.57	62.54
Microsoft	137 15/16	150.75	65.44	52.25	30.09
Odwalla	10 1/4	19.00	9.25	0.00	51.33
Larkspur Investment (Cash)					
Total Account Value:					

Figure 17-6: Ways of viewing a portfolio (from top to bottom): Holdings View, Performance View, Quotes View, Fundamentals View, and Positions View.

Positions View

Name	Latest Price	Quantity	Market Value
3Com	50 1/8	75.000	$3,759.38
AT&T	42 13/16	0.000	$0.00
Contoso Balanced Fund	18.730	200.000	$3,746.00
Contoso Growth Fund	32.800	100.000	$3,280.00
Duluth Mutual Biotech	49.000	50.000	$2,450.00
Duluth Mutual Select	34.620	60.000	$2,077.20
Microsoft	137 15/16	16.000	$2,207.00
Odwalla	10 1/4	50.000	$512.50
Stock	<no price>	0.000	
Wide World Importers	142 1/4	20.000	$2,845.00
Cash Balance:			$831.79

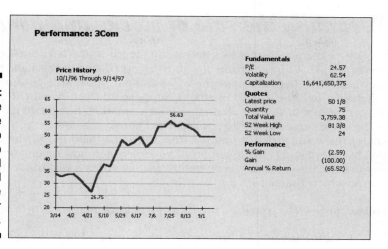

Performance: 3Com

Price History
10/1/96 Through 9/14/97

56.63

26.75

Fundamentals	
P/E	24.57
Volatility	62.54
Capitalization	16,641,650,375
Quotes	
Latest price	50 1/8
Quantity	75
Total Value	3,759.38
52 Week High	81 3/8
52 Week Low	24
Performance	
% Gain	(2.59)
Gain	(100.00)
Annual % Return	(65.52)

Figure 17-7:
Go to the
Performance
window to
get up
close and
personal
with one
of your
investments.

Recording a purchase of more stocks or more bonds

When you purchase more shares of a stock you already own or more bonds of a type you already own, follow these steps to record the purchase:

1. **Open the investment or retirement account register that holds the stock or bond whose purchase you want to record.**

2. **Click the New button.**

3. **In the Date text box on the transaction form, enter the date you purchased the stocks or bonds.**

4. **In the Investment box, click the arrow and select the security from the drop-down list.**

   The security's name should already be on the list, since you purchased it before.

5. **Select Buy from the Activity drop-down list.**

6. **Fill in the rest of the transaction form — the Quantity text box, Commission text box, Price text box, and Transfer from text box.**

   If you need help filling in these boxes, see the "Describing the securities in investment and retirement accounts" section, earlier in this chapter.

Recording the sale of stocks and bonds

Except for the problem of lots, recording the sales of stocks and bonds is pretty simple. A *lot* is a group of securities purchased at the same time for the same price (and also a nephew of Abraham whose wife got turned into a saltshaker, but that's another story). Suppose that you bought 10 shares of Burger Heaven at $10 per share in January, and then bought 10 more shares of the same company at $20 per share in February. In March, you sell 15 shares. How many shares you sell from the $10 lot and the $20 lot is important in determining how much profit you make and how much you have to pay in capital gains taxes. Fortunately, Money offers a wizard for helping you decide which shares to sell.

Follow these steps to record the sale of stocks or bonds:

1. **Open the investment or account register that holds the security that you sold.**

2. **Click the New button, enter the date of the sale, and select the name of the security you sold from the Investment drop-down list.**

3. **From the Activity drop-down list, select Sell.**

4. **In the Quantity text box, enter the number of shares or bonds that you sold; enter the price in the Price text box.**

5. **If a commission was charged on the sale, enter the amount of the commission in the Commission text box.**

   Money enters the total amount of the sale in the Total text box. If the figure is incorrect, double-check the Quantity and Price text boxes to make sure that you entered the numbers correctly.

6. **From the Transfer to drop-down list, select the account in which you deposited the profits from the sale.**

7. **Click the Enter button.**

That's all there is to it — unless you purchased the shares in different lots. In that case, you see the What Shares Should I Use? dialog box after you click the Enter button. Unless you tell it otherwise, Money assumes that you want to sell the shares in the lot that you purchased first. Follow these steps to tell Money which shares you want to sell:

1. **Click the Yes option button in the first What Shares Should I Use? dialog box and then click Next.**

   You see the Allocate Lots dialog box shown in Figure 17-8.

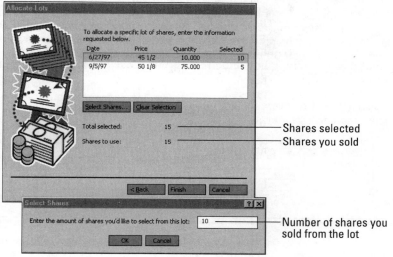

Figure 17-8:
Recording
which
shares
were sold
from
which lot.

2. **In the top of the dialog box, click one of the lots from which you sold shares.**

3. **Click the Select Shares button.**

   You see the Select Shares dialog box shown at the bottom of Figure 17-8.

4. **Enter the number of shares you sold from the lot and click OK.**

5. **Select another lot and repeat Steps 2 through 4 to tell Money how many shares you sold from it.**

   After you're done declaring which shares you sold, the Total Selected and Shares to use numbers in the dialog box should be the same.

6. **Click the Finish button.**

Be sure to notify your broker of which shares you want to sell. If you forget to do that, your broker may assume that you want to sell shares beginning with the first lot you purchased.

How to record brokerage account fees

Brokers charge fees. Not a few them have been known to nickel and dime their customers to death. How do you record brokerage fees in Money? The answer: You record transactions in the investment or retirement account register and select Other Expense from the Activity drop-down list on the transaction tab.

When you select Other Expense, category and subcategory drop-down lists appear so that you can categorize the brokerage fee. If the expense is associated with a particular security, select the security from the Investment drop-down list; otherwise, leave the Investment box blank. And make sure that the account from which you paid the fee appears in the Transfer from box. This figure shows a brokerage account fee of $55 in the Total text box on the transaction tab.

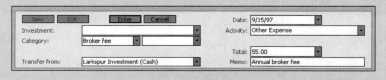

Recording and reinvesting dividends

Most stocks pay dividends, which means that you have to record dividends in the register as they arrive. And some stocks and mutual funds, instead of paying dividends, give shareholders the opportunity to buy more shares with their dividends as part of a DRIP (dividend reinvestment program). The advantage of reinvesting a dividend is that you often don't have to pay a broker's commission to purchase the new stock.

To record a dividend or the reinvestment of a dividend, start from the account register, fill in the transaction tab as you normally would, but select Dividend or Reinvest Dividend from the Activity drop-down list. Then do the following:

✔ **Recording a dividend:** In the Total text box, enter the amount of the dividend. Be sure to select the account into which you deposited the dividend from the Transfer to drop-down list. Click Enter after you are done.

✔ **Recording a dividend reinvestment:** Enter the number of shares you purchased with the dividend in the Quantity text box, the price per share in the Price text box, and any commission in the Commission text box. Make sure that the total in the Total text box is correct before you click the Enter button.

Recording stock splits, short sells, margin purchases, and other esoterica

The stock market, it seems, has a hundred different ways to trade stock, handle stock sales, and handle stock purchases. I suspect that the brokers like it that way because it makes them appear indispensable. Fortunately, you can use Money to record oddball stock trades and sales.

Stock splits

Occasionally, stock shares are split to lower the price of individual shares and make them more attractive to investors. In a 2 to 1 split, for example, investors are given twice as much stock, but the value of individual stocks is half what it was before, so the owner of 100 shares worth $2,000 now owns 200 shares worth the same amount, $2,000.

Follow these steps to record a stock split:

1. **Click Investments on the Navigation bar or choose Go⇨Investments to open the Portfolio window.**

2. **Click the Investments down arrow and select the stock that was split from the drop-down list.**

   You land on the Details window.

3. **Click the Split Shares button.**

   You see the Split Shares dialog box shown in Figure 17-9.

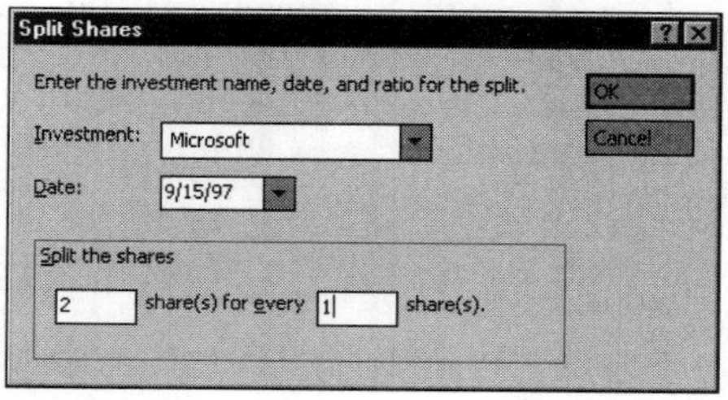

Figure 17-9:
Recording a
stock split.

4. **Enter the date that the stock was split in the Date text box.**

5. **In the Split the shares text boxes, enter the ratio of new stocks to old ones.**

   For example, in a 2 to 1 split, enter 2 in the first box and 1 in the second box.

6. Click OK.

On the Details window and on the Portfolio window, Money calculates and enters the number of shares you own. The total value of those shares, however, remains the same.

Short sells

A *short sell* is when you believe that a stock will fall in price and you attempt to profit by borrowing shares from a broker, selling them at a high price, and then buying shares when the price drops and using those low-priced shares to replace the ones you borrowed.

Suppose, for example, that you think that ABC Corporation's shares will fall below their current price of $20 a share. You borrow ten shares from your broker and sell those shares for $200. When the price drops to $15 a share, you buy ten shares on your own, pay $150 for them, and give the broker back his or her ten shares. By selling the shares that didn't belong to you first (for $200) and buying them later (for $150), you earn a $50 profit. Of course, if the stock rises in price, you end up paying the broker back out of your own pocket, not from the proceeds of the sale.

To record a short sell, fill in the transaction tab as you normally would, but select Short Sell from the Activity drop-down list. Typically, brokers charge interest for the shares you borrow. The interest is reported in the Commission text box.

Return of capital

A *return of capital* is a return of part of the price you paid for stock. Sometimes a return of capital is paid to investors in lieu of a dividend. You'll know when you have been paid a return of capital because your statement tells you so. To record a return of capital, select Return of Capital from the Activity drop-down list on the transaction form. Enter the amount of the return in the Total text box and select the account where you will stash it from the Transfer to drop-down list.

Margin purchases

Brokers gladly lend money to buy stocks and bonds. Buying a stock or bond with money you borrowed from a broker is called "buying on the margin."

To record stocks or a bond you purchased on the margin, record it as you would a buy, but select Other Expense from the Activity drop-down list. When you select Other Expense, category and subcategory boxes appear on the transaction form so that you can categorize the expense. Select an expense category from the category drop-down list to describe the interest you had to pay your broker for the loan.

Handling Mutual Funds

Mutual funds seem to be everybody's favorite investment. A *mutual fund* is an investment company that raises money from shareholders and invests the money in a variety of places, including stocks, bonds, and money market securities. With a mutual fund, you let experts do the work of deciding what to invest in. All you have to do is collect the profits, count them, and hide them under your mattress.

Recording the sale or purchase of mutual funds

You record the sale or purchase of a mutual fund the same way as you record the sale or purchase of stocks and bonds. Earlier in this chapter, the sections "Recording a purchase of more stocks or more bonds" and "Recording the sale of stocks and bonds" explain how.

When you buy shares in the fund, select Buy from the Activity drop-down list; when you sell shares, select (duh) Sell. Be sure to accurately describe the number of shares you purchased or sold in the Quantity text box. And don't forget to enter the price per share correctly in the Price text box, either.

Recording dividends and distributions

From time to time, mutual fund managers send dividend distributions. More than likely, however, dividends are paid in the form of *reinvestments*. Instead of sending a check for the profits that your shares have made, the profits are used to purchase more shares in the fund. The following are instructions for recording a dividend payment and for recording a mutual fund distribution.

Mutual fund dividend distributions

Follow these steps to record the receipt of mutual fund dividend distributions:

1. **Open the register of the retirement or investment account where you track the mutual fund.**

2. **From the Investment drop-down list, select the name of the mutual fund in question.**

3. **Enter the date that the dividend was disbursed in the Date text box.**

4. **From the Activity drop-down list, select the option that describes the dividend distribution.**

   Look on your mutual fund statement to find out which option to select:

   - **Interest:** An interest distribution.
   - **Dividend:** A dividend distribution.
   - **S-Term Cap Gains Dist:** A short-term capital gains distribution.
   - **L-Term Cap Gains Dist:** A long-term capital gains distribution.

5. **Enter the amount of the dividend in the Total text box.**

   The transaction tab should look something like the one in Figure 17-10. Make sure that the account into which you deposited the distribution appears in the Transfer to box.

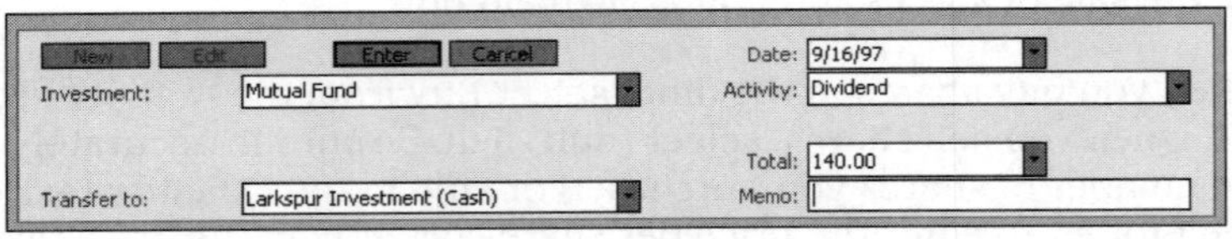

Figure 17-10:
Record a
mutual fund
dividend
distribution.

6. **Click the Enter button.**

Mutual fund reinvestment distributions

Follow these steps when the profits from a mutual fund are used to purchase more shares in the fund:

1. **Open the register of the retirement or investment account where you track the mutual fund and click New.**

2. **From the Investment drop-down list, select the name of the mutual fund in question.**

3. **Enter the date of the reinvestment in the Date text box.**

4. **From the Activity drop-down list, select the option that describes how the profits were reinvested.**

   Your mutual fund statement tells you which of these options to select:

   - **Reinvest Interest:** A reinvested interest distribution.
   - **Reinvest Dividend:** A reinvested dividend distribution.

- **Reinvest S-Term CG Dist:** A reinvested short-term capital gains distribution.

- **Reinvest L-Term CG Dist:** A reinvested long-term capital gains distribution.

5. **In the Quantity text box, enter the number of shares that the reinvestment purchased.**

6. **In the Price text box, enter the price of shares in the mutual fund.**

7. **If necessary, enter a commission you had to pay in the Commission text box.**

One of the advantages of reinvesting mutual fund profits is *not* having to pay a commission to purchase the shares. Most funds do not require you to pay a commission when you reinvest. If your fund makes you pay a commission, complain about it to the fund manager.

8. **Click the Enter button.**

Other Kinds of Investments

The tail end of this chapter is for investors who believe in precious metals and certificates of deposit. How do you handle those types of investment with Money? Read on.

Precious metals

To track precious metals in an investment account, treat the metal as you would stock shares and describe the investment by units of measurement. For example, to describe the purchase of two ounces of gold, record the purchase as you would a purchase of two stock shares.

You can use the same method to track commodities. For example, if you are the proud purchaser of five bushels of wheat, record the purchase as you would a stock purchase, and count the five bushels as five shares.

Certificates of deposit

You can track the value of a CD in an investment or retirement account by selecting CD in the Create New Investment dialog box. As the CD accumulates interest, record the interest payments by selecting Interest from the Activity drop-down list.

Part V

Money and the Small Business Manager

The 5th Wave   By Rich Tennant

"I just hope Microsoft Money can help us with this inventory."

In this part . . .

You can take care of business in this part of the book. In the next three chapters, filled with advice for tracking business finances with Money, you discover how to monitor bills and invoices and how to handle a payroll.

Money wasn't built specifically to track a business's finances, but you can do it. With a nudge here and twist there, Money works very nicely as a tool for managing your small business.

Chapter 18

Getting Ready to Record Business Transactions

Money was invented to help individuals track their finances, but with a push here and a pull there you can make Money work for tracking business finances as well.

This chapter examines the all-important question of whether Money will work for your business. Then it explains how to create a separate file, set up categories and accounts, and set up a cash account for a business. Finally, for the espionage fan, this chapter explains how to clamp a password on a Money file.

Is Money Right for Your Business?

Before you go to the trouble of finding out how to manage a small business with Money, you need to find out whether Money is the right program for you. Your business may be too complex or too big for Money. You may require a business accounting program, such as Peachtree or QuickBooks. You may require a living, breathing bookkeeper or accountant.

Following is a list of the things that Money can't do or can't do very well. Study this list. If two or three of these tasks describe what you do or do often in your business, then, frankly, you should consider using Money only to track your personal finances:

- **Generate invoices:** You cannot print invoices with Money. You can track invoices with Money (as I show in Chapter 19) and use a word processor to write and print them, but that is a lot of trouble if your business sends out many invoices each week. With a business accounting program, you can record an invoice and print it directly on a professional-looking business form. Can't do that with Money.

- **Keep inventory:** Money cannot in any way, shape, or form keep track of inventory. If yours is a retail business and you have to track inventory, don't bother using Money.

- **Store customer databases:** Sorry, Money can't keep a customer database and use it to prepare things like labels for mass-mailings. However, you can keep a customer database with a database program such as Microsoft Access and use Money to track the other aspects of your business. But don't do that if keeping a customer database is important to you.

- **Tracking employee pay and deductions:** As any business manager knows, tracking employees' deductions and taxes is a big drag. In Chapter 20, I show you how to handle the payroll with Money, but the program was not designed to do that. A business with many employees — especially employees who are paid hourly wages — is better off not using Money.

Creating a Separate File for Tracking Business Activity

You have to create a Money file for tracking a small business with Money. Self-employed people and people who operate very small businesses that require only one bank account can use their personal Money file, but all others need a separate file. As a rule, you need a separate file if you submit a separate income tax report for your business.

Read on to find out how to create a Money file and how to open a file. You can also discover how to open a file to switch back and forth between the Money file where you track your personal finances and the one where you track your business's finances.

Creating the separate file

Follow these steps to create a new file:

1. **Choose File⇨New or press Ctrl+N.**

   You see the New dialog box shown in Figure 18-1.

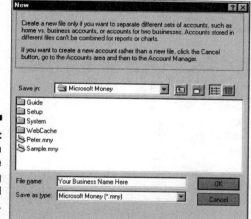

Figure 18-1: Creating a new file for tracking a small business.

2. **In the File name text box, enter a descriptive name for the new file.**

   Be sure to choose a name that is easy to identify. File names can be 255 characters long (though it's hard to imagine anyone that longwinded). File names *cannot* include the following characters: / \ [ ] : (* | <> = + ; , ? (if you saw these characters in a comic book, you would think that I was swearing at you).

3. **Click OK.**

   The Back Up dialog box appears. Money wants to close the file that is on-screen and open the one you just created, but before it closes files or closes the Money program, it always asks if you want to back up the file you have been working on. Chapter 12 explains the backup procedure in detail.

4. **Click the Back Up button.**

5. **If it appears, click Yes in the dialog box that asks if you want to overwrite the backup file that is on disk.**

   The new file appears on-screen. If you doubt me, look in the upper-left corner of the screen, where you see the name of the file you created.

Opening the file you want to work with

Follow these steps if you work with more than one Money file and you want to switch from one to another:

1. **Choose File⇨Open or press Ctrl+O.**

   You see the Open dialog box shown in Figure 18-2.

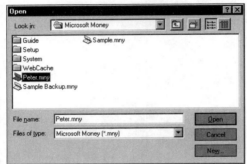

Figure 18-2:
Opening a
new file.

2. **Select the file you want to open.**

3. **Click the Open button.**

   Money insists on backing up a file when you close it to open another, so the Back Up dialog box appears. Chapter 12 explains all the details about backing up, but suffice it to say that you can click the Back Up button if you're in a hurry.

4. **Click the Back Up button.**

   The new file appears on-screen. You can tell which file you've opened by reading its name in the upper-left corner of the window.

Setting Up Accounts for Your Business

Set up one account in your business file for each of your business's bank accounts. Chapter 2 explains how to set up checking, savings, and credit card accounts. Track the business accounts exactly as you track personal accounts.

While you are setting up accounts, ask yourself whether your business needs to set up these kinds of accounts as well:

✔ **Cash account:** These accounts are for tracking a business's day-to-day cash payments. Taxi rides. Lunch for the employees. See the "Setting Up and Using a Cash Account" section later in this chapter.

✔ **Asset account:** The things you buy for your business — machinery, tools, furniture — are assets. In a pinch, you could sell them to fend off creditors. And if you take out a business loan, your assets can sometimes be used as collateral. By tracking assets, you make it easier to measure your business's worth. Chapter 16 explains how asset accounts work.

✔ **Line of credit account:** Perhaps you are a building contractor and you have a credit account with a lumberyard. Create a line of credit account for each store and supplier that your employees are authorized to make purchases from — purchases on credit, that is. See Chapters 2 and 3.

Creating the Right Categories for Your Business

Setting up the right categories and subcategories is especially important when you are tracking a small business's finances. For one thing, you need meaningful categories that tell you precisely what your sources of income are and where you spend money. You need meaningful categories so that you can measure the health of your business and plan ahead.

You also need the right categories for tax purposes. Did you know that almost every dollar you spend on your business is tax-deductible? When you set up a category, make sure that it's included on tax reports. For that matter, tag categories to tax-form line items — tag them to line items on Schedule C, the tax form reporting business income and expenses.

Chapter 4 explains how to set up categories, tag them for tax purposes, and tag categories to tax-form line items.

Setting Up and Using a Cash Account

The day-to-day cash spending you do for your business is tax-deductible. To track this money and to deduct cash payments from your gross income on tax returns, you need to set up a cash account.

When you withdraw cash from the bank or from an ATM machine, record it as a transfer from your business's checking or savings account to the cash account, as shown in the first entry in Figure 18-3. Then, as you spend the cash, categorize the expenditures and list amounts exactly as you would in a checking register. Record expenditures in the Spend column.

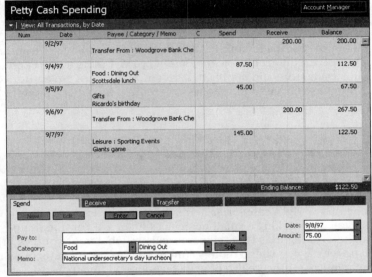

Figure 18-3:
Tracking
petty cash
payments
in a cash
account
register.

Don't be shy about using the Memo line on the transaction form. Except by describing how the money was spent, how else will you know where all the money in the petty cash drawer went?

To set up a cash account, follow the standard procedures for opening an account (see Chapter 2), but select Cash in the New Account dialog box.

Protecting Business Files with Passwords

Probably the last thing you want is someone snooping in your business file. To keep jealous colleagues, your spouse, future biographers, agents of Interpol, or anyone else from opening a file, you can protect it with a password. The following sections explain how to lock a file with a password, open a file that has been given a password, and change or remove passwords.

It almost goes without saying, but you must never, never forget a password. If you do, you can't open your Money file.

Locking a file with a password

Follow these steps to clamp a password on a Money file:

1. **If necessary, open the file that needs a password.**

2. **Choose File⇨Password.**

   You see the New Password dialog box shown in Figure 18-4. As the dialog box says, passwords can be as many as 16 characters long. It doesn't matter whether a password is uppercase, lowercase, or a combination of upper- and lowercase letters. If the password is Oaxaca, for example, it doesn't matter whether you enter oaxaca, OAXACA, or Oaxaca in the Password dialog box when you open the file.

Figure 18-4:
Clamping a
password
on a
Money file.

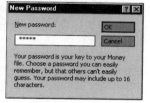

3. **Type a password in the New password text box.**

   Instead of letters, asterisks appear so that a spy looking over your shoulder can't read the password (a cunning spy, however, could watch your fingers to see what the password is).

4. **Click OK.**

   You see the Confirm New Password dialog box.

5. **Reenter the password.**

   If you reenter the password incorrectly, Money asks you to try again.

6. **Click OK.**

   It's settled: Whoever tries to open the file next time, or whoever starts the Money program next time, will need the secret password.

TIP

Some gratuitous advice about choosing passwords

Everybody has different advice for choosing a password that isn't likely to be forgotten or discovered, and everybody agrees that you shouldn't use your own name or the names of family members or pets, because devious souls try those names first when they try to crack open a file. Here's a good tip for choosing passwords: Pick your favorite foreign city and spell it backwards. My favorite foreign city is in Mexico. If I used a password, it would be **acaxa0**.

Opening a file that has been given a password

When you try to open a Money file that has been given a password, you see the dialog box shown in Figure 18-5. I hope that you know the password. If you do, enter it and click OK. If you don't, wag your head and proclaim, "Woe is me."

Figure 18-5:
This dialog box appears when you try to open a file that has been password-protected.

Password	? X
Please type the current password for 'Sample'	OK
	Cancel
Password: *****	

Changing and removing passwords

To change a password or remove a password from a file, choose File⇨Password. Then do the following steps when you see the Password dialog box:

- **Changing the password:** Enter the password and click OK. In the New Password dialog box, enter a new password and click OK. Reenter the password in the Confirm New Password dialog box and click OK.

- **Removing the password:** Enter the password and click OK. When the New Password dialog box appears, enter nothing and click OK. Then enter nothing in the Confirm New Password dialog box and click OK there, too.

Chapter 19

Paying and Sending Out Bills

• •

• •

*O*ne of the keys to running a successful business is keeping an eye on your cash flow. Obviously, you need to pay your bills on time, and just as obviously, you want others to pay you in a timely fashion.

Money can help you track the invoices you send out and keep on top of the bills you have to pay. In fact, Money offers some features that are more important to business users than to home users. This chapter shows you how to take advantage of those features and keep your business in the black.

Tracking What Is Owed Your Business

More than the bills you have to pay, I bet you are interested in tracking the bills you send to others. When your business sends an invoice, you need to keep track of when it was sent, to whom it was sent, and how much it was for. And you need to keep track of outstanding invoices so you can hunt down and throttle the people who haven't paid yet. Of course, you also need to record payments as the invoices roll in. The next sections explain how to accomplish these tasks.

Recording invoices as they are sent

As I mention at the start of Chapter 18, you can't create an invoice with Money. You need a spreadsheet or word-processing program to do that. What you can do with Money to track invoices is create an asset account like the one in Figure 19-1 and enter the invoices in the account.

Paid invoices   Unpaid invoices

Oustanding Bills						Account Manager
View: All Transactions, by Date						
Num	Date	Payee / Category / Memo	C	Decrease	Increase	Balance
	8/1/97	Marlin Gardens	R		1,450.00	1,450.00
		For work week of 7/24				
	8/6/97	Townhall Property Assoc.			875.00	2,325.00
		For repair to stage				
	8/12/97	The Toulleries			445.00	2,770.00
		Repair to kitchen				
	8/12/97	Marlin Gardens	R	1,450.00		1,320.00
		Payment received				
	8/19/97	Bodega Muneca			1,250.00	2,570.00
		Roofing work				
	8/21/97	Torre Pines			2,565.00	5,135.00
		Resanding the sand traps				
					Current Value:	$5,135.00

Decrease	Increase	Transfer		
New	Edit	Enter	Cancel	
			Date:	8/21/97
From:	Torre Pines		Amount:	2,565.00
Category:		Split		
Memo:	Resanding the sand traps			

Figure 19-1:
Track
invoices in
an asset
account.

Chapter 16 describes how asset accounts work in greater detail, but you can follow these steps to record an invoice in an asset register when the invoice is sent:

1. **Open the asset account in which you track invoices.**

2. **Click the Increase transaction tab.**

3. **Enter the date you sent the invoice in the Date text box.**

4. **In the From text box, enter the person or business to whom you sent the invoice.**

5. **Enter the Amount of the invoice in the Amount text box.**

6. **In the Memo text box, enter a few words that describe why you sent the invoice.**

Don't enter any categories or subcategories in the Category boxes. Leave them blank. When the person or company who receives your invoice sends a check and you deposit the check, then and only then will you categorize this transaction. If you categorized it now, the transaction would be categorized twice, once when you send the invoice and once when you deposit it in a bank account. You end up with double the amount of transactions in a category — not an accurate assessment of how much was really paid to you.

7. **Click the Enter button.**

   Your invoice is recorded in the asset account register. (If you see the Require a Category message box, click No to tell Money that you don't want to assign a category to this transaction.)

Recording payments as they arrive

When an invoice is paid and a check arrives, do the following to record the receipt of the payment:

1. **Open the asset account register in which you track invoices.**

2. **Click the De_crease tab to see the Decrease transaction form.**

3. **Enter the date that you received the invoice in the Date text box.**

4. **In the From text box, enter the person or business from whom you received the invoice.**

5. **Enter the Amount of the invoice in the Amount text box.**

   Don't categorize the transaction. You will do that when you deposit the payment in a bank account.

6. **In the Memo text box, enter a few words that describe why you sent the invoice.**

7. **Click the Enter button.**

   The last thing to do is reconcile the Decrease transaction you just entered and the Increase transaction by which you recorded the invoice when you sent it.

8. **Click the Decrease transaction you just entered and choose Edit⇨Mark As⇨Reconciled (R).**

   An R appears in the C (for Cleared) column of the register. Reconcile invoices and invoice payments in the asset register so you can generate reports and find out which invoices have not been paid. The next section of the book explains how to do that.

9. **Find the Increase transaction by which you recorded the invoice that has been paid, click it, and then choose Edit⇨Mark As⇨Reconciled (R).**

   An R appears in the C (for Cleared) column of that transaction as well.

Now all you have to do is record the check as a deposit in your business's savings or checking account. Categorize the check when you deposit it.

Staying on top of unpaid invoices

Your asset register for tracking invoices starts to get large and crowded after a while. Sure, finding unpaid invoices is easy when only a handful have been entered in the register. But when hundreds of invoices have been entered, how can you find the ones that haven't been paid?

To find unpaid invoices, generate an Account Transactions report and customize the report so that it shows only unreconciled transactions. If you followed my advice in the last section and marked paid invoices as reconciled, you can look for unreconciled invoice transactions in the asset account register to find the invoices that haven't been paid yet.

Follow these steps to generate a report that shows which invoices have not been paid:

1. **Click Reports on the Navigation bar or choose Go⇨Reports.**

2. **On the Gallery of Reports and Charts window, click the Spending Habits button, if necessary.**

3. **Double-click Account Transactions to generate an account transactions report.**

   The report appears on-screen. Now you have to customize it so that only unreconciled transactions in your asset account appear on the report.

4. **Click the Customize button.**

   You can find this button along the bottom of the screen. When you click it, you see the Customize Report dialog box shown at the top of Figure 19-2.

5. **From the From account drop-down list under Include transactions, select the name of the asset account in which you track invoices.**

6. **Also under Include transactions, click the Select transactions radio button.**

   As soon as you click that button, you see the Select Transactions dialog box shown at the bottom of Figure 19-2.

7. **Click the Details tab in the dialog box.**

8. **From the Status drop-down list, select Unreconciled Transactions and click OK.**

   Now the report shows only unreconciled transactions from your invoice asset account.

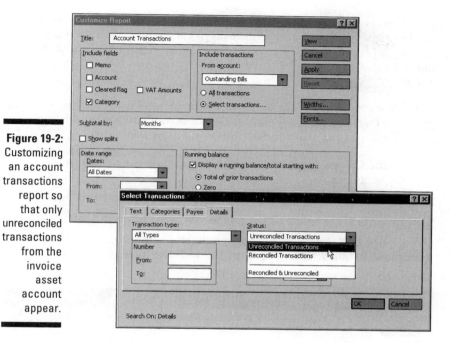

Figure 19-2:
Customizing
an account
transactions
report so
that only
unreconciled
transactions
from the
invoice
asset
account
appear.

9. Click the View button in the Customize Report dialog box.

The account transactions report shows outstanding invoices. Better call these people on the telephone and find out what's what.

While the account transactions report is on-screen, click the Add to Favorites button in the lower-right corner of the window. In the Add to Favorites dialog box, enter **Outstanding Invoices** (or another descriptive name) in the Report name box and click OK. Now all you have to do to generate your outstanding invoices report is choose its name on the Favorites menu or click the My Favorites button on the Reports & Charts window and then double-click your report's name in the Gallery of Reports and Charts.

Tracking Payments to Vendors

When you make a payment to a store, supplier, or business, simply record and categorize the payment as you normally do when you write a check. That's easy enough. As long as you select a meaningful category for the payment, you can generate reports that tell you how much you spent in a certain category and how much you paid to each vendor you do business with. Chapter 3 explains how to record and categorize a check payment, and Chapter 4 explains how to set up meaningful categories for measuring the health of your business.

In fact, the fastest way to find out how much you paid a particular vendor is to go to the Payees Details window and gaze at the bar chart and mini-register. To go to the Payees Details window, follow these steps:

1. **Click the Categories button on the Navigation bar or choose Go⇨Categories.**

2. **Click the Payees button on the Categories & Payees window.**

3. **Double-click the name of the payee you want to investigate.**

   As Figure 19-3 shows, you see a bar chart and mini-register that describe the transactions you recorded with the payee.

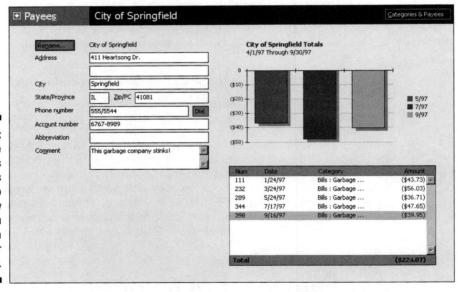

Figure 19-3:
Go to the Payees Details window to see how much you paid a particular vendor.

A trick for staying on top of unpaid bills

One of the problems of managing a business is that sometimes you get overwhelmed by bills and you can't pay them all at once. You have to pick and choose which ones to pay first. As long as you are printing checks with Money (and you ought to print checks if you manage a business), you can decide which bills to pay by recording printed checks in your checking account register.

Here's how the technique works: When you receive a bill, record a printed check payment immediately in the register. As Chapter 6 explains, the word *Print* appears in the Num column of checking registers when you record a check that is to be printed. However, you don't have to pay the bill right away. You can let an unprinted check sit in the register for weeks if you want to. By glancing down the Num column and looking for the word *Print*, you can see which bills need paying and decide which ones to pay.

When you give the command to print checks, specify which bills to pay by making selections in the Select Checks dialog box. Chapter 6 explains how to do this task, too.

Chapter 20

Handling the Payroll

• •

In This Chapter

▶ Using Money to handle the payroll

▶ Setting up liability accounts for tracking deductions

▶ Setting up categories and subcategories for tracking deductions

▶ Writing a paycheck

▶ Recording a check to federal and state governments for taxes owed and withheld

▶ Generating the numbers for W-2 and W-3 forms

• •

*E*conomists and politicians point out that small businesses create the majority of the new jobs in the United States. I'll bet that the payroll service bureaus that serve small businesses create a number of those new jobs. The amount of administrative work, knowledge, time, and effort that goes into handling a payroll is staggering. No wonder so many small businesses hire a service bureau to do it.

As I mention in Chapter 18, Money isn't built for handling a payroll, but that doesn't mean that you can't use Money to handle your business's payroll. As long as the number of your employees doesn't exceed five or six, Money can do the job.

To help you decide whether doing the payroll with Money is worthwhile, this chapter lays out all the tasks you have to do to handle a payroll with Money. If you decide to take the plunge, you can find out how to set up the accounts and categories you need, write paychecks, record tax payments to the federal and state governments, and calculate the numbers for W-2 and W-3 forms.

An Overview: Using Money to Track the Payroll

When you become an employer, you take on a bunch of new payroll responsibilities, including:

- ✔ Writing payroll checks to your employees, deducting the correct amounts for income tax withholdings, state tax withholdings, Social Security tax, and Medicare tax
- ✔ Making quarterly payroll tax deposits to the federal government
- ✔ Filing payroll tax returns to the federal government
- ✔ Making monthly or quarterly payroll tax deposits to the state government
- ✔ Filing payroll tax returns to the state government
- ✔ Fulfilling your tax obligations to local governments, if you have such obligations

As an employer, you are obliged to keep track of how much you deduct from employees' paychecks so that you can report the correct amounts on federal and state tax returns. Of course, you also have to track how much you deduct so that you can pay the correct amounts on your quarterly tax bills.

How can you track these deductions? The answer is to create liability accounts and new subcategories:

- ✔ **Liability accounts:** Create a liability account for each large deduction you make from employees' paychecks. In other words, create a liability account for federal income tax withholdings, for Social Security taxes, and so on. By putting aside money in these liability accounts, you make sure that you always have enough money on hand to meet your quarterly tax obligations. Chapter 16 explains how liability accounts work.
- ✔ **New subcategories:** Create payroll expense subcategories for employee's gross wages and for each minor deduction you make from paychecks. For example, depending on the minor deductions you make, you may have Payroll: Gross Pay; Payroll: Employer Social Security; and so on. Chapter 4 explains more about categories and subcategories.

When you write a paycheck, click the Split button. In the Split transaction dialog box, enter the gross wages, and either enter the deductions as transfers to liability accounts or categorize the deductions (Chapter 3 explains split transactions). Figure 20-1 shows how the split works.

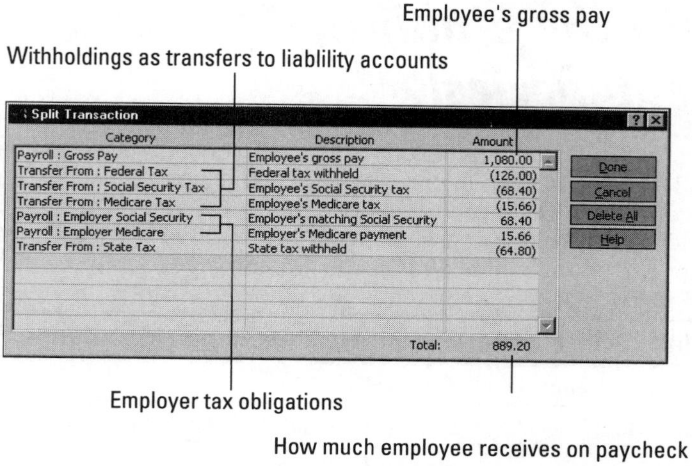

Employee's gross pay

Withholdings as transfers to liablility accounts

Figure 20-1:
Figure 20-1:
Use the
Split
Transaction
dialog box
to record
deductions
from the
employee's
gross
wages.

Category	Description	Amount	
Payroll : Gross Pay	Employee's gross pay	1,080.00	Done
Transfer From : Federal Tax	Federal tax withheld	(126.00)	Cancel
Transfer From : Social Security Tax	Employee's Social Security tax	(68.40)	
Transfer From : Medicare Tax	Employee's Medicare tax	(15.66)	Delete All
Payroll : Employer Social Security	Employer's matching Social Security	68.40	Help
Payroll : Employer Medicare	Employer's Medicare payment	15.66	
Transfer From : State Tax	State tax withheld	(64.80)	
	Total:	889.20	

Employer tax obligations

How much employee receives on paycheck

When the time comes to pay federal and state governments the amounts you withheld for taxes, for Social Security, for Medicare, and for what all, you can find out how much you owe by

✔ Looking at the balances in liability accounts, and

✔ Generating reports to see how much you spent in the different Payroll subcategories

You can also generate reports to find out the information you need in order to fill out W-2 and W-3 forms.

On becoming an employer

Governments are very eager to help employers file their taxes correctly. The IRS publishes a booklet called the *Employer's Tax Guide* that explains how much income tax, Social Security tax, and Medicare tax to withhold from employees' paychecks. State and local governments also publish booklets to help you file taxes correctly. And most governments offer payroll workshops for employers.

All the details of becoming an employer — the forms and returns to fill out, the deductions you must make from your employees' paychecks — are beyond the scope of this book. If you are an employer, however, you owe it to yourself to find out exactly what your tax and tax-reporting obligations are.

Setting Up the Liability Accounts and Subcategories

Table 20-1 and 20-2, respectively, list the liability accounts and categories that all employers need in order to handle the payroll. You are unique, however, and you may require more liability accounts and categories. Depending on where you do business, for example, you may have to track unemployment insurance and disability insurance requirements.

Table 20-1   Standard Liability Accounts for Handling a Payroll

Liability Account	For Tracking
Federal Tax	Employees' federal tax withholdings
Social Security Tax	Employees' Social Security tax withholdings
Medicare Tax	Employees' Medicare tax withholdings
State Tax	Employees' state tax withholdings

Table 20-2   Standard Payroll Categories and Subcategories

Payroll Expense Category/Subcategory	For Tracking
Payroll: Gross Pay	Employees' gross earnings
Payroll: Employer Social Security	Matching Social Security taxes to be paid by employer
Payroll: Employer Medicare	Medicare taxes to be paid by employer

Writing a Paycheck

Follow these steps to record a paycheck:

1. **Open the register of the checking account from which you pay your employees.**

2. **Click the Check transaction tab.**

3. **In the Number text box, either enter a check number or, if you print paychecks, select Print this transaction from the drop-down list.**

4. **Enter the employee's name in the Pay to text box.**

5. **Click the Split button. You see the Split Transaction dialog box shown in Figure 20-2.**

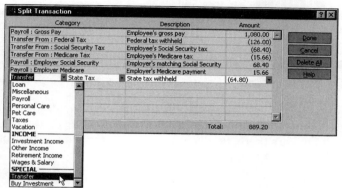

Figure 20-2:
The Split
Transaction
dialog box
is a handy
tool at
payroll time.

Now comes the important part. This is where you enter the employee's gross pay and withholdings and record what you owe in Medicare and Social Security payments as an employer.

6. **On the first line, enter the employee's gross pay by selecting Payroll from the Category drop-down list, selecting Gross Pay from the Subcategory drop-down list, and entering the gross pay amount in the Amount text box.**

Chapter 3 explains how to split a transaction and how to fill in the Split Transaction dialog box.

7. **Click the next line and either enter a transfer to a liability account or use a Payroll category and subcategory to describe amounts you will owe as an employer.**

   • **Transfer to liability account:** To record a transfer, go to the bottom of the Category drop-down list and select Transfer, as shown in Figure 20-2. From the Subcategory drop-down list, select the account that is to receive the money: Federal Tax, Medicare Tax, Social Security Tax, or State Tax. Then enter the amount you are withholding or deducting in the Amount text box. Enter the amount as a negative number. To do that, either enclose the amount in parentheses or put a hyphen before it.

   • **Payroll category and subcategory:** Select Payroll from the Category drop-down list and a subcategory from the Subcategory drop-down list.

8. **Repeat Step 7 until you have recorded all the withholdings and deductions.**

Strangely, Money puts the words Transfer From in the Category box when you transfer money *to* a liability account. Weird.

After you are done, the Split Transaction dialog box looks something like the one in Figure 20-1. The Total figure at the bottom shows you how much the employee will be paid.

9. **Click the Done button.**

10. **Back on the Check transaction form, click Enter.**

TIP

Printing checks is a big advantage when you prepare payroll checks because all the deduction and withholding information appears on the check stub or voucher. It appears there, that is, if you are printing on voucher or wallet-size checks. See Chapter 6.

Paying Taxes to Federal and State Governments

When the time comes to pay taxes, you can tell how much you owe by going into the liability accounts and by generating reports that show how much you spent in the Payroll expense subcategories. The Social Security Tax liability account shows how much you owe there, for example, and the Medicare Tax liability account shows how much you owe in Medicare taxes.

The only tricky part is remembering to split the transaction when you record the checks. To see what I mean, suppose that you owe $12,000 in federal tax withholdings, $1,000 in Social Security tax withholdings, and $500 in Medicare tax withholdings, a total of $13,500. When you record the $13,500 check to the IRS, split the payment and transfer $12,000, $1,000, and $500 respectively to the Federal Tax, Social Security Tax, and Medicare Tax liability accounts, as shown in Figure 20-3. By paying these taxes, you are no longer liable for them, and by transferring the amounts to the liability accounts you reduce your tax liability accordingly.

Figure 20-3:
Record a federal tax payment by splitting the total amount.

Category	Description	Amount	
Transfer To : Federal Tax		12,000.00	Done
Transfer To : Social Security Tax		1,000.00	Cancel
Transfer To : Medicare Tax		500.00	Delete All
			Help
		Total: 13,500.00	

Getting the Numbers for W-2 and W-3 Forms

A W-2 form lists each employee's gross pay and federal income taxes, Medicare taxes, and Social Security Taxes withheld. The W-3 form lists all the employees and summarizes information on the W-2 forms.

To generate the data for these forms, go to the Gallery of Reports and Charts, click the Spending Habits button, and double-click Who Is Getting My Money. You see a Who Is Getting My Money chart, which isn't worth much, so click the Report button in the lower-left corner of the window. Then follow these steps to customize the report and get the numbers for W-2 and W-3 forms:

1. **Click the Customize button.**

   You see the Customize Report dialog box.

2. **Select Subcategories from the Rows drop-down list.**

3. **Select Payees from the Columns drop-down list.**

4. **In the Dates drop-down list, select Previous Year.**

   If the report is not for last year, enter dates in the From and To text boxes.

5. **Click the Select transactions radio button at the bottom of the dialog box.**

   The Select Transactions dialog box appears.

6. **Click the Categories tab.**

7. **Click the Selected categories radio button.**

8. **Scroll down the list and click the Payroll category and all its subcategories.**

9. **Click OK.**

   You return to the Customize Report dialog box.

10. **Click the View button.**

    There it is — all the information you need to fill out W-2 and W-3 forms.

Chapter 13 explains how reports work, how to customize reports, and how to print them. Print a copy of the report so you can fill in the W-2 and W-3 forms.

Part VI
The Part of Tens

In this part . . .

*E*ach chapter in Part VI offers ten tidbits of good, rock-solid advice. With four chapters in this part, that makes 40 — count 'em — 40 tidbits in all.

You'll find suggestions for staying on top of your finances, improving your financial health, using Money when you are self-employed, and converting from Quicken to Money.

Chapter 21

Ten Things You Should Do Periodically

*T*his little chapter explains ten things you should do from time to time with Money. Do these ten things, and you will live happily ever after.

Back Up Your Data File

Whenever you shut down Money, the Back Up dialog box appears, and you get an opportunity to back up your data file. Seize this opportunity! Grab it by both ears and shout, "Yes, I want to back up my data file." If you don't back up your file and something bad happens to your computer, you may lose all the financial data you so carefully assembled.

Chapter 12 explains how to back up a file — and how to restore a file from its backup copy. Be sure to back up your file to a floppy disk. The data needs to be outside your computer, preferably in a hidden place that is safe from hurricanes, tornadoes, and earthquakes.

Update Your Savings and Checking Account Registers

When it comes to entering the checks you've written in a checking account and the transactions you've made in a savings account, falling behind is easy.

But if you procrastinate, you fall further and further behind. Soon, updating your savings and checking accounts seems overwhelming. You stop updating your accounts, and not long after that you stop using Money.

Set aside ten minutes in the middle of the month and ten minutes at the end of the month to update your account registers. Twenty minutes a month isn't that bad, is it? Okay, you may miss two-thirds of an *I Love Lucy* rerun, and that could be the death of you, but life isn't exciting unless you take a few risks.

Reconcile Your Bank Statements

Reconciling your bank accounts is another task that you should do each month when the statements arrive. Reconciling is easy to put off until tomorrow. However, if you keep putting it off, you end up with a stack of unreconciled bank statements and a bad case of the blues.

In Chapter 5, I explain a few tricks for recognizing and fixing reconciliation problems. After a while, you get good at reconciling. Not that you enjoy it, but you do start to understand it. Eventually, a minute or two is all it takes to reconcile. No kidding.

Enter Your Credit Card Transactions

Isn't it a drag when you get a credit card statement with a page or two of transactions on it? "Did I spend all that?" you ask yourself.

You did spend all that, and, if you're like most people, you now have to record all the credit card transactions you made in the past month. Most people don't record credit card purchases in the credit card register after they make each purchase. Instead, they record the purchases from the credit card statement after the statement arrives.

It's tempting to not record each credit card purchase and simply fire off a check to the credit card company. But by doing that you can't keep accurate records of how much you spend in different areas. When you record a credit card purchase, you get the chance to categorize it. If you don't record credit card purchases, you don't get the chance, and you never know precisely where you spend all your hard-earned money.

Reconcile Your Credit Card Statements

Not only do you have to record credit card purchases from the statement if you don't record purchases throughout the month, but you also have to reconcile your credit card statement when the statement arrives. Reconciling a credit card statement, like reconciling a bank statement, is one of those monthly jobs that's easy to put off until next month. Try to do it each month. If you don't, you get behind, become discouraged, fall into a state of despair, stop grooming yourself, stare at the ground a lot, and wear a permanent grimace on your face.

Generate a "Where the Money Goes" Chart

One of my favorite Money charts, and the chart that is probably the most revealing, is the "Where the Money Goes" chart. This pie chart shows in no uncertain terms where you spent all that money.

Chapter 13 explains how to generate and customize reports and charts. The "Where the Money Goes" chart shows spending in the past month, but you can customize the chart to show where the money went last year or in the last six months, for example.

Print Your Account Registers

When you file your income tax return in April, print a copy of your account registers and put them away with the rest of your income tax stuff — copies of your returns, receipts, and bank statements. I explain how to print an account register at the end of Chapter 3.

You don't have to print the entire register. Just print transactions from the previous year. That way, you leave behind a wide, easy-to-follow paper trail that the IRS posse can follow if you get audited.

Make an Archive File and Put It Away

Besides filing away a printed copy of your registers, make an archive file and put it away, too. An archive file is a file on which you store transactions from a certain time period. Make an archive file of transactions from the past year and file it away with copies of your tax returns and other important tax records. That way, you have a file of one year's records that auditors can examine at their leisure.

Prune Your Payee List

Once in a blue moon, go into the Payee list and remove the names of payees you no longer write checks to or receive money from. Money enters payee names automatically in the Payee box on transaction forms. Type the first few letters, and Money immediately enters a name for you.

When the Payee list gets too long, however, Money throws outdated names in the Payee box. To keep from seeing the names of people and companies you haven't dealt with for months, prune the Payee list. Chapter 11 explains how to do it.

Stop and Smell the Roses

I'm going to propose a radical idea: Computers aren't as wonderful as many people make them out to be. Even when you're surfing the Internet or exploring new cyberspace worlds, all you're really doing is staring into the glare of a monitor.

Getting carried away with all the features that Money has to offer is easy. If you own stocks and track them with Money, you may be tempted to download stock quotes each day from the Internet. If you read Chapter 14 of this book, you know how to forecast your future income, and you may be tempted to find out, for example, how rich you'll be in the year 2011.

Money is simply a tool to help keep your financial house in order. It simplifies the task of tracking your finances so you can devote time to other things. So do those other things! Stop and smell the roses. Money isn't another computer toy that distracts you from the rich and intriguing real world, the one that begins just outside your computer screen.

Chapter 22

Ten Ways to Good Health —
Financially Speaking, That Is

• •

In This Chapter

▶ Record credit card transactions as you make them

▶ Pay off all your credit cards

▶ Leave your plastic at home

▶ Create a "Where the Money Goes" chart

▶ Create a monthly cash flow report

▶ Create a budget

▶ Plan ahead for your retirement

▶ Set aside money for a rainy day

▶ Make like a new dog — learn new tricks

▶ Take the day off

• •

*W*arning: The Surgeon General has determined that not being in good
financial health causes undue stress and worry and can lead to other
health complications. The ten tidbits of advice in this chapter will improve
your financial health.

Record Credit Card Transactions
as You Make Them

You can very, very easily run up a credit card debt. A purchase here and a
purchase there, and pretty soon you owe $3,000, $4,000, or $5,000. Ouch!

To keep from spending so much with a credit card, record the transactions as you make them. After you buy the expensive piece of stereo equipment or the designer-label jacket, carry the credit card receipt home, lay it flat on your desk, and record the purchase in a credit card register. Watching the amount that you owe climb higher can discourage you from buying so many things with your credit card.

Pay Off All Your Credit Card Debt

Paying down or paying off a large credit card debt isn't easy, but it's worth it because credit card companies charge outrageous interest rates on credit card debt. Unless you pay off your credit card each month, you're paying extra for everything you buy with your credit card.

Look at it this way: If your credit card company charges 18 percent interest (the common rate in the United States) and you don't pay off your credit card debt, you pay an extra 18 percent with every purchase you make. The fancy handbag on sale for $180 doesn't really cost $180; it costs $212.40 after you add the 18 percent. The two tires don't really cost $112; they cost $132.16.

Leave Your Plastic at Home

Do you notice a theme developing in this chapter? Sorry for harping on credit card debt, but it is the single most daunting obstacle that comes between people and their financial well-being. If you have trouble keeping credit card spending in check, try leaving your credit card at home. Studies show that people are far more apt to spend with a credit card than they are to spend cash.

Create a "Where the Money Goes" Chart

I can't get enough of Money's "Where the Money Goes" chart. It's easy to generate, and it shows so plainly and nakedly where you spend money. The first time I saw the chart was a revelation. "Eureka!" I shouted. "So that's where all the money went — to ice cream!" Actually, my two biggest spending categories were Taxes and Home: Mortgage, which wasn't a very big surprise. It was surprising, however, to discover what a large chunk of my income I spent in those two categories.

Chapter 13 explains how to generate a "Where the Money Goes" chart. Money can generate 22 different charts in all. All the charts are revealing.

Create a Monthly Cash Flow Report

Another way to get a good look at your finances is to create a Monthly Cash Flow report. The report shows how much you earned in the last six months and how you earned it. It also shows how much you spent in each category and subcategory. Chapter 13 explains how to generate reports.

Reading down the Expenses list, you may find a few surprises. You may discover one or two categories in which you spent much more than you thought you spent. And next time you consider buying an item that falls into one of the categories, think twice about buying it.

Create a Budget

Chapter 10 explains how to formulate a budget with Money. Formulating a budget takes an entire evening, but if you have trouble keeping your spending in check, it is an evening well spent. Also, Money makes it very easy to find out whether you met your budget.

Plan Ahead for Your Retirement

Retirement is a dirty word in some people's books. They don't want to think that far ahead. But planning for your retirement is something that you really ought to do for two reasons. First, in order to spend your golden years comfortably you have to start saving now. Second, setting aside money for retirement is the best way to lower your tax bill. With 401 (k) plans, SEPs, and other tax-deferred investment plans, the federal government has made saving for retirement very practical as well as necessary.

Chapter 14 explains how to use Money to help plan for your retirement.

Set Aside Money for a Rainy Day

One of the first things that you realize when you read most financial self-help books is how important setting aside "rainy day" money is. Most authors recommend setting aside two month's income, the idea being that it usually takes two months to find a new job if you're bounced out of your present job.

Make Like a New Dog — Learn New Tricks

In Chapter 16, which describes how to set up an asset account, I explain that assets are things that add to your net worth — the money in savings and checking accounts, an object of value that you own, the equity in a house. However, your most important asset cannot be recorded in an account register. Your most important asset is *you*.

Your talents, your abilities, and your know-how are your most important assets. As such, you can make like a new dog and learn new tricks. Go back to school and acquire a few new skills. Or volunteer somewhere and learn new skills and acquire new experiences. By doing so, you can become a more valuable employee to others.

Take the Day Off

To use one of those man-as-machine metaphors, sometimes you have to relax and recharge your batteries. Take the day off. In fact (I'm writing this chapter late Friday afternoon), take the rest of the week off! You deserve it. The object of using Money is to get more free time to enjoy yourself.

Chapter 23

Ten Things to Do If You Are Self-Employed

As of 1998, I will have been self-employed for eight years. Not bad for a country boy from Idyllwild, California!

Being self-employed isn't for everyone. You need the right temperament, and you have to be willing to suffer the risks as well as reap the rewards. The following pages offer a few suggestions for self-employed people who use Money.

Diligently Record Your Financial Activity

One of the difficulties of being self-employed is that you have to account for all the money you spend. At tax time, your records, not those of an employer, are used to calculate how much income tax you owe. And because you can deduct certain expenses from your gross income on your income tax report, you have to record expenses as well as income carefully.

Money, of course, makes it easy to record income and expenses. But you have to stay on top of it. Don't let several weeks or months pass before you update your savings and checking account registers. Be sure to reconcile your account on a monthly basis, too. Falling behind is too easy.

Make Sure That All Tax-Related Expenses Are Marked As Such

Being self-employed, you can deduct certain expenses from your gross income when you file an income tax report. Office expenses, rent payments if you rent an office, and any payment you make on behalf of your business is tax-deductible.

To mark an expense as tax-deductible, you assign it to a category or subcategory that has tax-related status. Chapter 4 explains how to give categories and subcategories tax-related status. Give all categories and subcategories that have anything whatsoever to do with taxes a tax-related status.

Print a Tax-Related Transactions Report for Your Accountant

Transactions assigned to a tax-related category appear on the Tax-Related Transactions report. Under the name of each tax-related category and subcategory, the report lists transactions and gives the total amount that was spent. For example, the report lists each transaction assigned to the Charitable Donations category. At the bottom of the list is the total amount you spent on charitable donations.

Charitable donations are tax-deductible. An accountant who examines the Tax-Related Transactions report knows right away how much you can deduct for charitable donations. You don't have to pay the accountant to study your account registers and find charitable donations because the numbers are right there on the Tax-Related Transactions report.

Chapter 13 explains how to generate reports. You can save a lot of money on accounting fees by generating a Tax-Related Transactions report for your accountant.

Use the Memo Box Early and Often

As a self-employed individual, you have to track your own finances — your income, expenses, and so on. In account registers, you have to describe the money you spend and the money you take in. Usually, the Category boxes on transaction forms are adequate for describing your income and expenses, but consider using the Memo text box as well. When you record an odd expense, describe it in the Memo box in case you have to explain it to an accountant months from now when you will have forgotten what it was.

Set Aside a Tenth of Your Income in a Savings Account

Being self-employed takes discipline. Employers deduct income taxes, Social Security payments, and Medicare payments from the paychecks of wage earners and salaried employees. Not so with self-employed individuals. The self-employed are responsible for paying their own taxes and Social Security.

You have to make the payments four times a year: on January 15, April 15, June 15, and September 15. More importantly, you have to be ready to make these payments, which means setting aside some of your income throughout the year to meet your tax obligations.

I suggest stashing a tenth of your income in a savings account. If you're making more money than the previous year, set aside more than a tenth, because you'll owe extra when April rolls around.

Schedule Your Quarterly Tax Payments

It is a catastrophe if you miss or are late with a quarterly tax payment. Heads roll. There is much sorrow and gnashing of teeth. To make sure that you make the quarterly payments on time, schedule them. Chapter 11 explains how to use Money to schedule a payment. Scheduled bills appear very prominently on Money's Home screen under the word "Bills." You can't miss 'em.

Use Classifications to Track Business Expenses

One of the dilemmas of being self-employed is keeping your personal expenses separate from your business expenses. One way to keep them separate is to create a classification called Business and assign transactions that pertain to your business to the Business classification. See Chapter 4 for more about classifications.

Open a Checking Account for Business Transactions

Another way to keep business expenses and personal expenses separate is to open a checking account for business transactions. I got this idea from my accountant, who told me, mysteriously I thought, that I had "some ambiguity" between my personal and business expenses, but I could "re-solve these ambiguities" by opening a business checking account.

Now, all incoming checks are deposited in my business checking account. When I need money for my family's personal finances, I transfer it into the family checking account. Expenses for office supplies and such that fall in the business category are all paid out of my business checking account. I'm unambiguous. I'm as cut-and-dried as a salami sandwich.

Write a Check to Yourself Periodically

My accountant also told me that I need to spend more money on my busi-ness. "Why should I spend more money?" I asked. "I'm trying to save money." He said that my overhead was extremely low and that I should "beef it up." To do that, he suggested writing down all the piddley cash payments I make — for pencils, bus fare, and so on — in a book, and when the total expenses reach $100 or so, to write myself a check for that amount. By doing this, I can spend more money on my business and lower my tax bill.

I was surprised by how much the little expenses added up. Personally, I don't like having to write down payments in a book, but I do like saving money on taxes.

Keep Your Irons on the Fire

In the days before the electric iron, when people used irons that were made out of, well, iron to smooth the wrinkles from their clothes, the person whose job it was to iron clothes had to keep more than one iron on the fire. While one iron was in use, a second and third iron lay on the fire. That way, the person who ironed clothes never lacked a warm iron.

If you are self-employed, you also have to keep more than one iron on the fire. You need to devote an afternoon every other week to looking for work. Looking for work means sending out your resume, making phone calls, and maybe going to lunch. Looking for work does not pay well. In fact, the hourly wage for looking for work is zip. But looking for work is something you have to do if you expect to stay self-employed.

Chapter 24

Ten Things Ex-Quicken Users Should Know about Money

A couple of years back, on the idea that "if you can't beat 'em, buy 'em," the mighty Microsoft Corporation made a bold and underhanded attempt to purchase Intuit, the company that makes Quicken, Money's rival. Everyone shook hands and the deal appeared completed until the Federal Trade Commission stepped in. The FTC insisted that the deal created a monopoly and constituted unfair business practices.

After being rebuffed by the federal government, Microsoft redoubled its efforts to make a financial management program as good or better than Quicken. As the years go by and Money is revised, the program is sure to benefit from being in the Microsoft family of products. Already, Microsoft's Internet Explorer is included in Money 98.

This brief chapter is for people who have made the switch from Quicken to Money. I describe the chief differences between the programs and tell ex-Quicken users what to watch out for as they use Money.

Money Offers a Special Tour for Quicken Users

After you install Money 98, you have an opportunity to take a tour of Money that is especially designed for converts from Quicken. The tour touches on the most important parts of Money and explains where Money and Quicken differ.

Even if you didn't take the tour when you installed Money, you can still catch up with the tour bus. Take the tour whenever you want by putting the Money 98 CD-ROM in your computer and choosing Help⇨Product Tour. In the Tour dialog box, click the Tour for Quicken Users radio button, click Start Tour, and groove on the disco music and smooth-voiced narration. When the tour is over, don't forget to remove your belongings from the area around your seat and the baggage compartment.

You Can Use Your Old Quicken File in Money

Money offers a wizard that you can use to convert a Quicken data file to a Money file. Actually, the wizard doesn't convert the file. It makes a copy of the Quicken data file, converts the copy, and leaves the original data file intact. So if you decide after all that you like Quicken better than Money, you can go back to Quicken and continue using the data file as if nothing happened. After you convert a Quicken file, a new file called Qdata.mny opens on the Money screen. The file extension of Money files is mny.

As of this writing, Money can safely convert Quicken data files from Versions 4, 5, and 6, but not the newest version of Quicken, Quicken 98. However, even if you are using Quicken 98, you can convert your old Quicken data up to the date on which you converted it to Quicken 98. In the Quickenw folder where Quicken data files are kept, find a subfolder called Qw6files. This folder contains copies of your Quicken data files made on the day you converted from Quicken 6 to Quicken 98. Convert those files to Money, and you then have a fairly up-to-date Money file.

Follow these steps to convert a Quicken data file to Money:

1. **Close Quicken if the program is running, and open the Money program.**

2. **Choose File⇨Open or press Ctrl+O.**

   You see the Open dialog box.

3. **From the Files of type drop-down list, select Quicken files.**

4. **Find and select the Quicken data file.**

   Unless you tinkered with Quicken's default settings, the Quicken data file is called Qdata.QDB, and it is located in the C:\Quickenw folder. On my system, I can find it by clicking the Up One Level button twice, double-clicking the Quickenw folder, and clicking the Quicken.QDB file.

5. **Click the Open button.**

   The Back Up dialog box appears.

6. **In the Back Up dialog box, click the Back Up button to back up the Money file that was open, and then click Yes when Money asks if you want to overwrite the existing file.**

After the conversion is complete, a "Summary of the Conversion" window appears. It lists account balances in Quicken and account balances in Money. Compare the two to make sure that the Quicken data file was converted successfully.

Some Things Are Lost in the Conversion

The following elements are not converted from Quicken files because Money does not offer similar features:

- Memorized charts
- Transaction passwords
- A second or third budget
- Supercategories
- Savings goals

Some Quicken Features Have No Equivalent in Money

Besides savings goals, converts and forced converts to Money will not find equivalents to Quicken alerts and the financial planners such as the College Planner and Retirement Planner.

Purists will argue that the Money 98 Financial Suite offers financial planners on the Money Insider window. Maybe so, but the Money Insider window is so detailed that it isn't of much use for someone who simply wants to find out in a couple of minutes how much to save for college or retirement.

In Money, Transactions Are Entered on Forms

In my opinion, the biggest difference between Quicken and Money is that, in Money, you enter transactions on forms at the bottom of the account register. In Quicken, you enter a transaction by typing it directly into the register. The forms in Money take a bit of getting used to. Chapter 3 explains how forms work and how to record a transaction on a form.

You Get from Place to Place Differently in Money

In Quicken, you get from screen to screen by clicking buttons on the icon bar, by clicking Quick Tabs on the right side of the screen, and by clicking account buttons and activity buttons along the bottom of the screen.

In Money, the chief means of getting from place to place are the buttons on the Navigation bar. Click one and you move to a different window. You can also get from place to place by choosing commands on the Go menu. To move from one account register to another, click the arrow beside the word Accounts and select the name of the account you want to go to from the drop-down list. Chapter 1 has detailed instructions for getting around.

You Can Find Out Exactly How Quicken and Money Differ

The Help program in Money has a page that tells you in excruciating detail what happens when a Quicken data file is changed into a Money data file. To read the page, choose Help⇨Help Topics, click the Contents tab, scroll down the screen to Help for Quicken users, double-click the book icon beside Help for Quicken users, and double-click Details of Quicken conversion.

Your Quicken Checks Are Good in Money

Money puts Quicken check options in the Check Setup dialog box so that users who have switched from Quicken to Money can use their Quicken checks. As long as you printed checks with Quicken, you can find the following options in the Check Setup dialog box:

  ✔ Laser Standard (Quicken)

  ✔ Laser Voucher (Quicken)

  ✔ Laser Wallet (Quicken)

Chapter 6 explains how to reach the Check Setup dialog box and select a check option.

If the Quicken check options do not appear in the Check Setup dialog box, choose Tools⇨Options and click the Print Checks tab. Under Printing checks, click the Use my existing checks from Quicken check box.

Quicken's Online Banking Services Are No Good with Money

If you bank or pay bills online with Quicken, you can't pick up where you left off after you switch to Money. Sorry. You have to cancel the online services you use with Quicken, reapply for the services, tell your bank that you use Money now, and start all over again. Chapter 7 explains how to set up the online banking services in Money.

When I changed to Money, my bank let me keep the PIN number I used with Quicken. The switch was made in only three days.

Your Payee List Is Way, Way Too Long

Quicken has a very nice feature whereby payees whose names haven't been entered in account registers for a certain amount of time are dropped from the Payees list. Unfortunately, Money has no such feature. When you import a large Quicken file, you may end up with a Payees list as long as a brontosaurus's tail.

The only way to delete payees is to visit the Categories & Payees list and delete them one at a time. Chapter 12 explains how.

Appendix A

Installing Microsoft Money 98

••

*A*ppendix A explains how to install and reinstall Microsoft Money 98 on your computer. I'm happy to report that installing and reinstalling the program is as easy as falling off a turnip truck.

Microsoft recommends taking a few precautionary steps before installing a new program. This appendix explains what those steps are. It also shows you how to install Money. By the way, it doesn't matter whether an earlier version of Money is installed on your computer because the steps for installing a fresh copy of Money and an upgrade are the same.

Note: The instructions for installing the trial version of the Money 98 Financial Suite included on this book's CD are just a little different. To install the trial version of the program, read the next section, "Before You Install the Program," on the recommended precautionary steps, and then turn to the last two pages of the book.

Before You Install the Program

Before you install Money 98 or upgrade to Money 98 from an older version of Money, Microsoft recommends closing all applications that are running and making a backup copy of your old Money files.

In the course of installing the software, Money asks for your CD-Key if you install from a CD-ROM, or a Setup number if you install the program from floppy disks. Be prepared to type in these numbers.

Installing (Or Reinstalling) the Program

If you have already installed a computer program in Windows 95 or Windows 98, you probably don't have to read the following step-by-step instructions because you already know how to install new software. All you have to do is click the Add/Remove Programs icon on the Windows Control Panel and proceed from there.

Installing a brand-new copy of Money takes about ten minutes. It takes about three minutes to install Money if an older version of the program already resides on your computer.

Follow these steps to install Money 98 or the Money 98 Financial Suite:

1. **Click the Start button.**

   The Start button is located in the lower-left corner of your screen. When you click it, a menu appears.

2. **Choose Settings on the menu.**

3. **Choose Control Panel.**

   You see the Control Panel, a window with icons you can double-click to tell your computer how you want it to operate.

4. **Double-click the Add/Remove Programs icon.**

   You see the Add/Remove Programs Properties dialog box.

5. **Click the Install button.**

   The next dialog box asks you to insert either the Money 98 CD-ROM in the CD-ROM drive or the first installation diskette in the floppy drive.

6. **Insert the CD-ROM or first diskette and then click the Next button.**

   What happens next depends on whether your system is set up to start installing programs as soon as it detects a CD-ROM or floppy drive:

   • You see a dialog box that tells you that the Setup program has located the Setup file either on the CD-ROM drive where the CD is located, or on the floppy disk drive where you inserted the first floppy diskette.

   • You see a Welcome window.

If a dialog box tells you that "Windows was unable to locate the installation program," click the Browse button. In the Browse dialog box, click the arrow in the Look in box and click the drive icon that represents the location of the floppy disk or CD-ROM with the Money program, probably 3½ Floppy (A:) or Mny60_dlxen (D:). When you click, you see a program called setup. Click that program and then click the Open button.

7. **From this point forward, follow the on-screen instructions and press Continue, Next, I Agree, or OK as you do so (or click Reinstall if you want to reinstall the program). If you're installing the program from floppy diskettes, insert the diskettes when you are asked to.**

The Installation program asks you for your name, the CD-Key or Setup number that identifies your copy of the program, and the location where you want to install the program on your computer. You must also indicate whether you intend to use the online services, and whether you want to register the program online.

Unless you are competent enough or have a good reason to install the program elsewhere, be sure to install the program in the default folder that Microsoft recommends, C:\Program Files\Microsoft Money. To do so, click the OK button, as shown in Figure A-1. By installing the program in the default folder, you make sure that the program files that you install all work together.

Figure A-1:
Installing
Money to
the default
folder,
C:\Program
Files\
Microsoft
Money.

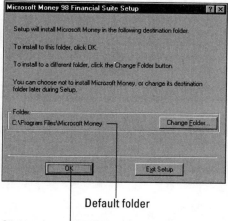

Default folder

Click to accept the default installation

8. **Click the Restart Windows button when the Installation program tells you that you must restart your computer in order to finish installing Money.**

Twiddle your thumbs while your computer restarts. That wasn't so bad, was it?

Appendix B

An Extremely Short Windows Primer

● ●

*W*indows, as the whole world knows by now, is the name of Microsoft's monolithic operating system. A little appendix like the one you're reading cannot possibly do justice to a monster as big as Windows 3.1, Windows 95, Windows NT, or Windows 98, so this appendix merely touches upon the Windows tips and techniques that you need to run Money 98.

In this installment of the Windows saga, you discover how to give commands, fill in dialog boxes, minimize and maximize windows, and switch between applications. If you're interested in delving into the Windows saga from start to finish, get a copy of *Windows 95 For Dummies,* 2nd Edition (published by IDG Books Worldwide, Inc.) by Andy Rathbone (no relation to Basil Rathbone).

Giving Commands

In a Windows-based computer program like Money 98, you can give commands in three different ways:

- ✔ Choose a command from a menu
- ✔ Press a shortcut key combination
- ✔ Click a button

Choosing commands from menus

Before you can choose a command from a menu, you have to *pull down* the menu so you can see the choices, or commands, that the menu offers. To pull down a menu on the main menu, either click its name with the mouse or press the Alt key as you press the letter that is underlined in the menu name. In computer jargon, the underlined key is called the *hot key.*

For example, to pull down the G̲o menu, you can either click the word Go or press **Alt+G**, *G* being the underlined letter in Go. When you do, a menu magically appears, as Figure B-1 shows.

After you pull down a menu, you have a bunch of different commands to choose from. To choose a command from a menu that you pulled down, either click the command name or press the letter that is underlined in the command name. To choose the Reports command shown in Figure B-1, for example, either click it or press **R**.

Pressing a shortcut key combination

Some people prefer to give commands by pressing keys, and for those people Money 98 offers shortcut keys. A *shortcut key* is a combination of keys that you can press to give a command. To tell which commands offer a shortcut key, look at the command name on a menu and see whether a shortcut key combination appears beside its name. In Figure B-1, for example, you can see that all the commands on the Go menu offer a shortcut key.

Lots of menu commands have shortcut keys that help you get your work done faster. If you find yourself using a command often, see if it has a shortcut key and start using the shortcut key to save time.

Clicking buttons

It may interest you to know that Money 98 is a state-of-the-art computer program. In the future, more and more programs will look like Money 98, whose design is modeled after a Web site.

Figure B-1:
Choosing a
command
from a
menu.

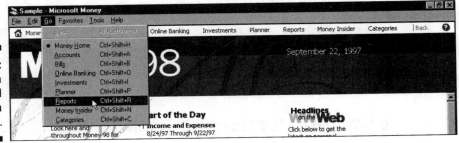

The mysterious shortcut menus

For your convenience, Money 98 and other Windows-based programs offer *shortcut menus* — menus that appear when you right-click part of the screen. *Right-click* means to click with the right mouse button instead of the left mouse button.

The makers of Money 98 have placed shortcut menus in strategic places, and you never quite know which menu commands you will see when you right-click. But right-click often — you will be pleasantly surprised by the menu commands that appear. For example, when you right-click a transaction on a register window, you get a bunch of useful commands for doing a bunch of useful things.

Woodgrove Bank Checking						Account Manager
	View: All Transactions, by Date					
Num	Date	Payee / Category / Memo	C	Payment	Deposit	Balance
344	7/17/97	City of Springfield		47.65		2,693.21
	7/18/97	Edit / Split... Ctrl+S		15.16		2,678.05
	9/2/97	Go to Payee: City of Springfield / Go to Category: Bills / Go to Subcategory: Garbage & Recycle		00.00		2,478.05
	9/2/97	Mark As	►	00.00		2,278.05
2349	9/2/97	Add to Bills Place... Ctrl+E / Move to Account...		1.00		2,277.05
	9/6/97	Delete		200.00		2,077.05
		Transfer To : Petty Cash Spending				
398	9/16/97	City of Springfield		39.95		2,037.10

You're thinking, "What do I care?" Well, the only reason you should care is that buttons in Money 98 appear all over the place — much like buttons and hyperlinks in a Web site. Click buttons on the Navigation bar to open new windows. Click buttons on windows to give commands. Click here and click there until your finger gets a blister.

In Money, you can tell when you've moved the pointer over a button because the letters in the button's name change color.

All about Dialog Boxes

Sometimes Money doesn't jump and do your bidding after you click a button or choose a command. When Money can't execute a command because it needs more information, it shows you a dialog box. Figure B-2 shows the Options dialog box. A dialog box is the program's way of gathering more information to complete a command.

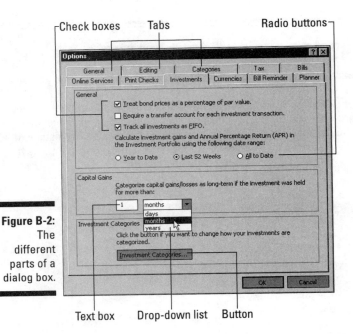

Figure B-2:
The
different
parts of a
dialog box.

Text box   Drop-down list   Button

All dialog boxes are different (the one in Figure B-2 happens to be very complex), but you usually find at least one or two of the following elements in each dialog box you encounter:

✔ **Tabs:** A tab in a dialog box is like another page. Click a tab name to move to a new page and see more options.

✔ **Check boxes:** When a check mark appears in a check box, the option is activated. For example, the check mark at the top of the Options dialog box in Figure B-2 tells Money to "Treat bond prices as a percentage of par value." Click a check box to remove a check mark; click again to enter a check mark. If you click the check box shown at the top of Figure B-2 to remove the check mark, Money no longer treats bond prices as a percentage of par value.

✔ **Radio buttons:** These buttons, also known as option buttons, appear in sets. The thing to know about radio buttons is that you can only select one in the set, just as you can only listen to one radio station at a time.

✔ **Text boxes:** A text box is simply a place to enter a number, a name, or another piece of vital information by wiggling your fingers over the keyboard.

- **Drop-down lists:** Click an arrow in a drop-down list, and you see a list of options that you can select from. In the dialog box in Figure B-2, the drop-down list offers days, months, and years as the means of categorizing capital gains and losses.

- **Buttons:** Buttons often appear in dialog boxes. Click a button and you go to yet another dialog box. Will this torment ever end?

- **OK and Cancel buttons:** All dialog boxes have an OK and Cancel button. Click OK (or press Enter) after you're done filling in a dialog box; click Cancel (or press Esc) if you get cold feet and want to start all over.

Minimizing and Maximizing Windows

In the Windows operating system, programs appear on — you guessed it — windows. By clicking the three buttons on the right side of the title bar in the upper-right corner of a program window, you can minimize, maximize, shrink, and restore it.

- **Minimizing:** To make a program leave the screen, click the Minimize button. To see the program again after you minimize it, click its name on the taskbar.

- **Maximizing/Restoring:** Click the Maximize/Restore button to make the window smaller. After you shrink the screen, the button changes from overlapping squares into a single square. Click the square "Restore" button again to make the window fill the screen.

Switching Applications with the Taskbar

Along the bottom of the screen is the taskbar. Thanks to the taskbar, you can run a bunch of different programs at once and switch back and forth among them. The names of all the applications that are running appear on buttons on the taskbar. To switch to a new application, click its button.

A Glossary of Financial and Computer Terms

401 (k) plan: A tax-deferred retirement plan by which a portion of an employee's pay is deducted from each paycheck and invested. Employees do not have to pay taxes on income from the plan until they start withdrawing it at retirement age.

amortized loan: A loan for which you make regular payments of the same amount. Part of each payment goes toward paying interest on the loan, and part goes toward reducing the principal (the amount you borrowed). See also *interest* and *principal.*

asset: Something of value that is owned, such as a house, stocks, or jewelry. Money that is owed to you is also an asset, as are savings and checking accounts. See also *liability* and *net worth.*

balance: The amount of money in a bank account. In the case of an asset, liability, or investment account, how much the thing being tracked in the account is worth.

bond: A paper promise to pay back a debt with interest by a certain date. Governments issue bonds, as do some companies. With a standard bond, regular interest payments are made to investors. With a discount bond, the buyer pays less than the face value (also known as the par value) of the bond. When a bond is redeemed, the owner receives the face value or more than the face value if the bond has increased substantially in value. Discount bonds are also known as "zero-coupon bonds."

browser: A computer application that connects to Web sites and displays Web pages. The term is not a contraction of the word "brown-noser."

CD (certificate of deposit): A bank deposit in which the depositor agrees to leave the money in the bank for a certain period of time. Banks guarantee a fixed rate of interest on CDs that is higher than the interest rate paid on savings accounts, for example.

check box: A square box inside a dialog box. Click an option's check box to place a check mark in the box and activate the option. Click again to remove the check mark and render the option dormant.

click: To press the left mouse button once. Not to be confused with "clique," a like-minded assortment of high school students who talk and dress alike. See also *right-click.*

cost basis: The total cost of purchasing a security, including commissions, fees, and mutual fund loads.

curb feeler: Before about 1963, luxury cars were fitted with curb feelers. A curb feeler was an antenna-like device that helped in parallel parking. When drivers backed too close to the curb, curb feelers scraped the cement and made a scratching noise. When drivers heard that noise they knew that they were too close to the curb and should stop backing up, lest they scratch the chrome on the fender of their cars.

dialog box: A box that appears on-screen when Money needs more information to complete a task. Fill in the dialog box and click the OK button to give a command. See also ***check box, drop-down list,*** and ***radio button.***

discount bond: See ***bond.***

dividend: From the word "divide." A portion of a company's earnings that is distributed to the holders of stock in the company. Usually, dividends are distributed quarterly.

double-click: To click twice very quickly, as though your life depended on it, with the left mouse button.

drop-down list: A menu box with a down arrow at its side. Click the down arrow, and a list appears with options you can select.

equity: A house's market value, less the amount that is owed on the house. For example, if $100,000 is owed on the house and its market value is $150,000, the owner has $50,000 equity in the house.

escrow account: An account that a mortgage company takes out on behalf of a borrower to make sure that property taxes, property insurance, and other such fees are paid.

hot key: The underlined letter in a command name. Press the hot key or Alt+ the hot key to execute a command quickly.

icon: In computerese, a visual image, or picture, that activates a command when you click it. Not so long ago, "icon" meant an object of religious devotion, but now anybody and anything can be an icon. I read the other day in *The New Yorker* that Barbra Streisand is a cultural icon!

index fund: A mutual fund that invests in all the securities in a market in order to provide returns similar to that by which the market grows.

interest: The cost, expressed as a percentage of the loan amount, for borrowing money. Also, money paid to a lender or bank patron for the use of his or her money. See also ***principal.***

IRA (individual retirement account): A tax-deferred retirement plan for employees. The maximum contribution is $2,000 per year. You do not have to pay taxes on income from an IRA until you start withdrawing income from it at retirement age.

Keogh plan: A tax-deferred retirement plan for self-employed individuals. Money invested in Keogh plans is tax-deductible. Withdrawals are taxed.

liability: A debt that you owe. Credit card debt is an example of a liability, as are taxes owed to the IRS. See also ***asset*** and ***net worth.***

lot: A group of securities purchased at the same time for the same price. Also a nephew of Abraham whose spouse was turned into a salt shaker.

money market fund: An interest-earning mutual fund that invests in Treasury bills and other short-term securities.

mouse: The soap-shaped thing on your desk that you roll to make the mouse cursor move on-screen. If you reach for your mouse and feel fur or hear a squeaking sound, stop eating at your desk. The mouse has a left and right button. See also *click* and *right-click.*

mutual fund: An investment company that raises money from shareholders and invests the money in a variety of places, including stocks, bonds, and money market securities.

Navigation bar: In Money, the area along the top of the screen on which Money Home, Accounts, Bills, and other buttons are found. Use the Navigation bar to get from window to window in Money.

net worth: What you are worth, not as a human being, but as a financial entity. Assets add to net worth and liabilities count against it. See also *asset* and *liability.*

P/E ratio: The price of a stock divided by its per-share earnings. If the ratio of price to earnings is high, the stock is being traded for its future value, not for its present value, which indicates that investors are expecting high earnings.

portfolio: The securities owned by an individual or investment firm.

principal: The actual amount of money borrowed on a loan. Principal is different from interest, which is the cost of borrowing the money. See also *interest.*

radio button: One of a set of two or more buttons, only one of which can be selected. A radio button is round. Sometimes called an "option button."

right-click: To click with the right mouse button.

rollover: When you transfer funds from one investment or retirement account to another. Also, what Beethoven did in an old Chuck Berry song.

scroll: To move through a register or menu by using the scroll bars along the right side or along the bottom of the screen.

security: Stocks, certificates, bonds, and other financial instruments that can be traded and whose values change over time.

SEP (Simplified Employee Pension): A retirement plan, similar to an IRA, for the self-employed and small businesses. Money invested in SEPs is tax-deductible. Earnings from SEPs are tax-deferred.

shortcut menu: A menu that appears after you right-click on-screen. Which shortcut menu appears depends on which part of the screen you click.

Start button: The button on the left side of the Windows taskbar. Click it and you see a menu for opening programs and documents, changing the computer settings, and shutting down the computer, among other things. See also *taskbar.*

stock: Shares of ownership in a company. Stocks pay dividends and can be bought and sold. See also *dividend.*

taskbar: The strip along the bottom of the screen in Windows. The names of computer applications that are running appear on buttons on the taskbar. Click a button to switch to another application. The Start button is on the left end of the taskbar.

tax-deductible: In income tax reporting, expenses that can be deducted from total income.

tax-deferred: Refers to income for retirement on which you don't have to pay taxes until you begin withdrawing it at retirement age.

wizard: In Microsoft programs such as Money, a series of dialog boxes in which the user makes choices in order to complete a task or set up a feature. Microsoft's wizards are a far cry from the wizards of yore, who used to make castles disappear and turn winter into summer. I'd like to see a Microsoft wizard do that.

Index

(continued)

(continued)

• H •

• I •

• J •

• K •

IDG Books Worldwide, Inc., End-User License Agreement

READ THIS. You should carefully read these terms and conditions before opening the software packet(s) included with this book ("Book"). This is a license agreement ("Agreement") between you and IDG Books Worldwide, Inc. ("IDGB"). By opening the accompanying software packet(s), you acknowledge that you have read and accept the following terms and conditions. If you do not agree and do not want to be bound by such terms and conditions, promptly return the Book and the unopened software packet(s) to the place you obtained them for a full refund.

1. **License Grant.** IDGB grants to you (either an individual or entity) a nonexclusive license to use one copy of the enclosed software program(s) (collectively, the "Software") solely for your own personal or business purposes on a single computer (whether a standard computer or a workstation component of a multiuser network). The Software is in use on a computer when it is loaded into temporary memory (RAM) or installed into permanent memory (hard disk, CD-ROM, or other storage device). IDGB reserves all rights not expressly granted herein.

2. **Ownership.** IDGB is the owner of all right, title, and interest, including copyright, in and to the compilation of the Software recorded on the disk(s) or CD-ROM ("Software Media"). Copyright to the individual programs recorded on the Software Media is owned by the author or other authorized copyright owner of each program. Ownership of the Software and all proprietary rights relating thereto remain with IDGB and its licensers.

3. **Restrictions on Use and Transfer.**

   (a) You may only (i) make one copy of the Software for backup or archival purposes, or (ii) transfer the Software to a single hard disk, provided that you keep the original for backup or archival purposes. You may not (i) rent or lease the Software, (ii) copy or reproduce the Software through a LAN or other network system or through any computer subscriber system or bulletin-board system, or (iii) modify, adapt, or create derivative works based on the Software.

   (b) You may not reverse engineer, decompile, or disassemble the Software. You may transfer the Software and user documentation on a permanent basis, provided that the transferee agrees to accept the terms and conditions of this Agreement and you retain no copies. If the Software is an update or has been updated, any transfer must include the most recent update and all prior versions.

4. **Restrictions on Use of Individual Programs.** You must follow the individual requirements and restrictions detailed for each individual program on the installation page of this Book and the CD label. These limitations are also contained in the individual license agreements recorded on the Software Media. These limitations may include a requirement that after using the program for a specified period of time, the user must pay a registration fee or discontinue use. By opening the Software packet(s), you will be agreeing to abide by the licenses and restrictions for these individual programs that are detailed on the installation page and on the Software Media. None of the material on this Software Media or listed in this Book may ever be redistributed, in original or modified form, for commercial purposes.

5. **Limited Warranty.**

   (a) IDGB warrants that the Software and Software Media are free from defects in materials and workmanship under normal use for a period of sixty (60) days from the date of purchase of this Book. If IDGB receives notification within the warranty period of defects in materials or workmanship, IDGB will replace the defective Software Media.

   (b) **IDGB AND THE AUTHOR OF THE BOOK DISCLAIM ALL OTHER WARRANTIES, EXPRESS OR IMPLIED, INCLUDING WITHOUT LIMITATION IMPLIED WARRANTIES OF MER-CHANTABILITY AND FITNESS FOR A PARTICULAR PURPOSE, WITH RESPECT TO THE SOFTWARE, THE PROGRAMS, THE SOURCE CODE CONTAINED THEREIN, AND/OR THE TECHNIQUES DESCRIBED IN THIS BOOK. IDGB DOES NOT WARRANT THAT THE FUNCTIONS CONTAINED IN THE SOFTWARE WILL MEET YOUR REQUIREMENTS OR THAT THE OPERATION OF THE SOFTWARE WILL BE ERROR FREE.**

   (c) This limited warranty gives you specific legal rights, and you may have other rights that vary from jurisdiction to jurisdiction.

6. **Remedies.**

   (a) IDGB's entire liability and your exclusive remedy for defects in materials and workmanship shall be limited to replacement of the Software Media, which may be returned to IDGB with a copy of your receipt at the following address: Software Media Fulfillment Department, Attn.: *Microsoft Money 98 For Dummies,* IDG Books Worldwide, Inc., 7260 Shadeland Station, Ste. 100, Indianapolis, IN 46256, or call 800-762-2974. Please allow three to four weeks for delivery. This Limited Warranty is void if failure of the Software Media has resulted from accident, abuse, or misapplication. Any replacement Software Media will be warranted for the remainder of the original warranty period or thirty (30) days, whichever is longer.

   (b) In no event shall IDGB or the author be liable for any damages whatsoever (including without limitation damages for loss of business profits, business interruption, loss of business information, or any other pecuniary loss) arising from the use of or inability to use the Book or the Software, even if IDGB has been advised of the possibility of such damages.

   (c) Because some jurisdictions do not allow the exclusion or limitation of liability for conse-quential or incidental damages, the above limitation or exclusion may not apply to you.

7. **U.S. Government Restricted Rights.** Use, duplication, or disclosure of the Software by the U.S. Government is subject to restrictions stated in paragraph (c)(1)(ii) of the Rights in Technical Data and Computer Software clause of DFARS 252.227-7013, and in subparagraphs (a) through (d) of the Commercial Computer–Restricted Rights clause at FAR 52.227-19, and in similar clauses in the NASA FAR supplement, when applicable.

8. **General.** This Agreement constitutes the entire understanding of the parties and revokes and supersedes all prior agreements, oral or written, between them and may not be modified or amended except in a writing signed by both parties hereto that specifically refers to this Agreement. This Agreement shall take precedence over any other documents that may be in conflict herewith. If any one or more provisions contained in this Agreement are held by any court or tribunal to be invalid, illegal, or otherwise unenforceable, each and every other provision shall remain in full force and effect.

Microsoft Money 98 Financial Suite Trial Edition Installation Instructions

This book does more than just tell you about Microsoft Money — the CD inside the back cover includes a trial edition of the Microsoft Money 98 Financial Suite!

This trial edition of Microsoft Money 98 Financial Suite only allows you to enter transactions within a 90-day window. When you upgrade to the full retail release of the product (and Microsoft has a special rebate offer to make that easier for buyers of this book; see the other side of this page), you can open and view all data entered in the trial edition.

To install the Money 98 Financial Suite Trial Edition:

1. **Insert the CD-ROM in your computer's CD-ROM drive.**

   After a few moments, the installation program automatically runs. If the installation program does not automatically run, use Explorer or the Desktop browser to display the CD-ROM icon, and then double-click on the icon. This action runs the installation program.

2. **Follow the instructions that appear on your screen.**

To run the Money 98 Financial Suite Trial Edition after installation:

1. **Click the Start button and choose Programs.**
2. **Click Microsoft Money.**

Due to differences in currency formats, data entered into this trial version is compatible with U.S. versions only. Compatibility with international versions of Money 98 (including the Canadian version) does not apply. A special Canadian edition of this Money 98 Financial Suite trial version is planned; if you have Internet access, go to the www.microsoft.com/money/ site and select Canada to find out more.

To use Microsoft Money 98 Financial Suite, you need:

- A personal computer with a 486/50 MHz or higher microprocessor (Pentium/90 MHz or higher recommended)
- Microsoft Windows 95 operating system or Microsoft Windows NT Workstation 4.0 or higher (the suite will not run on earlier versions of Windows)
- 12MB of memory (RAM) on Windows 95 or 16MB RAM on Windows NT. Microsoft recommends that you have 16MB on Windows 95 and 24MB on Windows NT.

- 25–55MB of available hard disk space. The higher amount is required if Microsoft Internet Explorer 3.02 or higher and the ActiveMovie API are not already installed; both are required and contained on the enclosed CD.
- A CD-ROM drive
- A VGA graphics card or compatible video graphics adapter and 256-color monitor
- A Microsoft mouse or compatible pointing device
- An audio board and speaker or headphones required for audio
- A 9600 baud or faster modem (28,800 baud recommended) to use online features

Note: Internet functionality requires an Internet service provider (ISP) and browser. (MSN trial offer and Internet Explorer 3.02 provided.) Connect time charges may apply. All software required is included in Microsoft Money 98. Compatible with all Windows-compatible ISPs. Online banking/brokerage options vary by financial institution. Some require Internet access, and others offer direct dial up. Contact your financial institution for program details. To use online bill payment, you need a checking account with any financial institution in the U.S.

Discover Dummies Online!

The Dummies Web Site is your fun and friendly online resource for the latest information about ...*For Dummies*® books and your favorite topics. The Web site is the place to communicate with us, exchange ideas with other ...*For Dummies* readers, chat with authors, and have fun!

Ten Fun and Useful Things You Can Do at www.dummies.com

1. Win free ...*For Dummies* books and more!
2. Register your book and be entered in a prize drawing.
3. Meet your favorite authors through the IDG Books Author Chat Series.
4. Exchange helpful information with other ...*For Dummies* readers.
5. Discover other great ...*For Dummies* books you must have!
6. Purchase Dummieswear™ exclusively from our Web site.
7. Buy ...*For Dummies* books online.
8. Talk to us. Make comments, ask questions, get answers!
9. Download free software.
10. Find additional useful resources from authors.

Link directly to these ten fun and useful things at
http://www.dummies.com/10useful

For other technology titles from IDG Books Worldwide, go to
www.idgbooks.com

Not on the Web yet? It's easy to get started with *Dummies 101*®: *The Internet For Windows*® *95* or *The Internet For Dummies*®, 4th Edition, at local retailers everywhere.

Find other ...*For Dummies* books on these topics:
Business • Career • Databases • Food & Beverage • Games • Gardening • Graphics
Hardware • Health & Fitness • Internet and the World Wide Web • Networking
Office Suites • Operating Systems • Personal Finance • Pets • Programming • Recreation
Sports • Spreadsheets • Teacher Resources • Test Prep • Word Processing

IDG BOOKS WORLDWIDE
BOOK REGISTRATION

Register This Book and Win!

We want to hear from you!

Visit **http://my2cents.dummies.com** to register this book and tell us how you liked it!

- ✔ Get entered in our monthly prize giveaway.

- ✔ Give us feedback about this book — tell us what you like best, what you like least, or maybe what you'd like to ask the author and us to change!

- ✔ Let us know any other ...*For Dummies* topics that interest you.

Your feedback helps us determine what books to publish, tells us what coverage to add as we revise our books, and lets us know whether we're meeting your needs as a ...*For Dummies* reader. You're our most valuable resource, and what you have to say is important to us!

Not on the Web yet? It's easy to get started with *Dummies 101®: The Internet For Windows® 95* or *The Internet For Dummies®*, 4th Edition, at local retailers everywhere.

Or let us know what you think by sending us a letter at the following address:

...*For Dummies* Book Registration
Dummies Press
7260 Shadeland Station, Suite 100
Indianapolis, IN 46256
Fax 317-596-5498

BUSINESS AND
GENERAL REFERENCE BOOK SERIES FROM IDG

COMPUTER BOOK SERIES FROM IDG